SIGNS IN SOCIETY

ADVANCES IN SEMIOTICS

Thomas A. Sebeok, *General Editor*

SIGNS IN SOCIETY
Studies in Semiotic Anthropology

Richard J. Parmentier

Indiana University Press

Bloomington and Indianapolis

The paper used in this publication meets the minimum requirements of
American National Standard for Information Sciences—Permanence of
Paper for Printed Library Materials, ANSI Z39.48-1984.

♾™

Manufactured in the United States of America

Library of Congress Cataloging-in-Publication Data

Parmentier, Richard J., date
     Signs in society : studies in semiotic anthropology / Richard J.
Parmentier.
         p.   cm.—(Advances in semiotics.)
     Includes bibliographical references and index.
     ISBN 0-253-32757-1 (cloth : alk. paper)
     1. Culture—Semiotic models.   2. Semiotics—Philosophy.   3. Signs
and symbols.   I. Title.   II. Series.
     GN357.P37   1994
     301—dc20   93-27758

1 2 3 4 5   99 98 97 96 95 94

For Nina and Emma

Contents

Acknowledgments

I WOULD LIKE TO thank Tom Kirsch, who advised my first foray into semiotic anthropology in an undergraduate reading course at Princeton University in 1969–70. Subsequent course work with Steve Barnett, Vincent Crapanzano, Mark Leone, Alfonso Ortiz, and Martin Silverman provided the impetus for my graduate studies and professional research in anthropology. The initial opportunity to carry out research on Peircean semiotics was provided by a postdoctoral fellowship (1981–82) at the Center for Psychosocial Studies in Chicago. In addition, the Center helped to fund my field research in Belau (1978–80), provided support during a sabbatical leave (1986), and sponsored many of the conferences where the chapters in this book were first presented. "Signs at the Center" would have been an equally appropriate title for this book. To Bernard Weissbourd and Ben Lee I extend my thanks.

That I still acknowledge the powerful influence of Michael Silverstein more than ten years after I ceased being his student is testimony both to the continuing relevance of my educational experience in his classes at the University of Chicago and to the constantly expanding corpus of his publications. All eight of the chapters as well as the overall organization of the volume are indebted to his pioneering efforts in anthropological linguistics and semiotically informed social theory. He has provided oral responses or written comments on most of the chapters in this book. Specifically, I acknowledge the importance of his work on the pragmatic codes of culture, on the contrast between explicit and implicit metapragmatics, on the limits to semiotic awareness, and on metasemiotic regimentation.

In the years that I have been working in the area of semiotic anthropology I have benefited from the insight, advice, conversation, and criticism of friends and colleagues in several disciplines who have been my "universe of discourse": Jim Collins, Craig Davis, Judy Irvine, Naomi Janowitz, Don Joralemon, Ben Lee, Laurie Lucking, John Lucy, Nina Kammerer, Beth Mertz, David Murray, Bob Petersson, Alfonso Procaccini, Nancy Rubin, and Benigno Sanches-Eppler. In addition, I gratefully acknowledge several individuals who provided sponsoring support, research assistance, and critical comments on specific chapters: Martha Denney and Deborah Toribiong (Ch. 3), Vincent Crapanzano and Anita Skang Jordan (Ch. 4), Roy Wagner and James Weiner (Ch. 5), Moise Postone (Ch. 6),

Frank Reynolds, Paul Powers, and Robert Hunt (Ch. 7), and Eric Reeves (Ch. 8). It is a great pleasure to thank the students who have studied symbolic analysis and semiotic anthropology with me over the years; many of the interpretations advanced in this book were developed in the dialogic atmosphere of my classes and seminars. Finally, I like to think that David Zilberman would have enjoyed this book.

The chapters included in this volume have been revised from their original presentation and publication forms. The sources are as follows:

Chapter 1 appeared originally as "Peirce Divested for Non-Intimates," *RS/SI: Recherches Sémiotique/Semiotic Inquiry* 7 (1987):19–39. Copyright © 1987 by the Canadian Semiotic Association. Reprinted by permission of *RS/SI*.

Chapter 2 was first presented at the Center for Psychosocial Studies (Chicago) on June 8, 1982. This chapter has been adapted and reprinted by permission of the publisher from "Signs' Place *in Medias Res*: Peirce's Theory of Semiotic Mediation," in *Semiotic Mediation*, ed. Elizabeth Mertz and Richard J. Parmentier (Orlando: Academic Press, 1985). Copyright © 1985 by Academic Press, Inc.

Chapter 3 was first presented at Brandeis University on March 4, 1988. It originally appeared as "Transactional Symbolism in Belauan Mortuary Rites: A Diachronic Study," *Journal of the Polynesian Society* 97 (1988):281–312. Copyright © 1988 by The Polynesian Society. Reprinted by permission of the *Journal of Polynesian Studies*.

Chapter 4 was first presented at The Graduate Center, City University of New York, on March 11, 1988. It appeared originally as "The Political Function of Reported Speech: A Belauan Example," in *Reflexive Language: Reported Speech and Metapragmatics*, ed. John A. Lucy (Cambridge: Cambridge University Press, 1993). Copyright © 1993 by Cambridge University Press. Reprinted by permission of Cambridge University Press.

Chapter 5 appeared originally as "Tropical Semiotics: Global, Local, and Discursive Contexts of Symbolic Obviation," *Semiotica* 79(1/2):167–95. Copyright © 1990 by Mouton.

Chapter 6 was first presented (in two parts) at meetings of the American Anthropological Association on November 19, 1988, and on November 15, 1989. It appeared originally as "The Semiotic Regimentation of Social Life," *Semiotica* 95(3/4): 357–95. Copyright © 1993 by Mouton de Gruyter. Reprinted by permission of Mouton de Gruyter (A Division of Walter de Gruyter & Co.).

Chapter 7 was first presented at the conference "Toward a Comparative Philosophy of Religions" at The Divinity School, University of Chicago, on May 9, 1992.

Chapter 8 was first presented at the symposium "Convention and Knowledge: The Anatomy of Agreement in Contemporary Intellectual Culture" on October 25, 1985, in Northampton, Mass. It appeared originally as "Naturalization of Convention: A Process in Social Theory and in Social Reality," *Comparative Social Research* 11 (1989):279–99. Copyright © 1989 by JAI Press. Reprinted by permission of JAI Press.

Introduction

IN REFLECTING BACK on the monuments of its intellectual heritage, modern semiotic anthropology gazes upon the twin peaks of Charles Sanders Peirce, the American scientist and mathematician, and Ferdinand de Saussure, the Swiss linguist. Among the many ironies of this dual heritage is a disjunction in the work of these theorists between the nature of the *facts* they proposed to explain and the potential of the analytical *tools* they developed. Peirce, in seeking to account for the homologous character of physical and mental realities, developed semiotic tools (especially his notions of indexical signs and chain-like semiosis) that have proved powerful for research into social, historical, and cultural phenomena, the study of which, for the most part, remained only an avocation for Peirce himself. Saussure, while attempting to justify historical linguistics by seeing language as part of the "life of signs in society" (1974:1.48), produced the framework for a linguistic theory that removes language from its social embeddedness. It is this disjunction that motivated me to title this collection of semiotic studies *Signs in Society*, for I follow Saussure in taking systems of signs as the data I am interested in explaining and yet I rely on Peirce for many specific analytical distinctions.

Anthropologists, at least in this country, have generally tended to see in Peirce's semiotics rather than in Saussure's semiology a suitable analog for the conditions and practice of fieldwork in other cultures. As in field research where the ethnographer tries to make sense of the sign systems of another culture through intense, often trying, interpretive abductions, so in Peirce's theory the meaning of a sign consists of the unforeseen succession of interpreting signs that serve to represent a common object (Daniel 1984:42). Peirce offers the possibility that meaning is more than an operation of mental decoding, since semiosis is an open-ended process in which each moment of interpretation alters the field for subsequent interpretations. In contrast, Saussure's theory focuses on the pre-established, fixed code shared equally by ideal speaker and ideal hearer (Ponzio 1984:274–75). And Saussure's effort to establish linguistic value without taking into account positive semantic meaning, the context of utterance, or worldly reference is countered by Peirce's close attention to the indexical anchoring of propositional reference and to the necessity of adequation between representation and reality (Steiner 1981:421).

At the level of the rhetoric of theory, Saussure's reliance on dichotomous oppositions (speech and system, signification and value, synchrony and diachrony, paradigmatic and syntagmatic) suggests the negative divisiveness of "difference," while Peirce's repeated use of trichotomous concepts (sign, object, and interpretant) points toward the positive richness of "mediation." Thus, Saussure has come to represent the status quo, immaterial abstraction, totalizing rules, and false equality, while Peirce stands as the champion of self-critical reflexivity, worldly engagement, and dialogic alterity (Boon 1990:65; Daniel 1989:96; Rochberg-Halton 1985:412).

From the fact that I open this book with an extended discussion of Peirce, however, it should not be concluded that I am an advocate of a "strong" Peircean theory of cultural semiotics. In fact, as the critical comments about "downshifting" and "transparency" in the opening two chapters should make clear, I think that Peirce's own philosophical approach is not well equipped to study the diversity of cultural sign systems, since it is primarily geared toward the understanding of scientific rationality and since its model of progressive consensus bears little resemblance to the cultural phenomena anthropologists encounter in the field, where "truth" is the premise rather than the conclusion of discourse. Rather, my attention to Peirce here is justified because his semiotic writings clarify a series of analytical distinctions in sign operation and structure that can be used as a starting point for cultural analysis. But just as the calculus, the indispensable mathematical tool for modern scientific research, makes no claims in itself about the laws which govern the physical universe, so Peirce's semiotic trichotomies enable the student of cultural codes to "calculate" many critical dimensions of "signs in society" only when applied to actual cultural phenomena. Moreover, I am not convinced of the necessity of bringing to our cultural analysis the entire panoply of Peirce's semiotic distinctions, especially the bewildering complexity of sign typology revealed in the late manuscripts. Trichotomous distinctions among interpretants, for example, may serve some logical or philosophical purpose, but I do not think that cultural analysis is yet prepared to fruitfully utilize them. I am, one could say, a "minimal Peircean."

Readers are, of course, welcome to enter into this book wherever their interests point them, but those who do follow the order of chapters will, I hope, discover that the overall organization constitutes a diagram of its semiotic argument: starting with analytical fundamentals in Part I, moving to ethnographic explications of text and context in Part II, then to the possibility of comparative typology of complex semiotic processes in Part III, and concluding with the broader issues of the pragmatics of social theory in Part IV.

Part I contains two complementary studies of Peirce's semiotic theory: Chapter 1 (Peirce Divested for Nonintimates) is designed to introduce readers to Peirce's fundamental concepts by showing how they form a coherent, interlocking pattern, while Chapter 2 (Peirce's Concept of Semiotic Mediation) traces the historical trajectory of the development of Peirce's ideas, especially his concept of "mediation." These two chapters suggest five specific areas where Peirce provides helpful analytical vocabulary and methodological orientations. First, Peirce's semiotic theory does not privilege spoken language as the "be all and end all" of sign phenomena, since it provides a generalized model in which linguistic and nonlinguistic signs can be included. This contrasts sharply with the fetishism of language which characterizes much semiotic and structuralist thinking in the Sausurrean vein (Márkus 1984:113). Second, Peirce's insistence on the full reality of generals or Thirds provides the ethnographer with a means of avoiding a naive empiricism or physicalism that systematically reduces cultural phenomena to recordable instances of social action. Third, Peirce rejected all forms of Cartesian introspection and argued that thinking, whether carried out within the mind or through the manipulation of artificial signs, requires some level of expressive form to convey information about the object. This notion of the "necessity of expression" moves anthropological theorizing about culture beyond attention to disembodied meanings to the exploration of the ways expressive vehicles constitute a collective "sensibility" (Geertz 1983). Fourth, his recognition that the indexical dimension of semiosis does not necessarily imply that contextually anchored signs are without type-level correlates opens the way for ethnographers to attempt cultural description of the pragmatics of social life. And fifth, Peirce's pathbreaking discovery of the "third trichotomy" (rheme, dicent, argument), involving how signs stipulate the way they are to be interpreted, suggests rich avenues for research into the complex semiotic processes of naturalization, conventionalization, metaphorization, and regimentation, where sign phenomena are inflected with power relations.

The ethnographic studies of Belau in Part II are inspired by the twin Peircean concerns for the structural patterning or "textuality" of signs and the temporal (both diachronic and processual) nature of semiosis. Chapter 3 (Transactional Symbolism in Belauan Mortuary Rites) is an analysis of the historical changes in the indexical and symbolic values of exchange valuables at funerals. It shows that various kinds of objects acquire specific meanings because of the kind of social "paths" followed by the people manipulating them and because of the presupposed modality of exchange relationship these objects realize, whether balanced reciprocity, asymmetrical payments, or transgenerational inheritance. A diachronic perspective, tracing the coding of exchange valuables from the earliest nineteenth-century references to the ethnographic present, reveals that the modern substitution of cash for certain traditional exchange objects makes it difficult for Belauans to conceptualize funerals as a consanguineal "family affair." Chapter 4 (The Political Function of Reported Speech) analyzes an instance of political oratory which tries to generate performative effectiveness by bringing into the context of the speech event highly valued rhetorical forms (such as proverbs) and by organizing them to make ongoing speech an icon or diagram of its political purpose. In this particular case, though, certain cultural assumptions about chiefly rhetoric which the audience brings to the event serve to defuse the speech's political effectiveness. Contextualized performance, as this example shows, entails risks, for the richness of metapragmatic signals in the speech becomes a liability in a culture caught between a traditional norm of chiefly "whispering" and a modern trend toward the explicit display of oratorical prowess.

The chapters in Part III focus on the question: to what degree can complex semiotic processes be used as the basis for cross-cultural typologizing? In other words, are there certain semiotic processes that distinguish kinds of social orders, in much the same way that some social researchers use the notion of modes of production to typologize the world's cultures (Jameson 1982:173)? Chapter 5 (Tropical Semiotics) investigates the process of metaphorization, that is, the construction of innovative tropes grounded in but creatively transforming literal or normative meanings. A reanalysis of tropes found in the myths and exchanges of the Foi people in Papua New Guinea provides the setting to evaluate one particular theoretical model, the theory of "symbolic obviation" developed by Roy Wagner and applied to the Foi by James Weiner. Whereas Wagner and Weiner insist that the cultures of New Guinea differ systematically from Western culture in the way that literal and tropic meanings are related, I challenge this global typologization with the claim that these processes can be found on both sides of the "great divide." This generally negative conclusion about the explanatory power of semiotic typology is supported in Chapter 6 (The Semiotic Regimentation of Social Life) by the three case studies of semiotic "regimentation," that is, the way one level of semiotic structure organizes, controls, or defines another level. I argue here that three kinds of regimentation—textual, institutional, and ideological—do not correspond to types of societies but rather are cross-culturally widespread in phenomena as varied as ritual, tourism, and advertising.

Finally, Part IV goes one step farther to examine the relationship between cultural processes and the theoretical discourse about them. The paradoxical claim advanced in these two concluding chapters is that theoretical discourse, whether in the comparative philosophies of religion discussed in Chapter 7 (Comparison, Pragmatics, and Interpretation) or in the social theories analyzed in Chapter 8 (Naturalization of Convention), shares many of the same semiotic structures and constraints as the cultural data under study. These chapters, following both Peirce's insight into the metasemiotic character of all semiosis and Silverstein's more detailed explication of the metapragmatic function, show that members of a society are constantly interpreting their social interaction and historical experience by constructing interpretive models or accounts that represent, in a limited way, the practices and conventions of the culture. Of course, philosophers and social theorists are extreme cases, since their work attempts to decontextualize the very grounds of their discourse—the philosophers by asserting the absoluteness of their truth claims and the social theorists by naturalizing the source of cultural conventions in extra-semiotic realms. The two examples chosen for study, comparative interpretation and naturalization of convention, reveal an unavoidable tension between the actor's point of view and the analyst's point of view. But since both decontextualization and naturalization are familiar cultural phenomena, the conclusion can be drawn that theoretical discourse is itself a cultural phenomenon subject to textual forms, pragmatic rules, and complex semiotic processes. This conclusion should not, however, be taken as a rejection of the possibility of comparative research but as a reminder that scholarly discourse can never escape its social groundedness.

Like a good Peircean diagrammatic sign, the organization of this volume is intended to represent its overall semiotic argument, beginning with the explication of its analytical foundations, followed by the study of the tension between text and context, then moving to the issue of comparative typology of complex semiotic processes, and concluding with the pragmatics of theoretical discourse. I have intentionally avoided programmatic discussion of the "semiotics of culture," not only because such position papers abound (Z. Bauman 1968; Boon 1982; Eco 1975; Herzfeld 1986; Mertz 1985; Posner 1988, 1989; Schwimmer 1977; Singer 1984; Winner 1988) but also because I believe that better theorizing must await additional semiotically informed ethnographic research. To the degree that these essays are effective in persuading others of the virtues of practicing a semiotic approach to cultural analysis, the volume will become, for its readers, an enacted indexical icon.

PART I

Foundations of Peircean Semiotics

1 | Peirce Divested for Nonintimates

> Truth as it walks abroad is always clothed in figures of which it divests itself
> for none but its intimates.
> —Charles Sanders Peirce (MS 634:18–19, 1909)

Sign, Object, and Interpretant

THE SEMIOTIC THEORY of C. S. Peirce (1839–1914) is an attempt to explain
the cognitive process of acquiring scientific knowledge as a pattern of communicative activity in which the dialogic partners are, indifferently, members of a
community or sequential states of a single person's mind.[1] In linking the acquisition of knowledge to the structure of communication, Peirce fuses together the
two poles of the classical semiotic heritage, the epistemologically focused tradition that studies the *semeion* or "natural" or "indicative sign" and the linguistically grounded tradition that studies the *symbolon* or "conventional symbol."[2]
He accomplishes this fusion by arguing that there is no inherent incompatibility
between logical inference through the manipulation of signs, which was the primary concern of the *semeion* tradition of the Stoics, for example, and the mediated communication of meaning by means of conventional symbols, a basic
concern of the *symbolon* tradition as expressed in Aristotle's *On Interpretation*
and *Poetics*.

For Peirce this knowledge-communication process involves a relationship of
progressive adequation between two fundamentally opposed elements, "objects"
and "signs." All knowledge at a given cognitive or historical moment must be
about something with which the knower is already acquainted to some degree
and in some respect. Opposed to this presupposed object are forms of representation (verbal, graphic, gestural, etc.) which stand for, substitute for, or exhibit
the object in such a way that the next stage of comprehension will consist of a
further developed representation of the same object. For Peirce the class of phenomena which can function as signs is extremely broad, including "pictures,
symptoms, words, sentences; books, libraries, signals, orders of command, mi-
croscopes, legislative representatives, musical concertos, performances of these,
in short, whatever is adapted to transmitting to a person an impression that vir-
tually emanates from something external to itself" (MS 634:17–18).[3] For our

cognitions to involve true knowledge, however, object and sign must be connected in such a way that the former "determines"—specifies or specializes—the character of the latter which represents it. So there must be some kind of principled linkage or reason, what Peirce calls the "ground," between the two if the sign is to become a mediate realization of the object in this process of constantly developing knowledge-communication.

There are, thus, two opposed yet interlocking vectors involved in semiosis, the vector of determination from object to sign and the vector of representation from sign to object. If these vectors are brought into proper relation, then knowledge of objects through signs is possible: "I shall endeavor consistently to employ the word 'object', namely, to mean that which a sign, so far as it fulfills the function of a sign, enables one who knows that sign, and knows it as a sign, to know" (MS 599:31–32).

The insertion of the phrase "and knows it as a sign" might seem at first to be introducing an unnecessary complexity into the situation. If a sign displays its object as the object has determined it to be represented for some further interpreting sign, why is it necessary that the knower need not only know the sign but also know it *as* a sign? Peirce's point is a subtle yet crucial one for his entire argument: "A sign does not function as a sign unless it be understood as a sign" (MS 599:32). In other words, two parts of reality might be in a relationship of mutual determination and representation, but unless the knower had some independent knowledge of this fact, there would be no sense in which one of the parts could function as a sign of the other part *for* this interpreter. So signs must be interpreted in order to be signs, but their "significant character which causes them to be so interpreted" (MS 462:86), namely, the ground, is the basis for this interpretation, when it occurs.

While I am out golfing the scorecard accidentally falls out of my shirt pocket and flutters several feet to the left; my partner drops bits of grass from her raised hand and carefully observes them flutter to the left. Now, the wind will act to blow both the scorecard and the grass to the left quite apart from my partner's interpretation of the movement of the grass as a sign of the wind direction so as to aim her tee shot with the proper compensation. In this elementary semiotic situation, the relationship between the object (the wind blowing in a certain direction) and the sign (the grass blowing in a certain direction) is useful only to the golfer who is already acquainted with the object (that is, that there is this physical phenomenon of wind) and who further understands the ground involved in the wind-grass connection, namely, a combination of physical connectedness between wind and grass, what Peirce calls "indexicality," and of formal resemblance between wind direction and grass direction, what Peirce calls "iconicity."

The importance of this point is that, for Peirce, the vectors of determination and representation are each more complex than suggested initially. Determination does not just flow from object to sign but from the object *through* the sign to some further action or mental representation, what Peirce terms the "inter-pretant," which is thus mediately determined by the same object (CP 6.347). The interpretant is the translation, explanation, meaning, or conceptualization of the sign-object relation in a subsequent sign representing the same object; a sign which is highly determined is one which offers little "latitude of interpretation" (MS 283:136) for the translating sign. In the golfing example, my partner's tee shot will be determined, that is, causally influenced, by the wind direction, but to the degree that her shot is directed by an aim corrected *because* of the knowl-edge afforded through the falling grass, the shot is mediatedly determined by the wind. Peirce's frequent metaphor for this mediate determination is skewing or slanting, so that the effect of the object operates on the interpreting sign through the mediating role of the sign.

What about the vector of representation? If the falling grass is known "as a sign," then the tee shot will also be a representation, but not simply of the phys-ical fact of wind direction (though the shot will, of course, be acted upon by the wind). It will display or exhibit—perhaps for the golfers waiting to tee off next—the complex semiotic relationship of "taking account of the wind." In other words, what is actually represented is the linkage or ground relating the wind and the grass: or, the object becomes the "grass taken semiotically." Thus, the vector of representation is also more complex than originally stated, since each subsequent representation in the semiotic chain represents the prior object-sign relation, taken itself as a higher-level semiotic object.

Symbols and Legisigns

The next step Peirce takes in the argument is truly revolutionary. He postu-lates that there is a kind of sign in which the ground between object and sign would not exist at all unless interpreted by a subsequent sign to be of some kind. Recall the previous example: the wind continues to determine the direction of falling grass whether or not we read it as a sign; when interpreted semiotically, the ground is understood to be the causal patterning of grass direction by wind direction. To repeat, the grass would not function as a sign unless interpreted semiotically, but *when* interpreted the interpretation is based on the indepen-dently existing grounds between object and sign (that is, the indexicality and iconicity). Now consider the example of the word *book*, a linguistic sign standing for a class of objects consisting (roughly) of printed pages bound together and found in libraries. What is the ground between this particular phonic shape and this particular class of objects? In what sense does this class of objects determine any of the identifying properties found in the word as a sign? Peirce's solution to these question is his concept of the "symbol," a kind of complex semiotic entity in which there is an irreducibly triadic relation among the sign, the object, and the interpretant such that the sign and object would not be in any particular relationship if not for their being represented *as* being so related. There is no reason inherent in the nature of the phonic form *book* why it should be appropriate for referring to this class of objects (indeed, other languages equally successfully use other linguistic forms), nor is there any physical connection to transmit the vector of determination from object to sign. A symbol is, thus, a fully "conventional" sign that "represents its object solely by virtue of being represented to represent it by the interpretant which it determines" (MS 599:43).

Our everyday experience as speakers of a language confirms this. A person who does not know a foreign language is able to hear the sounds of that language but has no grasp of the meanings of words or sentences and cannot utter sounds in functionally appropriate ways. So for linguistic signs, all very good examples of Peircean symbols, the interpretant consists of the rules of the relatively invariant linguistic coding shared by members of the language community. *Book* has the meaning it does for speakers of English only because the language community accepts this convention. Contrast this example with the previous example of the falling grass: if the golfer fails to recognize (to the detriment of his or her score!) the semiotic function of this sign, the grass will continue to be blown by the wind. But if a community of speakers does not accept a convention according to which *book* stands for bound printed pages found in libraries, this particular form has absolutely no status as a meaningful entity of any sort. As Peirce explains, symbols are

> those signs which are made to be signs, and to be precisely the signs that they are, neither by possessing any decisive qualities [i.e., icons] nor by embodying effects of any special causation [i.e., indices], but merely by the certainty that they will be interpreted as signs, and as just such and such signs. (MS 298:12–13)

As is clear from this quotation, Peirce envisioned the triad of icon, index, and symbol to form a nested hierarchical set. The internal construction of this set can best be understood from four perspectives. The first concerns the requirements for completeness found in the three members of the set. An icon "is fitted to be a sign by virtue of possessing in itself certain qualities which it would equally possess if the interpretant and the object did not exist at all" (MS 7:14); without its object an icon could not function as a sign, but as a sign it has the characteristics it does independently of any reason or force exerted by the object or by the interpretant. Next, an index has the qualities it does apart from its interpretant but not from its object, which must be in a relation of spatiotemporal contiguity with it. And finally a symbol would not have any of its characteristics if the object or interpretant were subtracted. Thus, the symbol, as a necessarily triadic relation, has the greatest internal complexity of the three signs. A second way of viewing the triad is to compare their respective foregrounded aspects. For an icon the ground appears most prominently; for an index the object attracts our attention; and for a symbol the interpretant is the focus of interest.

Third, the triad corresponds to Peirce's ontological triad of Firstness, Second-ness, and Thirdness, three degrees of reality which he believes exhaust the universe: Firsts are qualitative possibilities; Seconds are reactive objects; and Thirds are necessarily triadic phenomena, including rules, laws, mediations, and representations. The ground of an icon is a First, the ground of an index is a Second, and the ground of a symbol is a Third.[4] And, fourth, we can observe the compositional "syntax" (CP 2.262) of these three kinds of semiotic relations. Every index, in order to convey information, must embody an icon. The falling grass is an index of the wind, but it is also an icon in that the direction of the grass's fall resembles the direction of the wind. (Think of this in these terms: an index directs the mind to some aspect of reality and an icon provides some information about it.) And a symbol must embody an icon and an index, the former to express the information and the latter to indicate the object to which this information pertains.[5]

The postulation of the symbol as requiring the role of the interpretant's imputing a conventional relationship between sign and object introduces a further wrinkle involving the status of the sign itself, that is, viewed apart from the sign-object relation. There appears to be a fundamental difference in status between the action of falling grass and the action of uttering the word *book*, namely, that in the latter case the identity of the sign, as stipulated in the rules of the language, is not dependent upon any particular instance of uttering these sounds. The word I pronounce this morning is the "same" word you pronounce tomorrow; the word printed on the first line of a page is the "same" word when printed on the last line of the page. So linguistic symbols are "general signs," that is, signs which have the identity they have (in this case, specified by the code) independently of any concrete speech events or contextual application. The conventions of a language do not stipulate the meaning of *book* as dependent upon any particular circumstances of someone's using the word in conversation or in writing; and should no one pronounce the word for a year or should someone go around erasing all occurrences of it in written works, the word itself would continue to be part of the language:

> A *symbol* is itself a kind and not a single thing. You can write down the word "star" but that does not make you the creator of the word, nor if you erase it have you destroyed the word. The word lives in the minds of those who use it. Even if they are all asleep, it exists in their memory. (MS 404:45)

Contrast this with the grass example, where the sign is an actual physical event and is not an instance of a more general representational form.

Peirce developed a technical vocabulary to describe these phenomena: a sign which is an occurring event and for which "accidents of existence make it a sign" (MS 339:248r) is a "sinsign" (a sin-gular thing) or "token"; and a sign which is a "definitely significant Form" (CP 4.537) for producing and interpreting instances is a "legisign" (from the Latin word for "law") or a "type." The context-specific pronunciation of a word is a "replica," that is, a special kind of sinsign, namely, one which corresponds to a "type." It is important to see the peculiarity of linguistic utterances. Speakers and hearers cannot communicate with each other without producing physical events or sinsigns, yet these instances would have no meaning were it not for the system of conventional understanding operating at the type level. (Of course, in everyday conversation speakers often assume that the token utterance is directly linked to the contextually realized linguistic meaning.)

> A *Legisign* is a law that is a Sign. This law is usually established by men. Every conventional sign is a legisign. It is not a single object, but a general type which, it has been agreed, shall be significant. Every legisign signifies through an instance of its application, which may be termed a *Replica* of it. Thus, the word "the" will usually occur from fifteen to twenty-five times on a page. It is in all these occurrences one and the same word, the same legisign. Each single instance of it is a Replica. The Replica is a Sinsign. Thus, every Legisign requires Sinsigns. But these are not ordinary Sinsigns, such as are peculiar occurrences that are regarded as significant. Nor would the Replica be significant if it were not for the law which renders it so. (CP 2.246)

Despite these precise terminological distinctions it is easy to confuse a sinsign and a replica (which is a special kind of sinsign). Compare a footprint made in the sand and an utterance of the word *book*. Both are actually occurring events, both have the potential for functioning semiotically, and both are subject to regular repetition with similar significance. What, then, is the important difference? (It is not, by the way, that the footprint would retain the character it has even if no one interpreted it as a sign. This is very true, but has to do with its being an index rather than a symbol.) It is that the footprint is an actual phenomenon which, in certain contexts, can be used as a sign, whereas the utterance of a word could not possibly be interpreted as the sign that it is without the interpreter's recognition of its corresponding type: a footprint is *possibly* a sign; an utterance of a word is *necessarily* a sign. One interesting implication of this is that, while not all singular phenomena (what Peirce labels Seconds because they are essentially dyadic or reactive in character) are signs, *all* general phenomena—laws, habits, associations, evolutionary tendencies, abstractions, rules, logical arguments, and conceptions—are fundamentally semiotic entities.

A word, or any symbol, is thus a conventional sign in two interlocking senses. First, the semiotic identity of a given spoken or written instance of language is governed by a rule for recognizing each occurrence as a replica of a linguistic type, rather than as merely incoherent babble or meaningless scribbling. This rule of recognition gives users of a sign system the ability to evaluate various occurring phenomena to determine which are to be classified as proper signs. Of course, there needs to be a certain degree of flexibility built into this rule, however, since each replica of a word will be in some respects different—speakers talk with different pitches, accents, intonation patterns, and writers never produce exactly the same shape of handwritten letters. Second, the significance of a symbol is interpretable only because of the prior collective agreement or "habitual acquaintance" (CP 2.329) specifying the sign-object linkage. This imputed ground relating sign and object is provided by a general habit, rule, or disposition embodied in the interpretant. Thus, our ability to utter a linguistic sign on a particular occasion in order to communicate a meaning about some object to someone (or to oneself) presupposes the conventional rule associating sign and object. But note that, in the case of symbols, the sign and object cannot be singular things but must always be general, whether a general sign or legisign or a general object.

An important implication of this intersection of symbols and legisigns is that all symbols are legisigns but not all legisigns are symbols. In other words, all signs which represent their objects solely because they are interpreted to do so must also have the character of governing replicas in actual instances of communication. This is easily understood: a sign which is such because of a conventional ground must itself be of a general rather than a singular character and must also represent a general idea rather than a singular object. But there can be legisigns— signs which function only by governing replicas of themselves—which are not purely conventional. How is this possible? Consider the second-person singular personal pronoun *you*. This clearly is a legisign, since speakers of English recognize the same word in all the various contextual instances of saying *you*, but this legisign represents its object by virtue of a less-than-symbolic ground: *you* refers to whomever the speaker is addressing, an object which by this rule must be co-present in every successfully referring act of uttering a replica of *you*. There is a built-in indexical dimension in the meaning of *you*, a fact which can be quickly tested. Open a dictionary to the word *you* and ask: what is the object represented by this general sign? The answer is: that depends on whom the speaker is talking to when uttering a replica of the word. As Peirce observes, these indexical legisigns "do not possess the generality of purely conventional signs" (MS 748).

If all symbols are general signs, which signify their general objects by virtue of a general interpretant, it must be the case that all three components must be equally symbolic: the object of a symbol is a symbol and the interpretant of a symbol is a symbol. And if this is so, then there is no such thing as an isolated symbol. As Figure 1.1 illustrates, Symbol 1 has Symbol 2 for its interpretant, and this Interpretant 1 must in turn function as a symbol for its Interpretant 2, and so on infinitely. A similar expansion is found in the opposite direction: Object 1 of Symbol 1 is a symbol, so that it also stands for some general Object 2 by virtue of being represented to do so by its Interpretant 3 (which is identical with Symbol 1!). Thus, sign, object, and interpretant are not three distinct kinds of semiotic

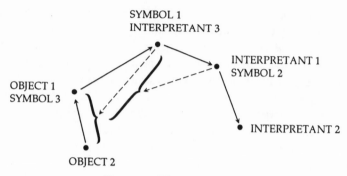

Figure 1.1. The sign relation

entities; they are dimensions of semiotic functioning. (Much confusion can be avoided if Peirce's notion of the object is not conflated with the Saussurean notion of the "signified" concept or "meaning." In Peirce's model the object is what the sign is about and the meaning is the "significative effect of a sign" [CP 5.473] embodied in the interpretant.)

The key point is that every symbol necessarily involves "two infinite series, the one back toward the object, the other forward toward the interpretant" (MS 599:38). Not only is there no ultimate object which could be represented in some symbol and not itself a representation, but there is no ultimate interpretant. Peirce clearly recognizes the almost incredible ramification of this theory: symbols are essentially alive. Not in the sense of having breath and locomotion but in the sense of having an evolving, growing, developing nature:

> Symbols grow. They come into being by development out of other signs, particularly from icons, or from mixed signs partaking of the nature of icons and symbols. We think only in signs. These mental signs are of mixed nature; the symbol-parts of them are called concepts. If a man makes a new symbol, it is by thoughts involving concepts. So it is only out of symbols that a new symbol can grow. *Omne symbolum de symbolo.* A symbol, once in being, spreads among the peoples. In use and in experience, its meaning grows. Such words as *force, law, wealth, marriage,* bear for us very different meanings from those they bore to our barbarous ancestors. (CP 2.302)

Peirce feels that this potential for growth or self-development in symbols is the central way in which reality and representation resemble each other, since both natural laws and logical conventions govern, respectively, the actions of objects and the course of ideas in reasoning, in essentially the same triadic manner.

Symbols appear to be wonderful entities indeed. But there is something extremely puzzling about Peirce's concept of symbol. A symbol, by definition, exists as a sign only because of the interpretant, which imputes a conventional relationship between sign and object. But, for Peirce, the object, through the medium of the sign, *determines* the interpretant. How can a symbol determine, that is, specify, an interpreting sign at the same time that it presupposes this same interpretant? Peirce himself was very conscious of this seeming paradox:

A *Symbol* differs from both of these types of sign [icon and index] inasmuch as it represents its object solely by virtue of being represented to represent it by the interpretant which it determines. But how can this be, it will be asked. How can a thing become a sign of an object to an interpretant sign which itself determines by virtue of the recognition of that, its own creation? (MS 599:43)

The solution to this paradox, like the solution to so many apparent paradoxes, is that the vector of determination operates at a lower logical level than the vector of representation: the interpretant represents the sign-object relation *as* capable of determining the interpretant that it in fact does. Peirce's own illustration is clear: a particular form of logical argumentation is a complex sign which represents the truth; but only when an interpreting mind acknowledges that argumentation *as* a sign of the truth, does it indeed function as a sign of that truth. An argument that, for its interpreters, fails to represent the truth is not a sign at all.

Language and Logic

Peirce rejects the assumption that the "law of thought" (MS 693:184) was stipulated by the grammatical or syntactical properties of European or "Aryan" languages, especially Greek and Latin (NEM 4:171). The subject (what Peirce prefers to call the "object") of a sentence need not be coded by the nominative case but appears in some languages, Gaelic for instance, in an oblique case; many "non-Aryan" languages display a marked paucity of "common nouns" (NEM 3/2:843) and use, rather, expanded verbal formulations in the predicate. And, most strikingly, the copula *is*, enshrined by Western logicians as an essential component of the categorical proposition, did not even appear normatively in Latin until the late Middle Ages. Yet people speaking languages without common nouns or copulas presumably "had probably not spoken in earlier times entirely without thinking" (MS 693:186).

Peirce attempts to replace these logocentric assumptions with an alternative approach to the relationship between thinking and expression that shows how different languages can be compared in terms of more fundamental semiotic functions which language shares with other sign systems: "The study of languages ought to be based upon a study of the necessary conditions to which signs must conform in order to fulfill their function as signs" (MS 693:188). This foundational science, termed by Peirce "speculative semeiotic," should not adopt the unreflective prejudice of language speakers—a person is, after all, "an animal that has command of some syntactical language" (MS 659:10)—who assume that language, or more accurately, their language is essential for thinking.[6] For Peirce, some "form of expression" is necessary for rational thought, but articulate or written language need not be elevated to this position of priority:

> It might be supposed that although such a study cannot draw any principles from the study of languages, that linguistics might still afford valuable suggestions to it. Upon trial, I have not found it to be so. Languages have never furnished me with a single new idea; they have at most only afforded examples of truths I had already ascertained by *a priori* reasoning. (MS 693:190–92)

Though human languages can well illustrate semiotic principles discovered by other means (primarily, for Peirce, logical analysis by means of his Existential Graphs), they must be treated with healthy suspicion. Precisely because language is "man's instinctive vehicle of thought" (MS 654:4), reasoning has a tendency to become "trammelled by the usages of speech" (MS 654:3). Even logicians have fallen victim to the "pernicious idleness of consulting ordinary language" (MS 559):

> I do not, for my part, regard the usages of language as forming a satisfactory basis for logical doctrine. Logic, for me, is the study of the essential conditions to which signs must conform in order to function as such. How the constitution of the human mind may compel men to think is not the question; and the appeal to language appears to me to be no better than an unsatisfactory method of ascertaining psychological facts that are of no relevancy to logic. (NEM 4:245)

Part of the danger involved in a logician's taking language as a guide is that there is a tendency to confuse the proposition itself with particular "lingual expressions" (NEM 4:248) of it. A logical proposition is a legisign, not a replica of a sign. It is the same proposition whether it "happens to have a replica in writing, in oral speech, or in silent thought" (NEM 4:248), or whether "one selfsame thought may be carried upon the vehicle of English, German, Greek, or Gaelic" (MS 298:7), that is, whatever the *form* of instances of its expression. And it is also the same proposition regardless of the particular purposive *function* intended or accomplished by its instantiation: "One and the same proposition may be affirmed, denied, judged, doubted, inwardly inquired into, put as a question, wished, asked for, effectively commanded, taught, or merely expressed, and does not thereby become a different proposition" (NEM 4:248). Furthermore, the symbols constituting language are logically defective in that they are involved in what we would today call "conversational pragmatics." As Peirce notes, "As little as possible is spoken, as much as possible is left to implication, imagination and belief" (NEM 3:140).

Abstracted from both expressive form and purposive function, a proposition is a complex symbol which represents to its interpretant that the qualities or characteristics signified in the predicate portion pertain to existing objects, the same objects denoted in the subject portion. These two components of a proposition can be classified as icons and indices: the predicate is an "image" and the subject is a "label," and when joined together in a full proposition these parts convey real information about the world, namely, that these qualities "iconized" apply truly to the objects indexed: "But the particular proposition asserts that, with sufficient means, in that universe would be found an object to which the subject term would be applicable, and to which further examination would provide that the image called up by the predicate was also applicable" (CP 2.369).

This should seem completely impossible! Having claimed in unequivocal language that a proposition is a symbolic legisign, that is, an abstract type distinct from its various modes of formal realization and contextual functioning, which represents its general object only on the basis of being interpreted to do so, Peirce then insists that a proposition must carry information about the world, that it is subject to being judged true or false. The path out of this perplexity lies in Peirce's observation that, although signs are related to their objects in diverse ways—by formal resemblance (icons), by contextual contiguity (indices), and by conventional attribution (symbols)—these same signs can determine their interpretants to represent them as being related to their objects *as other than* they are in fact related. We know that words and propositions are both symbols (and thus legisigns); but they differ radically in how they specify their interpretants to represent the relation with their respective objects: a single term (a common noun, for example) determines its interpretant to represent it as being merely an icon of its object (*book* or *is black* refer to any possible thing that has the qualities expressed by the sign), while a proposition, *the book is black*, determines its interpretant to represent it as being merely an index of its object. Now this is not to deny that the interpretant still represents both a term and a proposition to be conventionally related to their objects; the claim being made is that, in addition to this level of representation, interpretants have the power to apprehend semiotic grounds as being other than they are. And, of course, Peirce invented a set of technical terms for these distinctions: a "rheme" is a sign which is apprehended to be an icon; a "dicent" or "dicisign" is a sign which is apprehended to be an index; and an "argument" is a sign which is apprehended to be a symbol.

Cases in which a sign's actual relation to its object is identical with that relation as apprehended by the interpretant are easy to grasp but rather uninteresting. A weathervane is an index of its object, the wind, because it is in direct physical connection with it; a weathervane grasped semiotically as a dicent conveys the information it does only because it is apprehended to be in this relation of causal connection. For a farmer to interpret a weathervane as being merely iconic, that is, as a rheme, would be to form an interpretant representing the weathervane as standing for some possible wind condition—perhaps resembling yesterday's breeze. Obviously, this farmer could not rely on the weathervane to provide reliable information about the arrival of the storm clouds hovering in the western sky.

In contrast, cases in which a sign's actual relation to its object differs from the ground apprehended by the interpretant are fascinating precisely because they suggest the possibility for creativity built into semiotic processes. Take the linguistic sign *the king is dead*. Though clearly composed of purely conventional symbols, this complex sign is interpreted as a proposition when the subject, *the king*, is interpreted as referring to or denoting a particular person (e.g., Elvis, Louis XIV) with which the interpreter is in prior acquaintance; and the predicate, *is dead*, is interpreted to apply to that object. And the noun phrase *a tall man*, though a symbolic legisign, is also a rheme, since it is apprehended as an icon of its object (*the tall man* would, of course, be a dicent symbol).

And the argument, being a symbol taken as a symbol, is for Peirce the highest kind of semiotic entity. A series of propositions in syllogistic reasoning is an argument because the interpretant represents the syllogism as being related to its object by virtue of "the law that the passage from all such premises to such conclusions tends to the truth" (CP 2.263). As a symbol that compels an interpreting representation to represent it as a fully conventional sign, the argument is a particularly important feature of cultural phenomena that call attention to their semiotic shape or that impose constraints on the ability of members of a society to generate their own interpretations of messages (see Chapter 6):

> The argument is a representamen which does not leave the interpretant to be determined as it may by the person to whom the symbol is addressed, but separately represents what is the interpreting representation that it is intended to determine. (CP 5.76)

Thus, rheme, dicent, and argument form a logical sequence:

> Fully to understand and assimilate the symbol "a tall man," it is by no means requisite to understand it to relate, or to profess to relate, to a real Object. Its Interpretant, therefore, does not represent it as a genuine Index; so that the definition of the Dicisign does not apply to it. It is impossible here fully to go into the examination of whether the analysis given does justice to the distinction between propositions and arguments. But it is easy to see that the proposition purports to intend to compel its Interpretant to refer to its real Object, that is represents itself as an Index, while the argument purports to intend not compulsion but action by means of comprehensible generals, that is, represents its character to be specially symbolic. (CP 2.321)

It might appear that, in using English-language examples to illustrate the logical structure of the proposition, we have violated Peirce's firm warning against following the model of linguistic usage. But a moment's reflection on these examples will show that all linguistic usages, whether words, propositions, or arguments, can be reduced to the elementary principles of their semiotic functioning because they share these principles with all semiotic phenomena and not because any particular language's grammatical, syntactical, or lexical conventions are direct expressions of these principles. In fact, Peirce often remarks on the necessity of penetrating beneath these surface conventions in order to see logical regularity struggling to emerge. For example, diverse linguistic categories need to be reconceptualized in semiotic terms: proper names, personal pronouns (*you*), demonstratives (*that*), and locatives (*here*) are all "genuine indices" (CP 2.305). Many distinctions which would be essential for a perfectly logical language are missing entirely in many languages:

> If a logician had to construct a language *de novo*—which he actually has almost to do—he would naturally say, I shall need prepositions to express the temporal relations of *before, after*, and *at the same time with*, I shall need prepositions to express the spatial relations of *adjoining, containing, touching*, of *in range with*, of *near to, far from*, of *to the right of, to the left of, above, below, before, behind*, and I shall need prepositions to express motions into and out of these situations. For the rest, I can manage with metaphors. Only if my language is intended for use by people having some great geographical feature related the same way to all of them, as a mountain range, the sea, a great river, it will be desirable to have prepositions signifying situations relatively to that, as *across, seaward*, etc. But when we examine actual languages, it would seem as though they had supplied the place of many of these distinctions by gestures. The Egyptians had no preposition nor demonstrative having any apparent reference to the Nile. Only the Esquimos are so wrapped up in their bearskins that they have demonstratives distinguishing landward, seaward, north, south, east, and west. But examining the cases or prepositions of any actual language we find them a haphazard lot. (CP 2.290n)

Inversely, distinctions overtly expressed in languages often need to be nullified in semiotic analysis: in the proposition *John gives the book to Mary*, the semiotic object is a complex unit consisting of the denoted objects of *John, book, Mary*, despite the different case markings these may have.

If languages are such imperfect illustrations of semiotic functioning, why does Peirce persist in using linguistic examples? The answer to this question lies in the answer to a more general question: why analyze *forms* of expression at all, since they seem inevitably to muck up the logically precise picture? Peirce's answer is that, although "internal signs" (that is, mental ideas) and "external signs" (that is, representations clothed in perceptible forms) do not differ in principle, only the latter offer an opportunity to perform experimental manipulations.

Adopting as his maxim, "The function of reason is to trace out in the real world analogues of logical relations" (MS 278[a]:9), Peirce investigates the nature of semiotic relations in both naturally occurring and artificially constructed forms, and he argues that "the preference among different forms of signs should be given that one which is most easily examined, manipulated, preserved, and anatomized" (MS 637:30). On these criteria, particular natural languages present obvious difficulties (noted above), and human language in general seems to be a poor model: spoken language is spoiled by showing disparate significances of its forms in different contexts and having systemic ambiguities in its constituency hierarchies, and written language as well is too "encumbered with sensuous accessories" (NEM 3/1:270) to be useful to the logician. Even when language is revealing it is so to the degree that specific formal characteristics are ignored:

> A sign . . . perfectly conforms to the definition of a medium of communication. It is determined by the object, but in no other respect than goes to enable it to act upon the interpreting quasi-mind [the interpretant]; . . . other than that of determining it as if the object itself had acted upon it. Thus, after an ordinary conversation, a wonderfully perfect kind of sign-functioning, one knows what information or suggestion has been conveyed, but will be utterly unable to say in what words it was conveyed, and often will think it was conveyed in words, when if fact it was only conveyed in tones or in facial expressions. (MS 283:130–31)

What is called for is a system of signs which transparently convey the determination of their objects to their interpretants. If the primary function of signs is to be a "medium of communication," they fulfill that function more perfectly if the interpretant is determined to represent the complex semiotic object as if the mediating forms of representation were not there at all. Peirce does believe, however, that the "garment of expression" (NEM 3/1:406) can never be completely removed revealing "naked thought itself," since that would imply the collapse of fully triadic semiotic relationships: "The meaning of a representation can be nothing but a representation. In fact, it is nothing but the representation itself conceived as stripped of irrelevant clothing. But this clothing never can be completely stripped off; it is only changed for something more diaphanous" (CP 1.339).

The Trichotomies

Peirce's distinctions among kinds of signs can be summarized by returning to the elementary model of semiotic relations: a sign stands for an object in some respect to some interpretant. If signs are analyzed in themselves as they belong to one of Peirce's three degrees of reality (Firstness, Secondness, Thirdness), one can distinguish

(1) qualisigns, qualities or Firsts that are signs,
(2) sinsigns, existent objects or events, Seconds, that are signs, and
(3) legisigns, general laws or regularities, Thirds, that are signs.

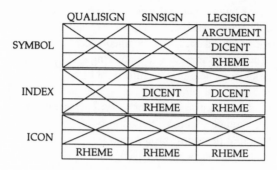

Figure 1.2. The three trichotomies

But signs can also be considered in terms of their relations to their objects, in other words, in terms of their respective grounds. On this criterion, Peirce also distinguishes

(1) icons, signs whose grounds involve formal resemblance,
(2) indices, signs whose grounds involve actual connection, and
(3) symbols, signs whose grounds involve conventional associations.

Finally, signs can be viewed in terms of how they are represented in their interpretants:

(1) rhemes are signs whose interpretants represent them as being icons,
(2) dicents are signs whose interpretants represent them as being indices, and
(3) arguments are signs whose interpretants represent them to be symbols.

Each of these sets of triple divisions Peirce calls a "trichotomy" (see Savan 1987–88). And these three trichotomies intersect in interesting ways so that not all twenty-seven possible combinations are realized semiotically. In fact, Peirce claims that the logical interaction of the three trichotomies yields only ten signs (CP 2.254–64), as shown in Figure 1.2.

Since symbols require interpretants to provide their grounds, they must be legisigns; so six possibilities on the top row are automatically eliminated. Similarly, since Firsts cannot have any degree of internal complexity, they cannot be indices or symbols; so six possibilities are eliminated from the left column. Peirce claims, further, that a sign cannot determine an interpretant to represent it as having a more complex ground than it actually has. Thus, an icon cannot be apprehended semiotically as an index or as a symbol; that is, an icon cannot be a dicent or an argument (thus blocking out six additional possibilites in the bottom row). Similarly, an index cannot be apperceived as a symbol; that is, an index cannot be an argument (blocking out two possibilites in the middle row). The resulting ten sign possibilities are given below, along with a concrete illustration for each class:

(1) (rhematic iconic) qualisign; feeling of red
(2) (rhematic) iconic sinsign; individual diagram
(3) rhematic indexical sinsign; spontaneous cry: *ouch!*
(4) dicent (indexical) sinsign; telephone ring
(5) (rhematic) iconic legisign; architectural order
(6) rhematic indexical legisign; type of shout: *hello!*
(7) dicent indexical legisign; vendor's cry: *beer here!*
(8) rhematic symbol (legisign); the noun *book*
(9) dicent symbol (legisign); proposition
(10) argument (symbolic legisign); syllogism

Placing certain words in parentheses indicates that they are not essential in defining a sign class because of certain logical implications (identical with the principles of exclusion used above). Thus a qualisign, being a First, must be an icon, and being an icon it can only be a rheme. Similarly at the other extreme of the hierarchy, an argument must be a symbol, and being a symbol it must be a legisign.

That this list of sign classes was generated by a method of exclusion should not be taken to imply that the resulting types do not have positive connections and interactions as well. Peirce specifies three such positive linkages (though not with these labels): replication, composition, and downshifting. Replication refers to the necessity that all legisigns generate replicas of themselves (in fact, to be a legisign is to be something that produces tokens of its type). If a sign is classed as an indexical legisign, for example, we know that its replica will be classed as an indexical sinsign—although, as noted previously, this replica will not have identical properties with the "run of the mill" indexical sinsign (e.g., telephone ring). Composition refers to the internal complexity of certain sign classes such that they necessarily contain or embody lower-ranking signs. The dicent symbol, a proposition for example, is built up of two rhemes, a rhematic symbol (common noun) as well as a rhematic indexical legisign (demonstrative pronoun), the former "to express its information" (CP 2.262) and the latter "to indicate the subject of that information." Finally, downshifting refers to the tendency of certain of the classes to be systematically apperceived by their interpretants as being lower-ranking signs. A rhematic indexical legisign will regularly be interpreted as if it were only a (rhematical) iconic legisign. The *that* in the phrase *that book*, though interpretable at all only because it is in proximity to its object, the book being denoted, functions to determine an interpretant which represents it as being related to this book by virtue of formal resemblance, thus not as picking out a particular object (the task of a dicent) but as stipulating a possible class of objects sharing the same feature, namely, whatever might possibly be "relatively far from speaker." In order to distinguish regular members of a sign class from other variants or varieties that fall into this class because of these processes of replication, composition, or downshifting, Peirce sometimes calls these latter instances "degenerate" signs—a term derived from mathematics rather than from morals.

An important implication of Peirce's third trichotomy (rheme, dicent, argument) for historical analysis is that the identical representamen can shift ranks in different periods. Jappy (1984:23–25) gives a particularly clear example of this: for a nonspecialist modern museum goer, the presence of ultramarine pigment on a Quattrocento altarpiece painting of a Madonna is interpreted as a rhematic iconic sinsign, that is, a sign that is a particular occurrence, that stands for its dark blue object by resemblance, and that can only be interpreted as representing some possible original object. For the contemporary viewer, however, this pigment generated several additional interpretants: knowing that this pigment was rare and expensive, the contemporary viewer would interpret its presence as a dicent indexical sinsign pointing to the wealthy patron who commissioned the work; and sensitive both to the place of ultramarine in the overall color code of the period and to the position of particular shades of ultramarine, the contemporary viewer would interpret the pigment as a replica of a dicent indexical legisign, since the color is part of a system of general regularities. Note that, in this example, the passage of time corresponds to a *lowering* of the rank of the sign, as the richness of "collateral knowledge" available to the viewer decreases.

Cultural symbols with embedded iconic properties are frequently interpreted as less than fully symbolic, that is, as "naturalized" signs that inherently, rather than conventionally, signal their object (Herzfeld 1992:69; Lotman 1985:56). One limitation of Peirce's view is that it does not allow for the possibility of the opposite to happen, the "upshifting" of signs as a result of the structure of interpretants. But this is precisely what happens in cases of the "conventionalizing" of relatively motivated signs (see Chapter 8).

Always sensitive to the difficulties involved in grasping these interlocking regularities among sign classes, Peirce tries to ease the student's mind: "It is a nice problem to say to what class a given sign belongs; since all the circumstances of the case have to be considered. But it is seldom requisite to be very accurate; for if one does not locate the sign precisely, one will easily come near enough to its character for any ordinary purpose of logic" (CP 2.265).

Scientific Knowledge and Cultural Belief

For Peirce, semiotic relations are anchored in the linkage between signs as constituents of cognitions and external reality, the character of the world "whatever you or I or any man or men may think of them to be" (MS 296:18). This linkage is not a static relationship, since human knowledge and belief about reality must be acquired through inferential processes in which signs and their objects come into truthful relation: "The whole effort in investigation is to make our beliefs represent the realities" (MS 379). Reasoning involves coming to believe true representations of reality. It is semiotically mediated in that all thought takes place through the medium of signs and it is realistically grounded in that the most perfect representations are those that depict reality so clearly that the semiotic means are not distorting factors.

The attainment of true opinion is a communal activity, since the inferential process arrives at "settled belief" among scientifically logical minds. But if the truth is what people ultimately agree on, it is not because a social group has collectively decided upon some belief but rather because a scientifically rigorous community of minds will ultimately agree on the representation of reality. So, that generations of people believe something to be true counts for nothing if "sufficient experience and reasoning" show this belief to be false. In other words, truth as the "final settled opinion" arrived at through scientific rationality is a future-oriented notion (in distinction to the past-orientation of historically inherited cultural beliefs). And yet truths are, in a sense, "predestinated" to reach the point they do in fact reach: "The method we pursue or the action of our will, may hasten or retard the time when this conclusion is reached; but it is fated to emerge at last. And every cognition consists in what investigation is destined to result in" (MS 379).

> So that the object of a final settled opinion not merely coincides with the truth, but is the truth by the definition of words. The truth is independent of what we may think about it and the object of an opinion is a creation of thought which is entirely dependent on what that opinion is. It exists by virtue of that opinion. There seems to be a contradiction here. But the secret of the matter is this. The final settled opinion is not any particular cognition, in such and such a mind, at such and such a time, although an individual opinion may chance to coincide with it. If an opinion coincides with the final settled opinion, it is because the general current of investigation will not affect it. The object of that individual opinion is whatever is thought at that time. But if anything else than that one thing is thought, the object of that opinion changes and it thereby ceases to coincide with the object of the final opinion which does not change. The perversity or ignorance of mankind may make this thing or that to be held for true, for any number of generations, but it can not affect what would be the result of sufficient experience and reasoning. (W 3:79)

Peirce consistently rejected the possibility of acquiring firm, scientific knowledge of anything nonreal, namely, whatever possesses the attributes it does solely because of the opinion of "any person or definite existent group" (NEM 3/2:881). The real does, however, correspond to the object of the opinion of a community if that opinion is the result of sufficient rational discussion. Of course, *that* a person or group has a false or nonsensical idea can be a true fact about that person or group. Peirce is quick to point out, however, that reality is not confined to the universe of existent objects (Seconds) but must include as well the class of *ens rationis* or "creations of thought" (Thirds). These general entities, including abstractions in metaphysics and linguistic types, are not "fictions" (NEM 3/2:918)—contrary to the physicalist or behaviorist prejudice against them (N 1:35)—because they are the "inevitable result of sufficient thought" (NEM 3/2:918).

Peirce's scientific realism, at first glance, leaves little room for the study of cultural units, categories, or entities which depend on the historically transmitted beliefs of a society and for which truth-value is not always relevant. He is careful, however, to indicate that the object of a sign can be real "as far as the action of the Sign is concerned" (MS 634:27), as long as the vector of determination still flows from object to sign:

> The word "witch" is a sign having a "real Object" in the sense in which this phrase is used, namely to mean a supposedly real Object, not the Sign, and in intention or pretension not created by the sign. . . . It is real in the sense in which a dream is a real appearance to a person in sleep, although it be not an appearance of objects that are Real. (MS 634:27)

A more complex example is the legal contract, obviously a social phenomenon dependent upon human agreement at two levels: agreement as to the general nature of binding, valid contracts and agreement between the parties to a particular contract. The issue is whether or not a contract is real, according to Peirce's definition. At first it would appear that the answer is "no," since every contract *depends* upon what people think—a contract is defined as something you must enter into intentionally. As Peirce tentatively concludes, "so that nothing which merely inheres in an agreement can be real" (MS 296). But Peirce proceeds to consider the question in greater depth. Imagine two persons, each dreaming of entering into a contract of identical specification with the other. Clearly these contracts are totally dependent upon the mental states of the persons involved and so would not be real, despite the historical fact of "judges deciding otherwise." So it seems that the contracting parties must come together in a genuine triadic way, such that each party assents to the agreement and, further, recognizes the other's assent as an essential reason for their assent. "I will say that there must be some voluntary, some deliberate molition of some kind, though it be merely mental, in which both parties shall be involved as agents" (MS 296). This contract now appears real, since it exercises an efficient force in coordinating the behavior of the parties according to the terms of the agreement. As Peirce concludes his discussion, "It is thus demonstrated that what is subjectively general is not thereby incapacitated for being real, that is, for holding its characters independently of thoughts of individual minds about its possession of them" (MS 296). This example is extremely important in that it shows how action deriving from social norms or cultural conventions can share Peircean reality—and thus openness to semiotic understanding—with the objects of physical laws and logical reasoning.

2 | Peirce's Concept of Semiotic Mediation

All my notions are too narrow. Instead of Sign," ought I not to say *Medium*?
—Charles Sanders Peirce (MS 339, 1906)

The Fundamental Model of Semiotic Mediation

ONE OF THE most significant contributions to semiotic theory made by Peirce is his conception of scientific epistemology as the study of the logic of signs.[1] For Peirce, human cognition, including sensory perception, emotive feeling, as well as inferential reasoning, involves "internal signs" linked, on the one hand, to each other in an endless series of states of mental "dialogue" and, on the other hand, to external reality represented as objects interacting in ways similar to the interactions among constituents of sign relations. In every mental act some feature of reality, defined as that which is as it is apart from any and all thought about it, is brought into connection with a chain of mental representations that has the unique power of interpreting reality in ways other than it is in itself. But since reality's objects possess the qualities or characteristics they do independently of human representation, the pattern of scientific representation is always "determined" or caused by natural regularities; resulting cognitions are true to the degree that the relations inhering among mental signs match the relations inhering among external signs. There is, to be sure, a world in itself *and* a world as represented, but Peirce's fundamental insight is that these two realms are brought into articulation by the mediating role of signs.

This chapter explores Peirce's theory of the semiotic mediation of thought and reality as it developed in the course of his persistent yet constantly shifting reflection on the nature of signs. Where possible the argument keeps close to Peirce's own words as found in his voluminous published writings and in the massive manuscript collection now available to scholars. After describing the essential features of the sign relation, the discussion examines the reciprocal vectors of determination and representation which constitute all moments of semiosis. A distinction between chains of semiosis and levels of semiosis then leads to a detailed consideration of Peirce's early views on the mediating function of thought in signs. A subtle shift in Peirce's point of view after his incorporation of the logic of relations is seen to have important implications for the theory of mediation taken more generally as the essential feature of the highest metaphysical category, which Peirce calls "Thirdness." The chapter concludes with an analysis of Peirce's notion of "medium of communication," which occupied his late thinking and which ironically implies a devaluation of the semiotic properties of expressive vehicles for the sake of a commitment to truth-functional epistemology.

In its most basic sense, the notion of mediation can be defined as any process in which two elements are brought into articulation by means of or through the intervention of some third element that serves as the vehicle or medium of communication. In billiards, for example, the action of the cue is capable of knocking the black eight ball into the corner pocket thanks to the white cue ball, which carries or transmits the directional impetus of the cue to the eight ball (CP 1.532; cf. Wild 1947:218). This simple account of mediation in which the cue ball mediates between the cue and the eight ball is, to use Peirce's term, "degenerate" for four reasons. First, in this case the process of mediation can be easily reduced to two independent dyadic moments, cue and cue ball, cue ball and eight ball. Second, the eight ball responds to the cue ball without taking into account or forming any representation of the initial impetus from the cue. Third, there is no dimension of relationship among the three elements involved other than that of dyadic physical connection, what Peirce calls "iconicity." And fourth, nothing of a general nature is transmitted in this sequence of stimulus-reactions that would be equivalent to the noetic quality conveyed when a speaker delivers words to a listener who understands thereby the speaker's meaning. These four observations suggest that the billiards model is only an example of degenerate rather than genuine mediation: the three elements are reducible without residue to independent dyads; there is no interpretation or representation by the resultant moment of the earlier moment; no symbolic or conventional relations exist among the elements; and no thought, idea, or meaning is embodied and transmitted in the process.

In order to understand how a genuine example of sign mediation would differ from the degenerate billiards example, we need to introduce Peirce's definition of the sign and the sign relation, since the sign is the most perfect example of "mediation" conceived of as a generalized category. In doing this we are operating in a fashion similar to Peirce's own style of argumentation, for he completes his deduction of his three fundamental ontological categories, "Firstness" or qualitative possibility, "Secondness" or existent otherness, and "Thirdness" or general regularity, by first generating a model of then necessary components of the sign relation. One of the clearest of Peirce's many attempts to define the sign relation is as follows:

> By a Sign I mean anything whatever, real or fictile, which is capable of a sensible form, is applicable to something other than itself, that is already known, and that is capable of being so interpreted in another sign which I call its Interpretant as to communicate something that may not have been previously

known about its Object. There is thus a triadic relation between any Sign, an
Object, and an Interpretant. (MS 654.7, 1910)

The sign relation, thus, necessarily involves three elements bound together in a
semiotic moment. The sign itself considered as the sensible vehicle or expressive
form, what Peirce often labels the "representamen," can be either an external
object functioning as a means of communication or an internal, mental representation conveying meaning from one act of cognition to the next. Second, the
object of the sign is that which the expressive form stands for, reproduces, or
presents "in its true light" (MS 599.28, 1902). And, third, the interpretant is a
resulting mental or behavioral effect produced by the object's influence on the
sign vehicle in some interpreter or interpreting representation. In more modern
vocabulary, the interpretant constitutes the "meaning" or "significance" of the
sign, while the object constitutes the "referent" or "denotation" of the sign.
Since these three elements can, in themselves, belong to various orders of reality,
such as single objects, general classes, fictions, mental representations, physical
impulses, human actions, or natural laws, what constitutes the sign relation is the
particular way in which this triad is bound together. Peirce expresses this unique
semiotic bond as a relationship in which the object or denoted entity "determines," specifies, or influences the sign vehicle or representamen to further determine the interpretant so that this interpretant comes to represent the original
object in the same respect as the representamen does:

> A *Sign*, or *Representamen*, is a First which stands in such a genuine triadic
> relation to a Second, called its Object, as to be capable of determining a Third,
> called its *Interpretant*, to assume the same triadic relation to its object in which
> it stands itself to the same Object. (CP 2.274, c.1902)

In insisting that the representamen and the interpretant are both signs representing the *same* object, although to different degrees of specificity, and that the object of the sign determines not just that first sign but, mediately, a second
interpreting sign, Peirce implies two things about the sign relation. First, the sign
relation is constituted by the interlocking of a vector of representation pointing
from the sign and interpretant toward the object and a vector of determination
pointing from the object toward both sign and interpretant. Second, one semiotic
moment in which the sign elements are in a genuine triadic relation requires an
infinite series of similar moments; in other words, the sign relation is a process.
I take up these two issues in turn.

Determination and representation are the opposed vectors in any sign relation. Determination, for Peirce, is the causal process in which qualities of one
element are specified, transferred, or predicated by the action of another element.
This process of adding to the determination of an element is equivalent to an
increase in the "depth" or intension of a term (CP 2.428, 1893); and the semiotic
transmission of this further determination is registered in the resulting characteri-

zation of the interpretant, so that the object is considered as the "determinant" and the interpretant the "determinand" (MS 499). Thus, color is a determination of an object, red is a determination of the color of an object, and scarlet is a determination of the red color of an object (CP 1.464, 1896; CP 8.177).

Representation, in this triadic scheme, works in the opposite direction from determination and is defined as the act or relation in which one thing stands for something else to the degree that it is taken to be, for certain purposes, that second thing by some interpreting mind. Because the representation substitutes or is regarded as substituting for the object, the interpreting mind acquires knowledge about the object by means of experience of the representing sign. Peirce's notion of representation includes a broad range of phenomena:

> The term representation is here to be understood in a very extended sense, which can be explained by instances better than by definition. In this sense, a word represents a thing to the conception in the mind of the hearer, a portrait represents the person for whom it is intended to the conception of recognition, a weathercock represents the direction of the wind to the conception of him who understands it, a barrister represents his client to the judge and jury whom he influences. (CP 1.553, 1867; cf. MS 389, c.1873)

Obviously there must be some constraint or limitation on the ability of an interpreting mind to form representations of aspects of reality if these representations are to afford true knowledge of that reality:

> If a thing has whatever characters it has utterly regardless of what any men existing either now or at any assignable future date may opine that its characters are, that thing is, by definition, perfectly real. But in so far as it is whatever the thinker may think it to be, it is unreal. Now I say that the object of a sign must resist in some measure any tendency it may have to be as the thinker thinks it. (MS 499)

This need for the object of the sign to "resist" the interpretant's powers of representation is answered in the definition of the sign relation cited earlier: the object specifies the sign in a particular way so that the sign determines a third element in a particular way, namely, that this third element (the interpretant) represents or stands for the *same* object in similar respects that the sign represents (see Figure 1.1).

It is important to note that the position of the sign or representamen is mediate between the object and the interpretant both for the vector of determination and for the vector of representation. Also, the triad of elements at one semiotic moment implies a constant expansion of the process of semiosis as the interpretant, in turn, acts so as to determine a further sign, becoming thereby a sign to that further interpretant. It is clear why Peirce says, first, that the action of the object upon the interpretant is "mediate determination" and, second, that the interpretant itself is a "mediate representation" of the object.[2] The first is the case since the specifying potential of the object must pass through the representa-men, which functions to convey or translate its determinate properties mediately to the interpretant. Wind blowing from the east determines a weathercock to point in that direction and mediately determines a cognition in the mind of an observer who understands the function of the instrument that the wind is from the east. The second is the case since the particular representation formed by the interpretant of the object is constrained by the "stood for" relation already ex-isting between the representamen and the object; the accumulation of determined qualities present in the object apart from all representation is attributed to the sign of that object by the interpretant in the case of a true representation. Thus the sign itself faces simultaneously in two directions: it faces toward the object in a "passive" relation of being determined, and it faces toward the interpretant in an "active" relation of determining (MS 793). This interlocking of the vectors of representation and determination implies that the three elements in the sign relation are never permanently object, representamen, and interpretant, but rather each shifts roles as further determinations and representations are realized. Semiosis is, thus, an "infinite process" or an "endless series" (MS 599.32, c.1902) in which the interpretant approaches a true representation of the object as further determinations are accumulated in each moment. This process operates in two directions, "back toward the object" and "forward toward the interpre-tant" (MS 599.38, c.1902).

> The object of representation can be nothing but a representation of which the first representation is the interpretant. But an endless series of representations, each representing the one behind it, may be conceived to have an absolute ob-ject at its limit. . . . So there is an infinite regression here. Finally, the interpre-tant is nothing but another representation to which the torch of truth is handled along; and as representation, it has its interpretant again. Lo another infinite series. (CP 1.339 = NEM 4.309; cf. MS 599.33, c.1902; MS 792)

An important implication of the processual nature of semiosis is that there is an inherent asymmetry in what can be termed the level of semiosis between the vector of determination and the vector of representation. This asymmetry derives from the fact that the representamen is fit to stand for the object in several distinct ways. The representamen can be taken for the object because of a par-ticular quality or form which both share, and so in that respect they are practi-cally interchangeable (CP 1.558, 1867; CP 3.362, 1885). Alternatively, the spa-tial or temporal position of a representamen may make it naturally fit to stand for some object in the same experiential field. But Peirce recognizes a third pos-sible mode of relation between representamen and object that transcends both the realm of common quality and the realm of common context, and this is what he calls a symbolic relation, in which the representamen and object are related *only because* the interpretant represents them as related.

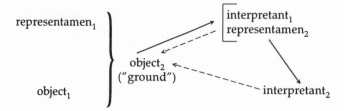

Figure 2.1. Hypostatic abstraction

It is this third symbolic[3] mode of relation between representamen and object that causes the asymmetry between determination and representation, since the first vector passes through the representamen to the interpretant at the same level of semiosis, while the second vector introduces a metasemiotic level at which the interpretant represents its object only by virtue of having formed a conception of the *relation* between the initial representation and the object. Because the interpretant is determined not just to represent the same object that the representamen represents but also to represent that object in the "same respect" and with the "same meaning" (although more highly determined), it must first form a representation of "second intention" in order to form a representation of first intention.[4] ("Second intention" [*intentio secunda*] is a term used by medieval philosophers to refer to knowledge involving not the thing itself but the mental or linguistic act of knowing the thing.) Figure 2.1 suggests an approximation of this essential asymmetry and is to be interpreted as follows: all the vectors of determination and representation that existed in Figure 1.1 are assumed to be in place linking the three elements labeled with subscript 1. The second level of semiosis occurs when the interpretant₁ functions as a representamen₂ by representing the *relation* between representamen₁ and object₁ as a new semiotic entity, namely, object₂. The solid and broken arrows depict, respectively, the vectors of determination and representation at this second level of semiosis.

Peirce has a technical term for what is labeled here object₂, namely, the "ground" of the relation between representamen and object. The ground is some respect, character, reason, or quality that brings the sign into connection with its object (CP 5.283, 1868; cf. CP 2.228, c.1897; MS 732, sec.6). The power of the interpretant to create this new entity is called by Peirce "hypostatic abstraction," since it involves taking a quality or predicate as an abstract subject. And this power is the key to the interpretant's capacity to fulfill its original charge of representing the same object with the same meaning that the first representamen does.

> That wonderful operation of hypostatic abstraction by which we seem to create *entia rationis* [mental entities] that are, nevertheless, sometimes real, furnishes us with the means of turning predicates from being signs that we think or think *through*, into being subjects thought of. We thus think of the thought-sign

itself, making it the object of another thought-sign. Thereupon, we can repeat the operation of hypostatic abstraction, and from these second intentions derive third intentions. (CP 4.549, 1906; cf. MS 283.146, 1905)

In shifting levels from *red* as a possible predicate or quality shared by representamen and object to *redness* conceived of as the ground of character of the sign relation between representamen and object, the interpretant exercises a synthetic function at the level of second intention. But, more important, in the special case described previously in which the sole relation connecting representamen and object is the relation of being represented by an interpretant, the ground of this relation is *necessarily* triadic, involving as it does the third element, the interpretant itself.

And so here we have finally arrived at the derivation of semiosis at the symbolic level as triadic in the genuine sense: the interpretant must form a conception of the semiotic process itself that is not reducible to any dyadic relations existing independently of semiosis. And this triadic structure is the result of fully symbolic representation, since the function of creating a ground at the second level of semiosis, which becomes the basis for the connection of object and representamen, opens up Peirce's system to a universe of semiotic entities (Thirds) whose character of being differs vastly from that of both qualities (Firsts) and existing objects (Seconds).

Semiotic Mediation and the Correlates of the Sign

Peirce's comments on the nature of semiotic mediation can be located in his manuscripts, published articles, and reviews stretching from the early attempts to construct the categories of Firstness, Secondness, and Thirdness through his late writings on Pragmaticism. Historical examination of these references shows that Peirce shifted the emphasis on mediation between two general poles. The first pole focuses on the synthetic role of the interpretant in forming a representation of the relation between the object and the representamen so that these two elements become linked in a semiotic web they would not be in by themselves; thus, the interpretant is said to be the "mediate representation" of the object of the sign relation taken as a whole. The second pole focuses on the idea of mediation by the representamen as the vehicle or medium of linkage between objects and further mental representation by interpretants. Thus, the sign itself, that is, the perceptible form, is said to mediate between object and interpretant, and the interpretant is mediately determined by the representation standing in place of the object. These two poles correspond to Peirce's twin concerns with, on the one hand, the level of semiosis and mediate representation and, on the other hand, chains of semiosis and mediate determination. Toward the end of his life Peirce gradually moved away from the doctrine of mediate representation and adopted a theory of "medium of communication" which, in some respects at least, nullifies the usefulness of the overall approach to semiotic mediation for disciplines other than formal logic.

In Peirce's early writings on semiotics the mediate position of the representamen between the object and the interpretant is partially obscured by his philosophical struggle to solve the essentially Kantian problem of how abstract forms can become realized in such a way that consciousness is modified to some degree. As early as 1861 he was convinced of the necessity for some level of expression in which "Form," quality, or pure meaning is united with substance or sensuous matter, a union roughly parallel to Kant's discussion of the "unity of apperception":

> If the object is expressed purely, all of the abstraction it contained (the expression) would be meaning. Pure expression therefore is pure meaning. But this the mind would not notice for the mind notices through resemblance & difference. . . . For an abstraction to emerge into consciousness, it is necessary that it should be contained in a manifold of sense. . . . Abstraction, therefore, to become modification of consciousness needs to be combined with that which modification of consciousness as yet unrelated to any abstraction is, that is to the perfectly unthought manifold of sensation. Well, how shall abstraction be combined with manifold of sensation? By existing as a form for matter, by *expression*. (MS 1105, 1861; variant in W 1:85)

Peirce found the "necessity of expression" not just in language but in other cultural forms as well: "Every religion must exist in some forms or rites in order to find the least realization" (MS 1105, 1861).

From this determination of matter according to form by expression Peirce deduced an ontology consisting of three elements, things, forms, and representations, related so that representations stand for things by virtue of or in respect to forms. Form or Logos is the quality or characteristic that, when linked with a representation, constitutes its "connotation" or "intension"; Object is some real or fictitious thing which, when linked with a representation, constitutes its "denotation" or "extension." Peirce's model of representation here is closely connected with his concern for the logical properties of propositions, in which the thing denoted by the subject of the proposition is said to embody the form connoted by the predicate (W 1:288, 1865). And from this ontological tripartition based on propositional form Peirce further deduced the three necessary "references" or "correlates" of every representation: a representation "stands for" its Object, it "realizes" its Form, and it "translates" an equivalent representation, as shown in Figure 2.2.

The third correlate of a representation is, thus, another representation in which the product of the first representation's denotation and connotation is translated or communicated; this product Peirce termed the "information" of the representation. And, finally, given the distinction between denotation and con-

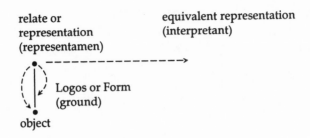

Figure 2.2. Correlates of representation

notation, that is, between that about which something is said and that which is said about something, Peirce produced a tripartition of types of representations. First, "copies" or "analogues" are representations that connote without denoting by virtue of resembling in themselves their objects (for example, pictures, statues, and hieroglyphs); second, "signs" or "marks" are representations that denote without connoting on the basis of some previous fixity of convention (as when a proper name is assigned in baptism); third, "symbols" are representations that denote by virtue of connoting and that, when presented to the mind, immediately call up a conception of the object, not because of previous convention or because of formal resemblance but rather by virtue of the equivalence relations to another representation or symbolic system (W 1:304, 1865).

The semiotic theory proposed by Peirce in the late 1860s stresses the role of cognitive representation as the synthesis of form and object and depends largely on the logical analysis of propositions, in which the form is an abstract quality predicated of an object denoted by the subject (CP 1.548, 1867). Although Peirce often made clear that his notion of representation included everything, mental as well as nonmental, that possesses attributes (WCP 1.326, 1865), he gave little attention to the sensible or material qualities of signs in the nonmental category, or what he later termed the representamen. In fact, the need for some "medium of outward expression" (CP 5.284, 1868) is admitted only as something that may be necessary to translate a "thought-sign" to another person; and these material qualities are, in themselves, only a residue of nonsemiotic properties of the sign that play no positive role in the sign's representational function.

It was from this theory of representation that Peirce developed the ontological categories presented in his 1867 paper "On a New List of Categories" (CP 1.545–59). The three correlates or references of a representation (form, object, and equivalent representation) become here the three universal conceptions or categories: reference to a "Ground," reference to a "Correlate," and reference to an "Interpretant." In this revised terminology, ground is the quality or respect in which the representation stands for its object or correlate; and the interpretant is the mediating representation that "represents the relate to be a representation of the same correlate which this mediating representation itself represents" (CP 1.553, 1867). There are, thus, three distinct levels of reference: *singular* reference to the ground of "Quality," *double* reference to the ground-correlate pair or "Relation," and *triple* reference to the ground-correlate-interpretant triad or "Representation." And these three levels, in turn, correspond to three fundamental categories, which Peirce labels Firstness, Secondness, and Thirdness.

> The conception of a *third* is that of an object which is so related to two others, that one of these must be related to the other in the same way in which the third is related to that other. Now this coincides with the conception of an interpretant. And *other* is plainly equivalent to correlate. The conception of second differs from that of other, in implying the possibility of a third. (CP 1.556, 1867)

This direct linkage of semiotic constituents and metaphysical categories depends not on isolated properties of the three terms of the sign relations, but rather on the necessarily hierarchical architectonic in which reference to the correlate or object presupposes reference to the ground and reference to the interpretant presupposes reference to both ground and correlate.

From this analysis Peirce proceeded to deduce that there must be three types of representation. In the first and simplest case, reference to the ground involves a quality that the representation and object share; in the second case, reference to a ground involves a quality that sets the representation over against the object so that their correspondence is a matter of fact; and in the third case, reference to the ground is impossible without (cannot be "prescinded" from) reference to the interpretant, which supplies the imputed quality founding the relation between the representation (relate or sign) and object (or correlate). These three cases correspond to the well-known trichotomy of icon, index, and symbol (although in the 1860s Peirce often used the terms "copy" and "likeness" for icon and "sign" for index).

Peirce summed up his early position on the semiotic mediation of cognition in the twin claims that there is no point in speaking about Being except as that Being is cognizable (CP 5.257, 1868) and that all cognitions are necessarily thought in sequences of signs (CP 5.251, 1868). Not just intellectual operations such as conceptions and judgments but also feelings and perceptions are all inherently semiotic, that is, involve the processual mediation of cognitions by subsequent representations, with each additional representation bringing about the synthetic unity of the previous one:

> In short, the Immediate (and therefore in itself unsusceptible of mediation—the Unanalyzable, the Inexplicable, the Unintellectual) runs in a continuous stream through our lives; it is the sum total of consciousness, whose mediation, which

is the continuity of it, is brought about by a real effective force behind consciousness. (CP 5.289, 1868)

By generalizing the Kantian notion of *Vorstellung* "representation" (W 1:257, 1865) to include all cognitive processes viewed from the point of view of propositional reduction, Peirce directed his philosophical attack in the late 1860s against all types of Cartesian intuitionism, which postulates the existence of immediate (and thus nonsemiotic) cognition (Buczynska-Garewicz 1978, 1979; Esposito 1979). Peirce's achievement here is no less than the synthesis of ontology (that is, the theory of categories), epistemology (that is, the theory of universal representation), and logic (that is, the analysis of representation-object relations) by the mediating unification of the semiotic perspective.

Thirdness as Mediation

Over the next forty-odd years Peirce modified this terminology frequently, substituting for the category of Thirdness or Representation labels such as Mediation, Branching, Synthetic Consciousness, Theory, Process, Law, Reason, Transuasion, Transaction, Betweenness, Continuity, and Regularity. There is a general tendency, however, for him to prefer Mediation for the most general characteristic of Thirdness in writings after the early 1870s, that is, after he fully integrated the "logic of relations" into his philosophy (CP 1.560–67; Murphey 1961:150–52; cf. Rosensohn 1974). But the common element tying together Peirce's various views is the fundamental idea that anything that either comes between two things in order to link them together, transfers a characteristic feature from one thing over to another, or synthesizes elements from disparate realms of reality must exist at a higher logical and ontological level than the initial two things. And it is this insight that led him to claim that there is more to reality than brute existence (Secondness) and qualitative possibility (Firstness). In fact, the genuine reality of Thirds or triads, including prototypically fully symbolic representations with their three references, implies that they are not reducible to either Seconds or Firsts, although they require these lower-ranking categories as much as they determine them. Peirce summarizes his view as of 1872–73 as follows: "A representation generally . . . is something which brings one thing into relation with another. . . . A representation is in fact nothing but *a* something which has a *third* through an *other*" (quoted in Kloesel 1983:115).

Having identified Thirdness on the basis of the triple references of a truly symbolic representation, Peirce generalized this highest level category to realms of experience not obviously thought of as semiotic. As early as 1875 the connection between Thirdness and a variety of processes of mediation is apparent, as in the fragment titled "Third":

By the third, I mean the medium or connecting bond between the absolute first and last. The beginning is first, the end second, the middle third. The end is second, the means third. The thread of life is a third; the fate that snips it, its second. A fork in a road is a third, it supposes three ways; a straight road, considered merely as a connection between two places is second, but so far as it implies passing through intermediate places it is third. Position is first, velocity or the relation of two successive positions second, acceleration or the relation of three successive positions third. But velocity in so far as it is continuous also involves a third. Continuity represents Thirdness almost to perfection. Every process comes under that head. Moderation is a kind of Thirdness. The positive degree of an adjective is first, the superlative second, the comparative third. All exaggerated language, "supreme," "utter," "matchless," "root and branch," is the furniture of minds which think of seconds and forget thirds. Action is second, but conduct is third. Law as an active force is second, but order and legislation are third. Sympathy, flesh and blood, that by which I feel my neighbor's feelings, is third. (CP 1.337, c.1875)

Two themes emerge from this fragment: first, Thirdness as pertaining to a middle position or term in a system, and second, Thirdness as pertaining to a rational or normative principle that regulates objects, perceptions, and events. Peirce's fundamental insight here is the linkage between what can be called the "cohesive principle" of Thirdness and the "regulative principle" of Thirdness—and this in turn suggests the continuing influence of Kant on Peirce's thought, since Kant stressed both the synthetic and the regulative functions of pure reason. There is, unfortunately, no clue in the fragment how Peirce would express the sign relation in terms of Thirdness as mediation; fortunately, he returned to this question in several manuscripts written after the late 1870s.

The explicit connection between Thirdness, mediation, and the elements of the sign relation occurs in an undated manuscript titled "The Categories," in which Peirce applies the logic of relations to distinguish systems with one object, systems with two objects in dual relation, and systems with three objects associated in pairs but in such a way that the "triad is something more than a congeries of pairs" (MS 717 = NEM 4.307, c.1893). A road that branches into two roads cannot be reduced to the sum of the two road segments, since the presence of the fork introduces a qualitatively new alignment whereby a traveler can pass along the main road, proceed along either fork, *and* return from one fork across the juncture to the other segment without ever traversing the undivided portion of the main road. Similarly, if A gives B something C, this cannot be reduced to the dyadic fact of A's giving up C and B's receiving C, for the process of giving is not two linked acts but a single act, as can be easily seen in the example Peirce gives in which A lays something down and then an hour later B comes by and picks it up, a sequence utterly devoid of triadic relations. Peirce then generalizes this analysis of triads to constitute the highest "formal ideal" or category:

It will, at any rate, be found a most helpful maxim, in making philosophical analyses to consider, first, single objects, then pairs, last triads.

We have already applied this maxim in Article 1, where Cunning is that skill that resides only in the single persons, Wisdom is that which can be stated to others, Theory is that which can be fortified by means (observe that a *means*, or *medium*, is a *third*) of a reason.

Art. 4. That above maxim crystallizes itself in the statement that there are three grand elementary formal ideas, as follows:

I. The *First*, or Original, expressed by the root AR. The plough goes first.

II. The *Second*, or Opponent, expressed by the root AN, as in Latin *in*, our *other*, and also more strongly, but with an idea of *success* in opposition, in AP, whence *ob*, apt, *opus, opes, optimus*, copy.

III. The *Third*, or Branching, or Mediation expressed by such roots as PAR, TAR, MA. These three ideas may be called the *Categories*. (NEM 4.308)

In another manuscript Peirce adds a brief comment on the notion of branching:

Namely, he must recognize, first, a mode of being in itself, corresponding to any *quality*; secondly, a mode of being constituted by opposition, corresponding to any *object*; and thirdly, a mode of being of which a branching line is an analogue, and which is of the general nature of a mean function corresponding to the sign. (MS 7.13)

He then goes on to address the sign relation as one of the "easiest" ideas of philosophical relevance in which this third category of branching or mediation is predominant. I have already cited the crucial passage from this manuscript, but it is important to recall that at this point in the development of Peirce's thinking the third is *not* the more familiar representamen, object, and interpretant, but rather object, meaning, and interpretant:

A sign stands *for* something to the idea which it produces, or modifies. Or, it is a vehicle conveying into the mind something from without. That for which it stands is called its *Object*; that which it conveys, its *Meaning*; and the idea to which it gives rise, its *Interpretant*. (MS 717 = NEM 4.309)

Clearly, the sign itself is conceived of as a nodal point analogous to the fork in the road, where the three termini of object, meaning, and interpretant (parallel to the three references or correlates of the sign from the 1860s: object, ground, and mediating representation) come together or, more accurately, are bound together. From the earlier notion that the interpretant functions as a synthetic power in uniting in a further representation of the sign both a meaning and an object (a logos and a correlate, in the earlier vocabulary), Peirce here focuses on the mediating role of the sign itself as constituting an irreducible triad.

A crucial modification in this model of Thirdness, mediation, and sign occurs about 1885 in a manuscript titled "One, Two, Three: Fundamental Categories of Thought and of Nature" (MS 901 = CP 1.369–72, 1.376–78) and in a published article, "On the Algebra of Logic: A Contribution to the Philosophy of Notation" (CP 3.359–403). In the manuscript Peirce stresses the synthetic function of consciousness as the key to the ability of the mind to learn, make inferences, and cognize relations of more than dual character. This consciousness of synthetic facts is clearly present in cognition through symbols, for in this class of signs there is a triadic system of elements parallel to the three termini of a forked road and to the three terms of the relationship of giving:

> We have seen that the mere coexistence of two singular facts constitutes a degenerate form of dual fact; and in like manner there are two orders of degeneracy in plural facts, for either they may consist in a mere synthesis of facts of which the highest is dual, or they may consist in a mere synthesis of singular facts. This explains why there should be three classes of *signs*; for there is a triple connection of *sign, thing signified, cognition produced in the mind*. There may be a mere relation of reason between the sign and the thing signified; in that case the sign is an *icon*. Or there may be a direct physical connection; in that case, the sign is an *index*. Or there may be a relation which consists in the fact that the mind associates the sign with its object; in that case the sign is a *name*. (CP 1.372, c.1885)

It is important to note that in place of the three references or correlates of the sign Peirce has substituted the triad of sign, thing signified, and cognition produced in a mind. In this semiotic model it is the sign relation itself rather than one element taken alone that reveals a triadic, synthetic, and mediational quality:

> It seems, then, that the true categories of consciousness are: first, feeling, the consciousness which can be included with an instant of time, passive consciousness of quality, without recognition or analysis; second, consciousness of an interruption into the field of consciousness, sense of resistance, of an external fact, of another something; third, synthetic consciousness, binding time together, sense of learning, thought.
>
> If we accept these [as] the fundamental elementary modes of consciousness, they afford a psychological explanation of the three logical conceptions of quality, relation, and synthesis or *mediation*. The conception of quality, which is absolutely simple in itself and yet viewed in its relations is seen to be full of variety, would arise whenever feeling or the singular consciousness becomes prominent. The conception of relation comes from the dual consciousness or sense of action and reaction. The conception of *mediation* springs out of the plural consciousness or sense of learning. (CP 1.377–78, c.1885; emphasis added)[5]

The "plural" character of mediation, Thirdness, and sign relation, and Peirce means by plural more than dual, is the test of "genuine" as opposed to "degenerate" triads.

In the paper "On the Algebra of Logic" Peirce notes that the triple relation of sign, object, and cognition in the mind is not equally genuine for the three classes of signs. Taken as the "conjoint relation" of sign, thing signified, and mind, the sign relation can be degenerate in two degrees: (1) if the sign has a genuine *dual* relation with its object apart from the mental association supplied by the mind, then the sign resembles a natural sign or physical symptom and is labeled an index; (2) if the sign has a degenerate *dual* relation with its object apart from any function of the mind, then the sign consists of mere resemblance between sign and object and is labeled an icon (CP 3.361, 1885). There are, obviously, two other dual relations, sign-mind and object-mind, which could possibly be either genuine or degenerate, but, as Peirce notes, without the presence of the sign and object dyad (in either degenerate or genuine status) there would be no question of a semiotic relation, since this would be the case of the mind thinking of both object and sign *separately*. Since plural relations have two degrees of degeneracy (index and icon) and since a dual relation can have only one degree of degeneracy (as in the combination of two independent facts about two subjects), the resulting possibilities form a system depicted in Figure 2.3.[6] Peirce finds these two degrees of degeneracy in many forms of experience:

> Among thirds, there are two degrees of degeneracy. The first is where there is in fact itself no Thirdness or mediation, but where there is true duality; the second degree is where there is not even true Secondness in the fact itself. Consider, first, the thirds degenerate in the first degree. A pin fastens two things together by sticking through one and also through the other; either might be annihilated, and the pin would continue to stick through the one which remained. (CP 1.366, c.1890)

> We now come to thirds degenerate in the second degree. The dramatist Marlowe had something of that character of diction in which Shakespeare and Bacon agree. This is a trivial example; but the mode of relation is important. . . . In portraiture, photographs mediate between the original and the likeness. In science, a diagram or analogue of the observed fact leads on to a further analogy. (CP 1.367. c.1890)

The stress on the essentially triadic or plural character of genuine Thirdness might seem to contradict Peirce's original definition of the categories as quality, relation, and representation, for triadic relations are clearly "relations" of some kind. In substituting a logic of relations for a logic grounded on propositional predication in the 1880s and 1890s, Peirce was able to realize that not all relations are dual and that the notion of mediation better expresses the reality of relations between a triad of elements. As he wrote in 1898:

> I did not then [in 1867] know enough about language to see that to attempt to make the word *representation* serve for an idea so much more general than any it habitually carried, was injurious. The word *mediation* would be better.

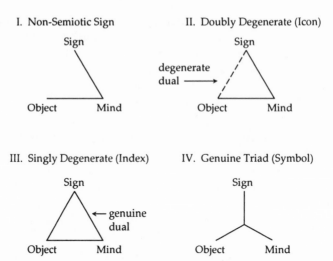

Figure 2.3. Semiotic degeneracy

Quality, reaction, and *mediation* will do. (CP 4.3, 1898; cf. MS 339, 1906, August 30)

Scholars disagree about the significance of this terminological shift (Murphey 1961; Rosensohn 1974:12–13): in the 1867 system the three categories were quality, relation, and representation, while in the 1898 paper Peirce prefers quality, reaction, and mediation. At least one significant implication of this terminological shift is that Peirce now comes to see representation as one species within the genus of mediation. In other words, the phenomenon of "standing for" is one variety of the broader phenomenon of "standing between." Thus, by 1890 Peirce defines his three categories as follows: First is being simply in itself; Second is that which is by force of something else; and "the Third is that which is what it is owing to things *between* which it mediates and which it brings into relation to each other" (CP 1.356, c.1890; emphasis added). This new definition of the Third as mediation occurs frequently in Peirce's work in the 1890s. In "A Guess at the Riddle" he links Thirdness, representation, and mediation:

> The third is that which bridges over the chasm between the absolute first and last, and brings them into relationship. . . . We have seen that it is the immediate consciousness that is preeminently first, the external dead thing that is preeminently second. In like manner, it is evidently the representation mediating between these two that is preeminently third. (CP 1.359–61, c.1890)

Similarly in a paper published in 1891 Peirce (1891:163) defines Third in terms of mediation or that "whereby a first and a second are brought into relation" and then generalizes this point to comprehend a range of sciences and disciplines:

First is the conception of being or existing independent of anything else. Second is a conception of being relative to, the conception of reaction with, something else. Third is the conception of *mediation*, whereby a first and second are brought into relation. . . . The origin of things, considered not as leading to anything, but in itself, contains the idea of First, the end of things that of Second, the process *mediating* between them that of Third. . . . The idea of the Many, because variety is arbitrariness and arbitrariness is repudiation of any Secondness, has for its principal component the conception of First. In psychology Feeling is First, Sense of reaction Second, General conception Third, or *mediation*. In biology, the idea of arbitrary sporting is First, heredity is Second, the process whereby the accidental characters become fixed is Third. Change is First, Law is Second, and tendency to take habits is Third. Mind is First, Matter is Second, Evolution is Third. (CP 6.32, 1891; emphasis added)

A second implication of this new terminology is that the concept of relation is freed from the limitations of Secondness and can be applied as well to Thirdness. The discovery of relations of greater logical complexity than dual or dyadic relations enabled Peirce to combine his earlier concern with propositional representation with a greater sensitivity to the Thirdness inherent in certain social acts, such as giving, concluding of a contract, and forming behavioral habits. A legal contract, to take one example, cannot be accounted for merely by the combination of two dyadic relations, the first being A's signature on document C and the second being B's signature on document C. The essence of the contract lies in the "intent" of the contract, which stipulates certain conditional rules governing the future behavior of A and B (CP 1.475, c.1896). Thus the act of making a contract cannot be reduced to the composition of the component dyads, and yet the function of Thirdness inherent in the contract itself is to bring these two dyads into a relationship binding for the future. In 1902 Peirce returned to this connection among Thirdness, intention, and mediation:

In all action governed by reason such genuine triplicity will be found; while purely mechanical actions take place between pairs of particles. A man gives a brooch to his wife. The merely mechanical part of this act consists in his laying the brooch down while uttering certain sounds, and her taking it up. There is no genuine triplicity here; but there is no giving, either. The giving consists in his agreeing that a certain intellectual principle shall govern the relations of the brooch to his wife. The merchant in the Arabian Nights threw away a date-stone which struck the eye of a Jinnee. This was purely mechanical, and there was no genuine triplicity. The throwing and the striking were independent of one another. But had he aimed at the Jinnee's eye, there would have been more than merely throwing away the stone. There would have been genuine triplicity, the stone being not merely thrown, but thrown *at* the eye. Here, *intention*, the mind's action, would have come in. Intellectual triplicity, or Mediation, is my third category. (CP 2.86, 1902; cf. MS 462.68–70, 1903)[7]

It is the intentional character of "throwing at," of "giving to," that constitutes these acts as examples of genuine Thirdness; the linkage of two dyads creates something that has reality only by virtue of the "bringing together" or mediation of component elements.

A few years after writing the passage just cited, Peirce took a further step in his generalization of Thirdness by combining his earlier insights into the nature of symbolic representation and his new discoveries about triadic relations. Put simply, Peirce claimed that Thirdness is that which brings together or mediates Firstness and Secondness. In 1902 the claim was that mediation is a modification of Firstness and Secondness by Thirdness (CP 2.92), and in 1903 again Thirdness is defined as the "mediation between Secondness and Firstness" (CP 5.121). And finally in 1904 Peirce stated explicitly: "A Third is something which brings a First into relation to a Second" (SS 31) and then glossed the sign relation in identical language:

> In its genuine form, Thirdness is the triadic relation existing between a sign, its object, and the interpreting thought, itself a sign, considered as constituting the mode of being a sign. A sign mediates between the *interpretant* sign and its object. . . . A *Third* is something which brings a First into relation to a Second. A sign is a sort of Third. (SS 31, 1904)

It would seem from this that Peirce is stressing the middle position of the sign vehicle or representamen rather than the function of mediate representation as exemplified in the work of the interpretant, which, as we have seen, characterized his earlier position.[8] Throughout the first decade of the century Peirce consistently held two doctrines about Thirdness and signs: first, this function of "bringing together" is grounded on a rational, intellectual, and law-like regularity that provides the common feature of natural as well as cognitive processes; and second, the sign itself is the middle, medium, means, or mediation that links object and interpretant in a communication system (SS 32, 1904).

Sign as Medium of Communication

Having established the third category in terms of bridging, bringing together, and coming between two other elements, Peirce extended this doctrine still further in his writing between 1902 and 1912 by focusing on the notion of communication as an essential feature of all semiosis. The endless series of signs stretching toward the object, on the one hand, and toward the interpretant, on the other, forms a unified continuum because throughout this process the "torch of truth" is passed on. That is, knowledge gained through the study of external and internal signs is not something which is later available for communication or transmission within the scientific community; rather, truth and communication in Peirce's view are completely isomorphic because the inferential character of argumentation is always dialogic—not between two different people who are "in communication" but between two different moments of the same mind in which the unity of the semiotic continuum is realized.[9] Now, in any process of communication there must be a medium, means, or vehicle through which the message is conveyed from one cognition to the next, and it is precisely the quality of signs as "mediating thirds" that enables Peirce to claim that a sign is a species of a "medium of communication" between two minds that are thereby brought to be one mind (MS 339, 1906; MS 498).[10] As he notes, a third or *tertium* is, etymologically at least, a middle or *medium*, and anything that functions in this capacity is properly a sign.[11] In the act of throwing a stone, for example, there is a genuine dyadic relation between the person who throws and the stone thrown, but there is also a triadic relation involved when the air, the medium through which the stone is thrown, is taken into account (MS 12.5–6, 1912). Though scarcely noticeable, the friction of the air exerts an influence on the stone's motion and thus on the character of the triad as a whole. Like the air in this example, a sign functions as the medium of communication and serves to transmit some form that it embodies:

> For the purposes of this inquiry a *Sign* may be defined as a Medium for the communication of a Form. It is not logically necessary that anything possessing consciousness, that is, feeling of the peculiar common quality of all our feeling should be concerned. But it is necessary that there should be two, if not three, *quasi-minds*, meaning things capable of varied determination as to forms of the kind communicated. As a *medium*, the Sign is essentially in a triadic relation, to its Object which determines it, and to its Interpretant which it determines. . . . That which is communicated from the Object through the Sign to the Interpretant is a form; that is to say, it is nothing like an existent, but is a power, is the fact that something would happen under certain conditions. This Form is *really* embodied in the object, meaning that the conditional relation which constitutes the form is *true* of the form as it is in the Object. In the Sign it is embodied only in a *representative* sense, meaning that whether by virtue of some real modification of the Sign, or otherwise, the Sign becomes endowed with the power of communicating it to an interpretant. (MS 793.1–3, c. 1905)

In this passage Peirce is clearly interpreting his new notion of medium of communication in terms of his earlier theory of semiotic determination and representation, but here the stress is on the function of "mediate determination" rather than of "mediate representation." The role of the sign is to mediately determine or influence the interpretant by functioning to "deflect the emanation from the object upon the interpreting mind" (MS 634.24, 1909; cf. NEM 3.839, 841, 1905).

In focusing on the sign's function as a medium of communication, Peirce is returning to an earlier concern, manifested in the earliest manuscripts from the 1860s, with the necessity of a level of expression for the modification of consciousness and to the problem of how to account for the transmission of Form from one moment of semiosis to the next. Throughout his life Peirce insisted on the necessity of studying expressive forms or external representations rather than attempting to examine thought itself through some kind of unmediated Cartesian introspection (CP 1.551, 1867; Buczynska-Garewicz 1984). The transmission of Form in the interpretant is likened by Peirce to metempsychosis: a soul passes from one body to another body, but the notion of a soul without some body is "simply an impossibility and an absurdity" (MS 2.98.11, c.1906); similarly a sign must have some interpretant to receive its "soul" as the sign is translated into another language. Peirce compares this translation to the act of pouring "idea-potential" or Form from one vessel into another, in which the vessel embodies but does not contribute to the determination of the Form (MS 283.102, 1905).

It is clear from these observations that Peirce's theory couples a notion of the necessity of expression with a notion of the ideal transparency of semiotic media, a goal of empirical semiotics since Aristotle's reflections on scientific language (McKeon 1946:195). That Form requires embodiment in some kind of expression does not imply that the quality of the embodiment contributes in any way to the determination of the Form. In fact, Peirce's lifelong struggle was to invent a form of logical notation that would be so iconically perfect that it would represent all and only logical relations among signs. The system of Existential Graphs he developed in the late 1890s is based on the need to translate the language of speech into a more intelligible, atomistic, and manipulatable symbolic medium (MS 637.30, 1909; MS 654.4, 1910). Yet Peirce was confident that the choice of medium does not affect the thought or Form embodied:

> Thinking always proceeds in the form of a dialogue—a dialogue between different phases of the *ego*—so that, being dialogical, it is essentially composed of signs, as its Matter, in the sense in which a game of chess has the chessmen for its matter. Not that the particular signs employed *are* themselves the thought! Oh, no; no whit more than the skins of an onion are the onion. (About as much so, however.) One selfsame thought may be carried upon the vehicle of English, German, Greek, or Gaelic; in diagrams, or in equations, or in Graphs: all these are but so many skins of the onion, its inessential accidents. Yet that thought should have *some* possible expression and some possible interpreter, is the very being of its being. (MS 298.6–7, c.1906 = CP 4.6)

The requirements for Peirce's logical graphs are narrow and more stringent than the requirements of natural languages, since logic deals only with fully symbolic diagrams and is unconcerned with either indexical categories or individual embodiment in sign tokens (MS 283.94, 1905). Whereas natural languages serve a multitude of functions—stating truths, commanding actions, expressing feelings—logical graphs consist of purely propositional diagrams that are matched only to a degree in grammar (CP 3.418, 1892).[12] And since logic deals with whether or not an argument is true, not with how we think an argument (MS 449.58, 1903), a proposition never "prescribes any particular mode of iconization" (MS 599.8, 1902), except that the signs employed accurately transmit to the interpretant the same determination that the object transmits to the sign. To the degree that a sign is "deceptive," it is not a sign (MS 637.36, 1909).

The combination of these two notions, the necessity of expression and the transparency of medium, implies that while the quest for "naked thought itself" is doomed to failure, since all thought is clothed in a "garment of expression" (NEM 3.406, 1903), the empirical study of various existing or possible systems of sign vehicles does not contribute to the goal of establishing an a priori and therefore universal typology of signs. Only when signs themselves vanish by being totally transparent to the logical relations of determination and representation they mediate does the science of signs become transformed into the science of thought. There is, in Peirce's position, no notion of the mutual delimitation of a Saussurean level of signifier and signified, that is, of expressive form and meaningful content, since there can be no such proportionality when the sign qua signifier is a medium of communication that does not meddle with what is being communicated.[13]

Peirce finds the vanishing signifier even in natural conversational language:

> A medium of communication is something, A, which being acted upon by something else, N, in its turn acts upon something, I, in a manner involving its determination by N, so that I shall thereby, through A and only through A, be acted upon by N. We may purposely select a somewhat imperfect example. Namely, one animal, say a mosquito, is acted upon by the entity of a zymotic disease, and in its turn acts upon another animal, to which it communicates the fever. The reason that this example is not perfect is that the active medium is in some measure of the nature of a *vehicle*, which differs from a medium of communication, in acting upon the transported object and determining it to a changed location, where, without further interposition of the vehicle, it acts upon, or is acted upon by, the object to which it is conveyed. A sign, on the other hand, just in so far as it fulfills the function of a sign, and none other, perfectly conforms to the definition of a medium of communication. It is determined by the object, but in no other respect than goes to enable it to act upon the interpreting quasi-mind; and the more perfectly it fulfills its function the less effect it has upon the quasi-mind other than that of determining it *as if the object itself* had acted upon it. Thus, after an ordinary conversation, a wonderfully perfect kind of sign-functioning, one knows what information or suggestion has been conveyed, but will be utterly unable to say in what words it was conveyed, and often will think it was conveyed in words, when in fact it was only conveyed in tones or in facial expressions. (MS 283.128–31, 1905; emphasis added)

The perfect sign, then, resembles the mechanical translating machine Peirce envisioned which translates from one language to another without going through the intervention of the human mind and which perfectly transmits the meaning from the first language into the second (MS 283.102, 1905). Although he founded his semiotic philosophy on the notion of the mediation by signs of thought and reality, Peirce in the end reduced the role of signs to being blind vehicles for communication of meanings that they do not influence.

PART II

Signs in Ethnographic Context

3 | Transactional Symbolism in Belauan Mortuary Rites

We people are clever in fixing what is becoming too long
We lessen what is getting too big, and what is growing too long we cut short
This making smaller and making shorter balances out
But death is the one thing about which there is nothing that can be done
When I was growing up I yearned to see the world
Cursed and now dead, death is all that remains
If it was human, seen by us, we would lash the canoe board and
    anchor the world
These houses and the *chebtui*-tree on the hillside are just the same
Who is going to sneak away, passing by this way or that?
If one goes around death, then we just travel in circles
Death still tips us over in the end
These mothers who bore us exhausted themselves giving answer to
    the falsehood
That we would not become people wiped out together by sickness
Death is all that remains
If it was human, seen by us, we would lash the canoe board and
    anchor the world
These houses and the *chebtui*-tree on the hillside are just the same
Who is going to sneak away, passing by this way or that?
If one goes around death, then we just travel in circles
Death still tips us over in the end

—Augustin Krämer (1917–29, 4:297–98; my trans.)

Responses to Death

THE DEATH OF a mature, married person in Belau (Palau) in western Micronesia sets into motion a series of ritual processes which regulate the successive termination of four aspects of the deceased's social status: as a "titleholder" (male
rubak and female *mechas*), as a living human being, as a senior kinsperson, and
as a "spouse" (*buch*).[1] Correspondingly, the ritual action, lasting in some cases
as long as six months, (1) transfers the male or female title (*dui*) to a successor,
(2) transforms the dead person's dangerously proximate "ghost" (*deleb*) into a
controllable yet distant "ancestral spirit" (*bladek*), (3) redraws the ties of kinship
solidarity and affection among the living, and (4) channels the inheritance of

47

valuables and real property by finalizing the exchange balance between affinal sides. These four tasks are accomplished by the highly prescribed activity of individuals and social groups, action focusing primarily on the manipulation of four classes of meaning-laden objects: various kinds of food, "male valuables" in the form of ceramic and glass beads (*udoud*), "female valuables" in the form of hammered turtleshell trays and oystershell slicers (*toluk* or *chesiuch*), and funeral mats (*badek* or *bar*). In the contemporary period, additional Western items have become included in these four traditional categories. And, finally, the interplay between the presupposed symbolic meaning of these objects and the interpersonal and intergroup relationships activated at the moment of death is pragmatically mediated by several distinct modalities of transaction, including asymmetrical exchange, reciprocal gift-giving, and transgenerational inheritance. This third analytical variable is designed to integrate what Bloch and Parry (1982:6) call the "sociological" and the "symbolic" dimensions of funerals.

The full course of the mortuary sequence can be divided into two complementary segments, the first being the week-long "funeral feast" (*kemeldiil*) and the second being the final "death settlement talks" (*cheldecheduch*) held several months later in cases where the deceased leaves a surviving spouse. The first segment, primarily a female rite, focuses on the kinship relationships which the living have to each other by virtue of their links to the deceased; thus, consanguineal (and, in particular, matrilateral) ties play an extremely important role.[2] The second segment, primarily a male rite, focuses on negotiating the closure of affinal relations between husband's and wife's kin and on transmitting property (land, money, status) to the offspring of the marriage. This chapter is confined to the analysis of the first segment, which can itself be divided into four ritual components: the taking of the title, the burial proper, divination of the cause of death, and the paving of the grave. In all the funerals I witnessed, the third and fourth components took place together one week after the burial.

Funerals held in Ngeremlengui district differ from those described in the ethnographic record in five basic ways.[3] First, contemporary Belauan customs are completely infused with Christian symbolism, language, and sentiment. Also, the strength of Modekngei, a local syncretistic religious movement, colors the funerals of members of this group living in the district. Second, the events themselves are far more socially and financially elaborate than any described in the eighteenth and nineteenth centuries. This is partly because of better intervillage communication and transportation and partly because of the overall inflation of customary exchange which has occurred since the influx of American dollars into the economic system. Third, funerals and death settlement talks regularly take place in the district's chiefly meeting house (located in Ngeremetengel village) rather than in private houses. The ritual procedures begin, of course, in the house where the person dies, but soon thereafter the coffin and the mourners, along with piles of funeral goods, food, and mats, move to the meeting house. I think that this shift, which took place for Ngeremlengui district in the 1930s, cannot be attributed merely to the larger numbers of people attending funerals. Equally important is the fact that many houses of titleholders no longer stand on their ancestrally prescribed spot, so that senior people from these houses would rather use, or actually rent, the public meeting house to feed and honor distinguished invited guests.

Fourth, in the contemporary scene death no longer automatically entails the dissolution of the household. Prior to the colonial periods, residential houses (*blai*) were located on prescribed land parcels controlled by the senior members of the matrilineal group. At marriage, a woman went to live in her husband's village, and when her husband was mature enough to receive a chiefly title, the couple and their children moved to his matrilineal house. The result of this disharmonic pattern is that married women regularly lived in villages where they had no strong kin ties and where titleholding men ruled over houses in which they did not grow up. In fact, the higher the social rank the greater the disharmony, since chiefs try to use nonlocal marriages to form political alliances. Death or divorce, accordingly, meant that in-married women and their children no longer received the deference of members of the house and had, in fact, to struggle to protect forms of wealth (valuables and household items) from forced seizure by the deceased's younger brothers or mother's brothers. Kubary, the brilliant Polish ethnographer of Micronesia, describes the situation in the mid-nineteenth century:

> The wife living abroad with her husband manages his house and enjoys great respect from her husband's family as long as he lives. She is called *chedil* "mother" by everyone, but in many respects her influence is limited by the conditions maintaining inside the *blai*. She is watched in secret by the *ochellel* "younger brothers" of her husband, and special attention is paid to the *udoud* "male valuables" given by the husband. If the husband dies, and even before the corpse is buried, as much money as possible is squeezed out of her, this attaining particular prominence in the important houses, where greater values are at stake. She then remains for the whole period of mourning in the house, and leaves it, together with her children, after a formal *osumech* "departure payment" on the part of the dead man's relatives. (Kubary 1885:58)

With the introduction of private ownership of domestic houses in this century, men take steps to provide for their surviving wives and children, who frequently continue to live in the same house after the spouse's death. In Ngeremlengui at least, widowed women who were married to titled men continue to be called by the correlative female title, despite the fact that another woman (married to the successor to the male title) also commands the same respectful form of address.

And fifth, burial no longer takes place, as it did in precontact times, beneath the stone pavement in front of the house but rather in community graveyards located on the empty hillside behind the villages. This change was the direct result of orders from German (1899–1914) and Japanese (1914–44) colonial officials, whose fear of "public health" contamination parallels the Belauans' fear of spiritual contamination caused by the presence of death.

Immediately after a death many different groups spring quickly into coordinated yet seemingly undirected action. Close female kin who happen to be living nearby gather at the house of the deceased and attend to the intimate details of preparing the body for burial. In traditional times, a person who became seriously ill would move to the house of a senior member of his or her matrilineal group, to be visited there by the spouse. Even today terminally ill patients leave the hospital in Oreor town to die in their own houses, although women frequently die in the familiarity of their husbands' houses rather than move to another village. As the news spreads throughout the archipelago by means of repeated radio announcements, additional female kin will join this "mourning group" (*remengeung*). Three sorts of messages are common: the first in the name of the deceased's eldest male child,[4] the second in the name of the close male matrilineal relatives of the deceased, and the third in the name of the titleholder of the deceased's spouse's house. While the second solicits aid from relatives of the deceased, the third summons titleholders from many other districts who are linked by the complex system of "house affiliation" (*kebliil*) (see Parmentier 1984).

The women arrive carrying funeral mats of various sizes, weaving styles, and value, most of which are piled up in a corner of the house. Said to be "presents for the deceased," these mats will play an important role in the burial rites and subsequent distributions. Meanwhile, senior titled men from the village assemble together, either in a different partition of the house, in a nearby house, or else in the village meeting house. As the day wears on they too are joined by titleholders from affiliated houses in other villages. If the deceased is a woman, these titled men do not have much to do during the funeral, since the heaviest obligation falls upon the woman's brothers. If the deceased is a fellow titleholder, then they must engage in discussions about finding a suitable successor to the title. And if the deceased is the wife of one of the high-ranking titleholders of the village, this man will take responsibility for orchestrating the funeral sequence, although he is likely to ask a junior relative or friend to transmit his decisions, keep financial records, and oversee the timing of events. In this case there is also likely to be some tension between his decision-making role and that of the woman's brothers, especially if they too are high-ranking. This was exactly the situation at one of the more elaborate funerals I attended, where the surviving male titleholder warned his male associates, "Our responsibility is to be careful to help out those on the [wife's] side, but we should not take charge of anything. Together, we are all subject to debt [*obals*]." (The meaning of this last comment will be explained below.) Of course if the deceased is already a widow, then a senior matrilineal relative takes charge. But primarily, the senior men will spend the next few days sitting together, telling stories, chewing betelnut, giving orders, and being served meals.

Death has suddenly created a dangerous situation in the house and village, both because the ghost of the deceased has become separated from its physical body (the two are thought to be mirror images of each other) and because the malevolent spirit which caused the death continues to linger, identity still unknown, near the living. This situation requires several symbolic responses by female mourners and villagers. The former become "confined" (*chelsimer*) in the house, where they are prohibited from cooking or washing and where they spend their time weeping and singing "dirges" (*kelloi*). Cooking and other domestic activities are transferred to a small, makeshift structure near the main house. At the heart of this core group of mourners sits the deceased's oldest sister, who holds the handbag of the person Belauans say is "one of her." In this dangerous, isolated state, these women are labeled *meai* "taboo," a term connected to the word *meang* "sacred" (Parmentier 1987a:241). I was told by a mourning woman that their task is not only to stay close to the deceased but also to prevent strangers from being able to look upon the corpse:

> It is prohibited for a stranger to view the death of my relative, since then this person would have the opportunity at some later time to insult me by saying: "I held the dying person." I would be ashamed to hear a stranger say this. (F)

As close kin, these women have the obligation and the strength to withstand the pollution or contamination of the corpse/ghost disjunction, although they do take steps to protect themselves, the most important act being covering the corpse with layers of mats. In addition, women overtly signal the affection they have for the deceased by rubbing the body with oil and turmeric, which is said to represent the "feelings of the women." The ritual use of turmeric is widespread in Austronesian cultures (see Sopher 1964). In Belau the word for the plant, *reng*, is also the word for "contents," "core," and "inner feelings" (Krämer 1917–29, 3:347; Kubary 1969:1–2). An elderly man told me, "Women use a lot of turmeric on the corpse, until it is red all over. The turmeric [*reng*] represents the feelings of the women [*rengrir a mechas*]. And when women from related houses come to the village they will carry turmeric as a sign of their feelings." [5]

The village as a whole also reacts to the presence of contamination by beginning a period of funeral restriction (*taor*), during which time children may not play in the road and all loud noises are prohibited. The purpose of this imposed silence is not so much to show respect for the deceased but rather to avoid scaring off the hovering ghost before it can be properly sent on its final journey. [6] This period of restriction does not imply, however, that the village becomes still, for much intensive activity is taking place. The local men's club goes fishing to provide food for the funeral feast, village women start weaving food baskets and preparing large cauldrons for boiling taro and fish, and a group of young men digs the grave while another group kills one or more pigs.

Initial Funeral Transactions

The primary responsibility for providing betelnut and for preparing meals for mourners and visiting titleholders falls to the women who are categorized as "spouses of men" (*buch el sechal*), that is, women married to men belonging to the houses of the husband and wife. These women may be assisted by unrelated women from the local women's club. This food service is in accordance with the normal asymmetrical pattern of "affinal exchange" (*omeluchel*): aided by their children, sisters, and brothers, women prepare food for their husbands and husbands' sisters. Also included in this category of spouses of men are wives of male children of men and women related to the houses of the husband and wife. Additional food is supplied by the "female children" (*ngalek el redil*) of the deceased; these contributions, too, are consistent with the normal pattern in which young people provide food and service to senior kinspersons. These two groups of women may bring identical kinds of food (including sacks of rice, baskets of taro, bakery goods, sweets, and pigs), but their contributions are kept physically separate and are labeled differently, the spouses-of-men-food being called "boiled in water" (*ngeliokl*), while the female-children-food is called "carried on the shoulder" (*chelungel*).[7] This distinction is important because the two kinds of food, which correspond to distinct paths of relationship, will merit different forms of repayment. Food and labor provided by women who are in-married spouses will be paid for by the women at the house (including relatives of *both* husband and wife), who present them with female valuables. These valuables may be turtleshell trays or oystershell slicers, and in the contemporary context store-bought items such as plastic basins, tin trays, utensils, soap, cloth, and glassware are also given. Although these modern items are simply called "goods" (*klalo*), it is clear that the traditional symbolism continues: all these objects are associated with the female sphere of activity, food preparation (cf. Traube 1980:100). In contrast, the female children will not be directly recompensed for their food and service, since that transgenerational financial settlement will be the subject of the second segment of the mortuary sequence:

> These kinds of food [*ngeliokl* and *chelungel*] are identical; they just have different names. The reason that they have different names has to do with the goods which will be distributed after the customary event is over: those who are female children will not receive any goods, while those who are spouses of men will receive goods afterward. But those who bring *chelungel* do not receive anything, since they just "carry" the food as the proper duty of being children of the house. And so this is why we notify those women who are in charge of

the distribution how many spouses of men there are and that the other women are just female children who are not to receive anything. (F)

Another slight difference between *ngeliokl* and *chelungel* is that the former category is used up first, and the latter is cooked only if there is a shortage. The point of this difference is that *chelungel* is seen as uncooked food (i.e., "just carried"), since the labor of cooking (i.e., "boiling") is the responsibility of the spouses of men.

The use of female valuables (generally called *toluk*) to pay for the funeral food follows the usual pattern according to which women reward service, whether from unrelated friends or from their husband's sisters, with valuables:

Toluk are the real money of the women of Belau. Let's say I am living right here, and the wife of one of my brothers comes here and cleans up the front yard of my house. When I go to say goodbye to her I will take a *toluk* and give it to her and that would be enough. And if she clears weeds from my garden, I will also give her a *toluk*, saying, "Thank you very much." This is women's money. . . . It is completely impossible for a man ever to give a *toluk*, and yet women carry them to give to the spouses of their brothers, though she is equally capable of giving them to any other woman who has expended effort on her behalf. And the husband of a woman is very happy to purchase these turtleshell pieces and to give them to people skilled in making them into trays. He purchases them and gives them to another person skilled in polishing them, and he purchases them again and then gives them to his wife. So if we know that a woman has lots of female money, then people are eager to help her, since they will be able to say, "Give me one of those." And, inversely, if a woman does not have any of this kind of money, no one will want to help her, because these *toluk* do not automatically go to our brothers but rather become the possessions of us women. *Toluk* presented by my husband's sister are my personal possession, and I do not give them to my brother; my brother just uses male money. However, should his wife encounter a customary obligation requiring a *toluk*, he can say, "My wife does not have a *toluk*," and then I will give him one. On the other hand, if she is energetic in helping me, then I will be constantly giving her *toluk*. (F)

These payments to food workers are not the only presentations at the funeral. Visiting women not directly related to the deceased who spend time comforting the close mourners and who sing dirges honoring the memory of the deceased's ancestors are also given female valuables. This is called "giving presents" (*mengebar*), and the objects given include turtleshell trays and oystershell slicers. Women sometimes refer to this gift-giving as "laying down funeral dirges" (*olekerd er a kelloi*): one mourner leads the singing until all the women have joined in, and then one of the mourners presents her with a valuable, saying, "I am giving you this for the funeral dirge, since it is the dirge of our relative who is dead."

When the women come to attend a funeral in Ngeremlengui and sing dirges and songs which praise the ancestral titleholder of the house (or his sister), the women of the house will be very pleased. And so they will prepare a female valuable and give it to these visitors. This presentation is called "gifts of women." . . . This female valuable is truly the money of women, and this is an authentic practice from ancient times in Belau. (M)

Note that the same "female" objects are involved in very different kinds of transactions, the affinal payment to in-married women and the emotionally charged gift to female friends (a third usage will be discussed below). What links them, of course, is that the exchange objects flow between women.

Food and labor provided by villagers (*uus er a kemeldiil*) are not paid for, since these local people know that their efforts will be reciprocated when a death occurs in their houses. One exception to this is that pigs are purchased by the deceased's kin, usually from young men who raise them commercially for just this purpose; the cost of these pigs, in fact, constitutes one of the major expenses of the funeral. Figure 3.1 summarizes the pattern of contributions described so far.

Burial Practices

Constantly attended by female mourners and carefully wrapped in a shroud made of six to a dozen fine mats stitched together,[8] the body is placed in a wooden coffin, which replaces the traditional bier made of bamboo or betelnut sticks. Formerly, the unburied corpse (*klloi*) of a titled individual remained on display for a period of time commensurate with his or her rank. Semper (1982:79–80) provides important details concerning the demeanor of the mourning party seated around the corpse of the wife of the chief of Ngebuked village in the 1860s:

"Do you see," he [Semper's friend] said, lifting the curtain which temporarily divided our little room from the rest of the house, "all those women there? There are more than twenty from Ngkeklau, Chelab, and even Melekeok, all relatives of my mother and Mad. They're staying in the house for twenty days. During this time, I must always be ready to serve them and make sure that my own people and the rest of the villagers provide enough to eat. The death of such a woman caused much work in the state. She was the highest-ranking woman here, Mad's sister, and considered here what you call a queen." . . . At the time of the mourning ritual at Ngiralulk's house, I again had an opportunity to admire the dignity with which the assembled women took up their apparently quite boring business. My mother sat in front opposite Mad's wife. Each of the two had gathered ten or twelve women around her, so that they formed an open halfcircle around the doorways. They wore their best clothes, whose hems they had dyed black as an external symbol of mourning. Red and white stones [male valuables] stood out brilliantly against their dark necks; they were carried to proudly display proof of their families' wealth.

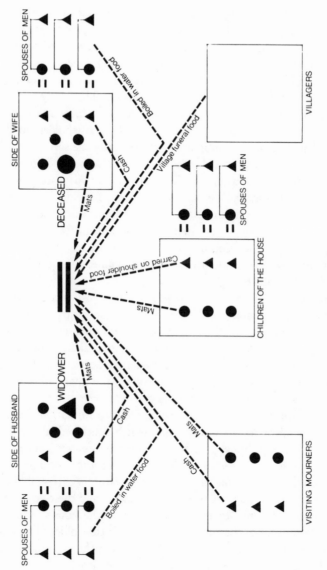

Figure 3.1. Initial funeral contributions

I was told that, in Ngeremlengui, the mourning period at the death of the first-ranking male titleholder, Ngirturong, would be ten days, for the second-ranking male titleholder, Ngiraklang, nine days, and for the third- and fourth-ranking titleholders seven days. Also, elderly informants recall funerals of high-ranking individuals at which the bier itself became an elevated platform (also called *toluk*), constructed not of bamboo but of solid wood.[9] The family of the deceased did not bear this expense, however. At the funeral of the first-ranking titleholder, senior women from the house of the second-ranking titleholder purchased the platform from the local men's club; and at the death of the second-ranking titleholder the tribute was reciprocated. Mention must also be made of the remarkable andesite sarcophagus which Hidikata (1973:85–91; see also Osborne 1966:206, fig. 64) found in Ollei village (northern Babeldaob) in 1939.[10] Although this is a unique object in Belau, its original placement does suggest that mortuary practices have long been used to mark rank differentiation (Osborne 1979:270). Today, this gradation in social rank is more clearly demonstrated by the length of time the female mourners remain confined after the burial and by the number of pigs killed for the various feasts.

According to pre-Christian cosmological notions, just as the corpse must be shielded so as not to contaminate the living, the ghost must be prepared for the journey which results in its final transformation into an ancestral spirit. Ethnographic information on concepts of ancestral spirits is sketchy but sufficient to point out that they were considered intermediaries between living people and more formally recognized, named gods (*chelid*), and that only high-ranking houses generated significant spirits. This is one reason that these houses require extensive and expensive funeral feasts, since the transformation from personal ghost to ancestral spirit results in an entity which continued to exert powerful forces in the village's political life. In the domestic context, ancestral spirits played a positive role as guardians of the house, as sources of information and good fortune, and as guarantors of generational continuity (resembling to some degree the famous *baloma* spirits of the Trobriands); and their cooperation was secured by regular offerings of food and prayer at the house's altar (Kubary 1969:6–7). Indeed, part of the authority of the male titleholder of a house rested in his role as the officiant of this domestic cult and in the fact that, through his carrying the house's sacred title, he was closer to the ancestral *bladek*, who held the same title in previous generations (Kubary 1900b:25–26).

Personal ghosts from all over Belau travel in a southerly direction, first to Melachel island (near Oreor), where they are purified in a bathing pool, then to the southern coast of Beliliou, and finally to Ngedelech beach on Ngeaur island, the "dancing place of ghosts," from which place they cross a bridge to the spirit world in a westerly direction (Krämer 1917–29, 3:348, 4:195). The belief was that the ghost takes along the spiritual image or shadow of items placed near the corpse. Alongside a female corpse might be placed her finest female valuables, whereas a male corpse might be adorned with male valuables and his favorite handbag. Kubary (1900a:38) writes:

> Women's corpses are covered with turtleshell trays, which are the principal kind of female money. According to the wealth of the house, these extend up to the hips, and the trays lean on the legs, or they may be placed as far up as the shoulders, if the family is rich. If a man has died, his handbag is placed at his left side, it is filled with fresh betelnut and tobacco, and the native *udoud* ([male] money) is piled up on its outer edge. His shoulder axe, which was his inseparable companion, rests on the body, and his battle lance stands against the door.

These particular beliefs have faded today, though I have seen photographs of the deceased placed on top of the coffin, and people still talk, though in a Christian idiom, of the "journey" of the dead.

These beliefs and other graveside rituals are well summarized in Captain Barnard's description of a funeral he witnessed in 1832:

> In a few days after, his brother was taken sick and soon was very sick. My friend came to the Prophetess with a piece of money for her to cure him, but he soon died. I was then told the cause of his death. It was because his brother, belonging to another town from where I was, had become my friend, and the prophetess being the wife of my friend in Ngebiul, she had spoken to her God and he had caused his death. I attended his funeral and witnessed that ceremony; after his death he was taken to his brother's house. When I entered the town it appeared like a fair; many little huts were stuck up, large enough to hold three or four individuals. The large *bai* [meeting house] was filled with Chiefs cooking a hog, and a sack of tobacco ready for distribution, at the house of mourning, for such it was in reality. The Corpse was laid within the door, the head on the sill. Red paint [turmeric] was strewn over the body. By his side lay his basket with nut leaves, fireworks, etc., and a sword belonging to his brother. According to the universal custom, a grave was dug a few feet from the door into which the body and its ornaments were placed. On the tenth day after, stones were placed over the grave. Then all mourning ceases, except that the females do not wash themselves for three Moons. (Barnard 1980:29; spelling and punctuation modernized)

One specialized practice pertains to funerals of unmarried women, who by definition no longer have affinal relatives to provide active financial assistance. These women require an additional piece of male money called *diall* "ship" to accompany them on their journey.[11] People explained that the woman's ghost travels with this piece of money to Ngeaur, where she confronts Orrekim, the guardian of the bridge to the spirit world. Without the *diall*, the woman would not be allowed to pass over this bridge to attain the status of ancestral spirit (Force and Force 1981:87). Today things have become even more confusing because most people no longer cite this traditional justification for the practice and because, now, married women too are presented with the *diall*. Prior to the introduction of Western currency, the *diall* was a very small piece of Belauan money, or even a piece of polished glass. This is not to be taken as an insult to the woman, but is typical of financial dealing with spirits, who are always presented with low-valued or even counterfeit pieces. Though Belauan money is still used at funerals, more commonly the *diall* consists of a sum of American cash collected during the funeral, which is put to use in paying off the incurred debt.

In Ngeremlengui, a distinction is made between the *diall* collection at a funeral of a widowed woman and that at the funeral of a woman with a surviving spouse. In the former case, the *diall* is collected principally from the deceased's male and female children and from the children of her male brothers. In the latter case, it is collected from the "senior men" (*okdemaol*) of the house of the deceased. These men are quite happy to contribute this cash because they know that, in so doing, they are marking themselves out as people entitled to receive a portion of the money at the affinal death settlement talks several months later.

At this point the focus of activity shifts to the meeting house, where visiting men and women have been waiting. They have not been unattended, however, since local women and children have been entertaining them with comic dances and singing intended to lift their sorrowful state of mind. These dancers and singers are rewarded for their efforts by small gifts of money (*sengk*) provided by the senior men of the house. In addition, visiting mourners are thanked for their patience by the presentation of "food for sitting so long" (*kallel a kltom el but*), which is more properly called "traveling food" (*ukerael*):

> We call this "food for sitting so long" because these women have been in the meeting house all day and night, and so the food is to thank them. . . . But if a person joins the mourners at the house, they do not receive this. In olden times this would consist of taro and coconut syrup [*ilaot*], but today it is just rice, biscuits, soy sauce, and sugar. Also, there is something called "food of the village" [*kallel a beluu*]. If a lot of food is left over from the evening meal, it is divided up and sent to houses in each village. Even if people did not attend the funeral, it is taken to them. They will not receive the food for sitting so long, however, since they did not stay in the meeting house. (F)

This traveling food is provided by the female children of the house (and thus specifically *not* by the spouses of men), who are thereby thanking these women for helping them mourn *their* dead kinsperson. These gifts of cash and traveling food exactly parallel the presentations described by Kubary (1900a:40–41) over one hundred years ago:

> Custom demands that the mourning house distribute something to drink to everyone present, and the first task of the relatives [at the house] is to purchase stone pitchers of coconut syrup [*ilaot*], in a number commensurate with the importance of the family. This syrup is mixed with water, and everyone drinks it, but it is chiefly given to the visitors and the mourners. Then the women,

who sing during the night, receive *Gekur*, a present made of turtleshell objects.[12]

With the coffin now resting in the meeting house, all is set for the next two stages of the funeral, the "taking the title" (*omelai er a dui*) rite and the "burial" proper (*omelakl*). At one of the funerals I attended, however, it was already growing dark by this time, and people were afraid that it would be difficult to proceed any farther. Everyone simply stayed put until morning: the visiting male and female mourners crowded at opposite ends of the meeting house, the close female mourners sitting inside the house of the deceased, and the male titleholders affiliated with the surviving spouse gossiping in front of his house. I must confess that at about 1:00 a.m. I returned to my house to type fieldnotes and to sleep. Men in the village, however, told stories together through the night.[13]

The funeral resumes in the morning with the final expressions of grief on the part of relatives of the deceased. Dressed in black, the close female mourners come slowly out of the house and take their place near the coffin in the center of the meeting house. Several emotional eulogies are delivered by spouses, sisters, adult children, ministers, and others linked to the deceased; some of these utterances resemble Christian prayers, while others directly address the deceased. I was impressed by the degree to which men joined women in overt emotional display—the ethnographic record is consistent that such public expressions of grief were confined to women.

Then the coffin is carried to the central door, where the taking-the-title rite is performed. A minor titleholder known to be a specialist in this practice stands at the head of the coffin and, slowly waving a coconut frond wrapped with wild taro leaves back and forth three times, quickly recites formulaic words, such as the following:

> I am going to take this sacred title [*meang el dui*]. The person who carried this title was unfortunate. She did not have a *mur*-feast in her honor, and now she has nothing at all. But there were plenty of pieces of *orau*-valuables. And so now she is dead and takes all this misfortune and departs. Good luck now comes to the house, to all of us, and to myself.[14]

The symbolism here is complex. A male chiefly title is known as *dui*, which is the word for coconut frond, the idea being that a high-ranking man "carries the title" (*meluchel a dui*) on his head. In this portion of the rite, the coconut frond is wrapped in a wild taro leaf (*dudek el bisech*), since this is the same word for the white-tailed tropic bird (*dudek*), known to be a particularly strong flier.[15] So the frond, emblematic of the title, is taken by the chosen successor, who places it behind his or her heel, indicating thereby the closeness of the new titleholder to the maternal affection of the senior women of the house. This seemingly minor detail of ritual action is connected with an expression used to describe men who have close matrilineal relations to the senior woman (*ourrot*) of the house: *merrot a ochil a ourrot*, "pound the heel of the senior woman," that is, as small children these men slept against this woman's leg, so that their close kinship connection can never be doubted or challenged by other men who may have begun serving this senior woman later in life.

In the absence of a successor, the title is taken by a caretaker (usually a woman), who puts the symbolic coconut frond on the rafter beams of the house for temporary safekeeping until a suitable person can be found. On the other hand, in several cases where the title was transferred to the successor, I saw the coconut frond tossed carelessly on the meeting house floor, as if its symbolic properties were no longer significant. After the title transfer in the traditional funeral sequence a complex series of feasts begins which prepares the way for a successor to the chiefly title to take his place in the meeting house. Since these ceremonies are more properly analyzed under the rubric of chiefly installation rites, they are not discussed here (see Parmentier 1987a:69–70).

At this point in the funeral, traditional and contemporary practices begin to diverge most strongly. Formerly, the body was placed in the hole (*debull*) dug in front of the house, and then a layer of mats was added. Dirt was piled on top until a small mound was created. And this mound, in turn, was covered with additional mats. Above all this a small wooden structure was constructed to house close relatives of the deceased, who actually slept on top of the grave for the short period between the burial and the final paving of the grave nine days later. These details are significant because of the fact that the corpse is separated from its closest living kin by no less than four protective layers of "female" mats or cloth: the specially selected burial garments, the stitched body wrapping, the first mat layer, and finally the mats spread over the dirt mound (cf. Kaeppler 1978:185). The significance of mats in the funeral ritual is invoked in the popular love story about Oreng and Mariar (Kesolei 1971:11–12, 23–25; cf. Kubary 1969:2–3). Oreng was unhappily married to Osilek, the powerful chief of Ulong island. When her young lover, Mariar, realized the impossibility of their relationship, he died of a broken heart. At his funeral Oreng asked to be allowed to sleep beneath one of the funeral mats. Underneath the mat she died, united with her lover only in death.

Today, when graves are dug in village cemeteries or in hillside land parcels owned by the house, the power of this symbolism is less apparent. Graveside activity is brief and matter-of-fact, with the mourners who made the hike silently placing flowers in the grave, which is then filled with dirt. At several funerals I saw auspicious *sis* (*Cordyline* sp.) planted on top of the grave.

Back in the village the main concern is to cover the costs incurred thus far, including rental of the meeting house, gas for boats carrying mourners to the village, charges for keeping the electrical power running through the night, the coffin, and the cost of store-bought foods. A small funeral might total less than $1,000, but the most expensive one I witnessed ran over $4,000. What is important, however, is the pattern of money collection to settle this "debt" (*blals*). A small amount of money called *blekatl* (usually $10 or $20) is collected from all the men related to either husband or wife. That these senior men balance the debt together is taken to be a temporary sign of kinship solidarity, for everyone knows that difficult financial negotiations will be taking place several months hence, at which time these same senior men will sit on opposite sides of the exchange floor. Again, an obvious point needs to be made: exactly parallel to the transactions involving female valuables discussed above, all the cash collected so far (the presents for dancers, the "ship" money for unmarried women, and the debt of the funeral) is collected by men.[16]

The village gradually thins out as mourners travel home and as local people catch up on lost sleep. Despite the calm, however, much planning is going on behind the scenes in preparation for the next phase of the ritual sequence. Because the meeting house is needed for daily public business, close female mourners return to the house of the deceased's brother, and the widowed husband remains at his house, surrounded by his male and female children. Much evidence remains of the just completed funeral, such as the huge collection of funeral mats at the house of the deceased's brother and the equally enormous quantity of food and funeral goods stacked up in the kitchen area of the husband's house. And throughout the week especially well prepared food continues to pass from the house of the deceased to the house of the husband—food cooked, of course, by the relatives of the wives of the brothers of the deceased.

Final Transactions

One week after the burial, many of the mourners and all the immediate relatives of the deceased return to the village to participate in two additional ceremonial components, divining the cause of death (*sis*) and paving the grave (*omengades*), which have become combined in recent years. The *sis* rite is named after the *ti* plant, which used to be the instrument employed to divine the identity of the malevolent spirit which caused the death. Prior to the introduction of Christianity and Western notions of disease, this rite was a necessary intermediate step between the burial of the corpse and the final sending off of the personal ghost, after which point the grave can be safely sealed with stones. Four days after the burial, senior female relatives of the deceased would have prepared a bouquet of *ti* leaves rubbed with turmeric and coconut oil. Holding this bundle wrapped carefully in a small piece of cloth and standing on a protective woven mat, one of the women stood in the middle of the house while her female kin shouted out possible names of spirits that might have caused the death. The idea was that when the right name was called the *ti* plant bundle would start to shake, because the ghost was attracted by the fragrant display and was coaxed by formulaic language: "Could be this one, could be that one, or it could be you?" (cf.

Danks 1892:350). Having successfully captured the ghost, the *ti* bundle would be quickly transferred to the gravesite, where it would be placed on top of a bamboo pole covered with the deceased's clothing, carrying basket, and specially prepared food (*kallel a deleb*), spiritual images of which would accompany the ghost's final journey to Ngeaur. The silence of the mourning period would suddenly be broken with loud shrieks, which would send the ghost on its way (Kubary 1900a:46).[17] Keate (1788:163–64) records a slightly different form of divination after death, one which employs coconut shells, betelnut leaves, and turmeric.

> Previous to their departure, the next morning, for the King's island, Rechucher took Mr. Sharp and the boatswain to a house not far distant from the place where his son had been interred the preceeding evening; there was only an old woman in the house when they went in, who, on receiving some order from the General, immediately disappeared, and soon after returned with two old coconuts, and a bundle of betelnut with the leaves; she also brought some red ochre [turmeric]. He took up one of the coconuts, crossing it with the ochre transversely; then placed it on the ground by his side. After sitting very pensive, he repeated something to himself, which our people conceived was a kind of prayer, as he appeared a good deal agitated; he then did the same thing by the second coconut, and afterwards crossed the bunch of betelnut, and sat pensively over it; this done, he called the old woman and delivered her the two nuts, and the bundle of betelnut, accompanied with some directions.

I did not observe any of these divinatory activities in Ngeremlengui, and my impression is that only the name, *sis*, remains as a clue to the original meaning of this day's activities.

More in keeping with earlier customs, however, is the ceremony of laying stones or pouring cement on the grave. Given the exigencies of the modern work week, the combined *sis* and *omengades* rites usually take place on the weekend following the funeral. This rapid scheduling has upset one of the former meanings of *omengades*, since formerly this rite signaled the end of the period of confinement for the close female mourners. For a high-ranking individual the rite could be delayed as much as a hundred days, but today these mourners, keeping with the original intent of this custom, continue their confinement well beyond the paving of the grave. The labor itself is the responsibility of members of the local men's club, and other mourners in fact rarely accompany them to the cemetery. The kin of the deceased contribute a pig so that the men's club can enjoy a feast after their job is completed.

But, as in the earlier part of the funeral, a complex of food preparation and reciprocal prestations of various sorts are the focus of attention in the village. Three transactions merit particular attention: (1) the exchange of funeral mats among kin, (2) the payment of funeral goods to the spouses of men, and (3) the transmission of maternal gifts to the children of the deceased.

The previous discussion of the role of funeral mats as providing a multilayered protection between the dangerous corpse and living relatives did not sufficiently emphasize a complementary function, namely, the role of these mats as the material embodiment of kinship sentiment. I think that these two symbolic aspects work together, since the strength of mats as a protecting medium is proportional to the strength of the feelings sedimented in them. And at the occasion of *sis-omengades* these same mats are exchanged (*olteboid er a badek,* or more simply, *omadek*) in a chiasmic pattern so that mats from children on the husband's side are presented to the deceased woman and then passed on to this woman's brothers' children; reciprocally, mats from these latter children are presented to the deceased and then transmitted to the children of the widowed husband. Funeral mats, thus, pass not only across generations but also across the affinal tie. The point, however, is to emphasize the affective continuity *through the deceased* of these potentially factional social relationships. This pattern of reciprocity also reinforces the sentiment that consanguineal links to the deceased transcend, at least momentarily, the more fractious reality of the affinal division (cf. Traube 1986:211).

All mats are not alike. The largest, most expensive mats pass from the senior daughter of the couple to the senior daughter of the oldest brother of the deceased wife. These costly ones are placed inside the coffin, although people say that the reciprocal distribution of the smaller mats is necessary simply because they could not also fit inside. In addition, mats are exchanged between women of the same generational stratum; for example, the husband's sister and the wife's sister exchange mats. Small mats are also presented to the visiting mourners, especially to those who brought food and funeral goods to the previous week's ritual.

> Mats are brought to the funeral by female mourners, the children [of the deceased], and some of their relatives. In addition, people from Oreor village who were not able to attend the funeral send mats by other people. These are all distributed to members of the household of Tabliual. But there are also people in the village who have "paths" [of relationship] to this house, and so they are distributed to them, too. This is a very costly custom. And when there is another funeral, these people who took the mats home with them will reciprocate (*omtechei*), and so the mats will come back again. (F)

Presentation of mats (*badek*) is, in addition, a way women honor those who have raised their children. Two patterns common in Ngeremlengui are for grandparents to raise their grandchildren and for sisters to raise each others' children.[18] The natural parents prepare a mat bundle in the name of their child and present it at the funeral of the child's mother. This is done partly to thank the mother for her childrearing efforts and partly to ensure that the child will be included in the group called "children of the house" (*ngalek er a blai*), who stand to receive portions of the inheritance.

And, finally, mats (or small cash amounts referred to by the same label, *badek*) are presented to the widowed husband by his male friends and political allies "simply out of affection." These become his personal property and are not directly reciprocated, at least not until subsequent funerals involving these same male associates, at which time they will be returned.

Cash given as *badek* thus differs from cash given by a person claiming senior *okdemaol* status to pay the debt of the funeral. Semper (1982:175–76) comments on the strategic aspect of these prestations at the funeral of high-ranking titleholders. The two chiefs of Ngebuked village, where he was living, appeared to be hassled at having to deliver elaborate funeral mats at the rites following the death of Reklai Okerangel, the chief of powerful Melekeok village. "Krai [one of the chiefs from Ngebuked] is upset that he has to go to Melekeok, but he must pay his last respects to the dead chief. That is the custom here in Palau." I also observed several cases in which titleholders from different villages sent and received *badek* (in the form of cash) because the two villages are said to be "related villages" (*kauchad el beluu*). Titleholders who send cash *badek* are entitled to receive in return a portion of the funeral feast, even if they do not themselves attend; called *dikesel a rubak*, these portions used to be calculated by the graded division of the pig, but more recently they are simply combinations of rice, sugar, soy sauce, and instant coffee.[19]

> The significance of this custom [of *omadek*] is reciprocity. The money might be only $25, but it is a *badek* for me. It is given by a person who has affection for me. Lots of money arrived this way, perhaps about $400. Now I can use this money to help pay for the funeral, but this money is different from the money collected by the *okdemaol*. That money is just to pay the debt, so it does a different kind of work. (M)

People keep written records of all the funeral mats they have received, since, as should be obvious, the complexity of these transactions over a lifetime would defy even a Belauan's social memory. These transactions also severely challenge the ethnographer, since the prestations are very numerous, since people often bring or carry away mats on behalf of others, and since each gift presupposes a history of prior funerals.

> This is a very long-term affair. People definitely remember [who gave mats]. If they do not recall, and there is no reciprocity [*olteboid*] to those who once gave them mats, then they are to be pitied. People are extremely careful about this. . . . Women are especially skilled at this and rarely make a mistake. (M)

We are now in a position to appreciate the semantic motivation which connects the word *badek* "funeral mat" and the word *bladek* "ancestral spirit." The infixed -*l*- signals the state resulting from the operation or instantiation of the thing referred to in the base form, so that an ancestral spirit is an entity which is literally constructed through the reciprocal exchange of funeral mats among

kin of the deceased. And conversely, the social groups brought into high definition at funerals are perpetuated under the protective, generative guidance of this
collectivity of ancestral spirits (cf. Poole 1984:192). This analysis enables us,
further, to see that the correlation between the social rank of titleholders and the
ritual elaboration of their funerals is not simply a matter of conspicuous distribution, since a high-ranking person requires more expanded effort of social cooperation to construct him or her as a major ancestral spirit.

The second transaction that comes to a conclusion at the divination-grave-
paving rite is the distribution (called *mengesiuch* after the word for turtleshell
tray) of funeral goods to the spouses of men who have labored for the past week
to ensure a constant supply of food for the kin of the deceased and for visiting
mourners. As was explained above, this presentation involves various store-
bought goods useful in food preparation; to these are added more traditional
items such as female valuables (principally, turtleshell trays). Although this presentation of funeral goods to wives of men in payment for food and service follows exactly the directionality of normal affinal exchange, there is reason to believe that this is not the way people try to categorize the exchange in the funeral
context. First, it should be recalled that the main axis of affinity activated by a
funeral is the bond between husband's house and wife's house, *not* that between
men of these two houses and the houses of all in-married women. As one man
explained to me, there are really two important categories of people participating
in funeral rituals, those "who belong at the sorrowful event" (*ngar er a tia el
chelbuul*) and the spouses of men, who clearly are viewed as peripheral servers
entitled to payment for their efforts. Second, the many overt gestures of reciprocity and cooperation between "sides" of this main affinal axis suggest that the
ritual as a whole attempts to downplay this inevitable source of division. Everyone talks in consanguineal language (*tekoi er a klauchad*), saying that "we are
all children of the deceased" or "we are all mourning the loss of our mother/
father." [20]

Taken together, these two points help to explain what might seem to be a
peculiarity of the symbolic dimension of *mengesiuch* prestations, namely, that in
contrast to the norms of affinal exchange, food (here, *ngeliokl*) passes against
funeral goods (here, *klalo* and *toluk*) rather than against male valuables. In other
words, the fact that these women are given female valuables and other kitchen
equipment rather than objects which would emphasize the affinal character of
the relationship points to the conclusion that villagers conceptualize *mengesiuch*
payments by analogy to friendship-service gifts—women to women—rather than
by analogy to affinal payments of *orau* valuables—men to men. (Recall that women
give each other female valuables when they help each other in various domestic,
agricultural, or customary tasks, and that a man gives male valuables to his wife's
brothers.) This is an excellent example of the power of ritual objects to convey
their inherent symbolic meaning so that the context itself is transformed, here

through the female associations of turtleshell items—deriving, I am sure, from the facts that they are made out of the shells of animals which lay eggs on dry land according to lunar cycles and that the production process involves the softening of the shell material into a mold (cf. A. Weiner 1992:12–13).

This, in turn, allows us to unravel the mystery of one of Kubary's (1895:190) statements about nineteenth-century funeral customs, namely, that trays and slicers are "paid at funerals to the outsiders who have come to mourn." This is confusing, since in the modern context these two kinds of objects are given not to "outsiders who have come to mourn" but rather to the wives of men, people not technically considered to be mourners. And as we have seen, visiting mourners are given traveling food rather than tokens of female wealth. The solution seems to lie in the fact that neither Kubary nor Semper observed an important role for wives of men at funerals; in fact, both state clearly that *relatives* of the deceased prepare food for visiting mourners and that these mourners receive coconut syrup (destined to be the principal ingredient of traveling food) purchased by women of the house.

The historical development appears to be this: that the gradual inflation of funeral rituals in the modern period led to the increased involvement of wives-of-men houses, people who seize upon funeral service as one more way to obligate their in-laws to contribute male valuables to them in the future. But, in order to downplay the affinal nature of these activities and to stress the "female" quality of the rite itself, mourners gave them *female* valuables rather than male valuables, thus putting them in the category of friendly female helpers rather than greedy male affines. So Kubary's observation about turtleshell trays most likely refers to reciprocal presentation (*mengebar*) of female valuables among dirge singers, who perfectly fit the description of being "outsiders come to mourn."

The final irony of this development is a new pattern which I witnessed in 1979, when the female relatives of the husband and of the deceased wife decided to give the spouses of men cash amounts graded by the closeness of their link to the deceased's brothers: wives received $150, more distant relatives such as sisters, cousins, and children of these wives received $100, $50, and $30. One of the women involved in this explained to me:

> Yes, this is very new. The women said, "We have to go all the way to Oreor and purchase these plastic basins and soap and carry them all back here, and then we give these goods to the spouses of men, who must pack them up and carry them right back to Oreor. This is a lot of extra work. So they decided just to put cash in their handbags, so they could depart carrying only a light load." . . . They said that it would be good if this became the custom in Belau. I think that Belauan customs have started to change, and I think that at some point [these prestations] will be just cash, with no goods at all. . . . I have a whole room full of these funeral goods, and yet every time I go to a funeral I

feel that I need to purchase new ones. My shower room is full of them; my garbage area is full of them. I have so many basins that I should open a store! So I think it is much better what [personal name] began, that is, just using money. We can take the money and use it to buy food and drink. And that is a lot better than plastic basins. (F)

And, as if to compensate for the intentional modernism of this substitution, the women in charge of this funeral tried to prepare traveling food baskets with locally produced items such as taro, tapioca, fish, and coconuts, rather than with store-bought food.

Considered in diachronic perspective, this change is laden with additional significance, since it is one of the first instances where women use cash, normally parallel to but not intersecting male valuables, in their transactions. The first substitution, that is, the use of store-bought kitchen goods in place of turtleshell trays and oystershell slicers, retains the "female" symbolic meaning. But the second substitution, cash for goods (*klalo*), cannot maintain the gendered differentiation of exchange objects, thus undermining the parallelism between male and female valuables (cf. Barnett 1949:56) and making it more difficult to overlook the penetration of affinity into the funeral context. The presentation of cash opens these exchanges to the interpretation that they are, after all, just like financial presentations in the affinal exchange system.

The third and final transaction to be completed is the gift to the children of the deceased. Gender differentiation becomes important once again, since male children are given carved wooden plates (*ongall*), while female children are presented with one of a variety of turtleshell items, either a hammered tray (*chesiuch*), a large spoon (*terir*), or an elongated ladle (*ongisb*). These objects are the personal possessions of the deceased, who leaves careful instructions with her sisters as to the eventual disposition of the treasured objects. Every senior woman would have had only one each of these plates and trays, and so the children who inherit them are thereby acknowledged to be the "real" children of the house. The wooden plates are given to male children at the death of a senior man by his closest sister, while turtleshell objects go to female children at the death of their mother. The plates and trays are functionally distinguished by gender in that wooden plates are used to hold "protein food" (fish, fowl, pig), the collection of which is the task of men, whereas turtleshell objects are used by women in food preparation. Furthermore, the individuality of the present is signaled by the fact that a titleholder eats off a single wooden plate, and no one else (with the exception of very small children) is permitted to use it. So the presentation of this object to a son implies that the child will some day become a titleholder with his own reserved plate. (Although titleholders eat off china and plastic dishes today, the practice of reserving a bowl for the "father of the house" still remains.) While this pattern of transgenerational inheritance certainly identifies the young heirs with their parents through the continuity of inheritance of these gendered objects, it also suggests a hierarchical relationship between the subordinated recipients and their generational superiors (cf. Munn 1970:158).

Now, with the techniques for carving wooden plates a lost art, both male children and female children receive similar turtleshell trays, although the linguistic differentiation still remains firm. It is clear that this transgenerational transaction symbolizes the continuity of maternal kinship, expressed, it must be noted, by the same objects that are employed in asymmetrical affinal exchanges with the spouses of men. Given the completely different emotional attachment found in the maternal bond, however, no one in Belau would confuse the distinct meaning adhering in these objects functioning in the two disparate social contexts. And, in contrast to the chiasmic, reciprocal exchange of funeral mats, the *ongall* and *chesiuch* gifts to children are intended to be the permanent, personal possessions of the heirs. Last, whereas both mats and funeral goods for spouses of men have undergone substitution by American cash, these intimate forms of maternal inheritance maintain their attachment to the traditional turtleshell form.

Conclusion

From the foregoing analysis, it is clear that both traditional and contemporary variations in Belauan funerals rites closely parallel the well-documented patterns of funerals in the Indonesian and Oceanic worlds.[21] We have noted widespread themes such as the journey of the ghost to a western land of spirits, the role of mats and cloth in sedimenting the affect of kin, the imposition of silence and inactivity during the mourning period, the use of mortuary practices to signal differential social rank, the lengthy period of delay between the burial and the final settlement of affinal obligations, and the transformation of the dead into fructifying ancestral spirits. Although these general areal similarities are worth noting and do aid our understanding of the Belauan case, I think that each society needs to be studied in terms of specific patterns of intersection involving kinds of meaningful objects, social roles and groups brought into play during the ritual, and modalities of transaction or exchange which couple these objects and these social relations.

But the ethnographic evidence from Belau suggests that it is impossible to simply read off the understood meaningfulness of exchange events from the presupposed symbolic meaning of transacted objects. We have seen examples where identical objects carry different meanings when they are present in social contexts requiring distinct transactional modes: baskets of taro being both *ngeliokl* and *chelungel*; and, inversely, radically distinct objects, such as mats and cash, can be categorized as *badek* for senior men. Clearly, it is the social relationships themselves which provide the contextual specification of the meaningfulness of objects. Yet we have also seen instances where changes in the character of ex-change media make it nearly impossible for particular symbolic meanings to be differentiated, especially where one ritual practice adopts an object already asso-ciated with a polar meaning, as in the example of women substituting (male) cash for (female) kitchen goods. In other words, the vectors of intersection of these three analytical distinctions cannot be predicted prior to empirical research. In fact, the assignment of fixed symbolic meaning to objects, the *ti* plant and tur-meric for instance, may be an indication that these objects have lost the power to create social contexts, a power still maintained by male and female valuables.

And, by looking at the funeral data from a diachronic perspective, it is pos-sible to see how different aspects of the society are intertwined. For example, the abrupt termination of the practice of burial in front of houses (in favor of com-munity graveyards) correlates with the increased importance of intervillage af-filiative relations, so that "lateral" rather than "vertical" paths of relationship contribute to social identity; this lateral expansion also correlates with the infla-tion of the importance of spouses-of-men houses. Together these two develop-ments in turn link up with the gradual severing of Belauan social groups from their prescribed land parcels (cf. Bloch 1982:212–13). Thus, social identity is almost entirely a product of customary transactions like the ones described above rather than, as was the case in the traditional situation, of presupposed territori-ally anchored hierarchies. Whereas, in the traditional situation, a person's strong-est claim to status at a given house was to say (actually, to insult) "My mother is buried here," social status today is roughly calculable by the number of visitors from affiliated houses who attend a funeral. Thus, the irony is that, despite the apparent commercialization of funerals and the gradual loss of cosmological groundings for many of the ritual actions, the mortuary sequence is destined to play an even greater role in Belauan social life.

4 | The Political Function of Reported Speech

Authoritative Speech

In the course of his discussion of discourse in the novel, Bakhtin (1981) points out that the social-historical fact of the "internal stratification" of language into dialects, jargons, and speech genres is the prerequisite for the stylistic "heteroglossia" of the modern polyphonic novel, in which authorial speech, narrator's speech, and the speech of characters enter into complex "interanimation." Many of Bakhtin's specific analyses of literary techniques found in novelistic heteroglossia can be transferred to the anthropological study of language in its social context. In particular, in the novel as in social life, speech constantly takes as an object of reference or representation previous speech, as in direct and indirect quotation of the actual utterances of others. As Bakhtin notes, "The topic of a speaking person has enormous importance in everyday life. In real life we hear speech about speakers and their discourse at every step. We can go so far as to say that in real life people talk most of all about what others talk about—they transmit, recall, weigh and pass judgment on other people's words, opinions, assertions, information; people are upset by others' words, or agree with them, contest them, refer to them and so forth" (Bakhtin 1981:338). But in addition, as Jakobson (1980b), Sanches (1975), Silverstein (1976, 1981b, 1985b, 1993), and others have argued, metalingual activity goes beyond reporting token utterances, since language also has the potential for becoming a comprehensive metalanguage with respect to higher-level semiotic phenomena such as semantic and pragmatic meaning (as in glossing), conventional rules of speaking (as in performatives), and the parameters of the contexts of speaking (as in deixis). In this broader sense Silverstein (1976) has distinguished the realm of "metasemantics," that is, language about the relatively decontextualized meaning of forms, and the more encompassing realm of "metapragmatics," that is, language about the indexical or pragmatic relationship between linguistic signals and their contexts of use. Rather than being highly unusual aspects of language use, these two types of metalinguistic representation are more accurately seen as statistically widespread and structurally crucial in language. In other words, it is not merely a social fact that dialogicality characterizes linguistic utterances but it is also the case that linguistic structure and use depend essentially on language's ability to refer to itself along many dimensions.

Although it was not his primary focus of interest, Bakhtin recognized the importance of examining what he called "authoritative utterances" as one pole of the continuous interaction between an individual's speech and the language of others:

> In each epoch, in each social circle, in each small world of family, friends, acquaintances, and comrades in which a human grows and lives, there are always authoritative utterances that set the tone—artistic, scientific, and journalistic works on which one relies, to which one refers, which are cited, imitated, and followed. In each epoch, in all areas of life and activity there are particular traditions that are expressed and retained in verbal vestments: in written works, in utterances, in sayings, and so forth. There are always some verbally expressed leading ideas of the "masters of thought" of a given epoch, some basic tasks, slogans, and so forth. (Bakhtin 1986:88–89)

In another passage Bakhtin comments on the resistance of authoritative speech to being creatively assimilated by another speaker or author:

> The authoritative word demands that we acknowledge it, that we make it our own; it binds us, quite independent of any power it might have to persuade us internally; we encounter it with its authority already fused to it. The authoritative word is located in a distanced zone, organically connected with a past that is felt to be hierarchically higher. It is, so to speak, the word of the fathers. Its authority was already *acknowledged* in the past. It is a *prior* discourse. It is therefore not a question of choosing it from among other possible discourses that are its equal. It is given (it sounds) in lofty spheres, not those of familiar contact. Its language is a special (as it were, hieratic) language. It can be profaned. It is akin to taboo, i.e., a name that must not be taken in vain. (Bakhtin 1981:342)

As language clothed in "verbal vestments," authoritative speech confronts speaker and writers as unquestionable, distant, and powerful. For Bakhtin, such language exists at the opposite end of a continuum from the rich, multivoiced quality of novelistic discourse, since it not only blocks any modification or "analysis" by an authorial intention but also projects its own worldview upon the reporting voice (Morson and Emerson 1990:220–21). This point is taken up specifically by Vološinov in his work on reported speech:

> Political rhetoric presents an analogous case [to judicial language]. It is important to determine the specific gravity of rhetorical speech, judicial or political, in the linguistic consciousness of the given social group at a given time. Moreover, the position that a specimen of speech to be reported occupies on the social hierarchy of values must also be taken into account. The stronger the feeling of hierarchical eminence in another's utterance, the more sharply de-

fined will its boundaries be, and the less accessible will it be to penetration by retorting and commenting tendencies from outside. (Vološinov 1973:123)

Fictional discourse as well as conversational and rhetorical speech are character-ized by a complex interplay between reporting and reported speech, between an outer authorial frame and an inner represented image of another's speech. The basic difference between novelistic discourse and the rhetorical genres is that in the former the stronger vector of influence is the "penetration" or "incursion" of the author's ideological perspective into the speech being reported, whereas in the latter the fixity, objectivity, and authority of the reported speech enables it to resist this manipulation and to assert its own independent power upon the outer frame.

This opposition between the transforming effect of fictional representation in novelistic discourse and the ideological determination of authoritative speech harnessed in various rhetorical genres suggests, then, a sharp distinction between the two genres in the hierarchical ranking of reporting and reported speech. The Russian novelist's authorial voice dominates the reported speech of the novel's characters as surely as the priest's report during the Mass of Jesus's words at the Last Supper is dominated by that divinely endowed discourse. An obvious impli-cation of this analysis is that there is a link between the presupposed authority of a segment of speech and the tendency for reports to retain its linguistic shape or canonical form, that is, for it to be reported in direct discourse rather than in indirect discourse. Or to put the argument the other way around, in the rhetor-ical genres the power of ideological determination of reported speech is propor-tional to the degree of iconicity of the relationship between the original utterance and its subsequent linguistic representation.

Although I feel that Bakhtin's general distinction between these two genres is basically sound, there is danger in underestimating the creative role the political speaker can play in reporting authoritative discourse. First, in contrast to the highly prescribed genres such as ritual language and judicial formulae, political oratory described for many societies quotes authoritative speech—gems from traditional wisdom, historically memorable utterances, proverbial expressions, legitimzing statutes—for creative, contextually specific rhetorical effect.[1] The politician's aim is to harness these "words of another" for the purposes of the moment, and this is frequently accomplished by submitting instances of quoted speech to the regimenting organization imposed by the unfolding of the reporting or framing speech. In a sense, then, the quotation of authoritative discourse sur-renders only momentarily to the hierarchical rank inherent in this reported dis-course, for these official or traditional words are in fact put to uses unintended by their original authors or not implied in their initial contexts. Second, the use of direct rather than indirect quotation, while certainly demonstrating appropri-ately reverential obeisance, can also be a mechanism for transferring the aura of historical objectivity and representational naturalness from the inner to the outer frame of discourse. Here it is precisely the presumed "distancing" (Sherzer 1983:213) of the reported utterance that allows the speaker to harness the authority attaching to the quotation without calling attention to the creative, rhetorical purpose of doing so. In other words, speakers can induce legitimacy upon their own speech through the juxtaposition of iconically represented authoritative speech.

In this chapter I explore these issues through an analysis of the political function of reported speech in a specific ethnographic example of oratory I witnessed during fieldwork in Belau (Parmentier 1987a). While I realize the limitations of using a single speech event as the sole datum for analysis, the speech and events surrounding it are such an important signal of political transformation that I feel justified in treating it as a privileged "diagnostic event" that, as Moore (1987:730) puts it, "reveals ongoing contests and conflicts and competitions" and "display[s] multiple meanings in combination" (735). The analysis will consider the relationship among three levels of linguistic phenomena: (1) formally explicit devices for metapragmatic representation belonging to paradigmatic sets of the code, (2) text-internal pragmatics generated by the syntagmatic unfolding of the rhetorical architecture of the speech as performed, and (3) the encompassing cultural principles and norms about the linkage between the use of language and chiefly authority. My goal is, on the one hand, to illustrate the creative avenues open to the orator in manipulating and framing authoritative speech and, on the other hand, to demonstrate that the performative effectiveness of speech is constrained by norms of language presupposed in actual events of speaking.

Ethnographic Context

Belau is an Austronesian culture occupying a group of islands in the western corner of the Pacific Ocean, approximately 550 miles east of the Philippines and 600 miles north of New Guinea. After several millennia of relative isolation, Belau became the locus of successive colonial regimes, starting with the British in the late eighteenth century and followed by Spain, Germany, Japan, and the United States. As a Trust Territory formally under the jurisdiction of the United Nations, Belau has been dominated by United States' political and military interests for the past fifty years, although in the last decade the people have made great strides toward independent self-governance. The islands are divided into political districts (also called municipalities and states), some occupying separate islands and some located on Babeldaob, the largest island in the archipelago. Districts, in turn, are made up of spatially distinct villages, though Belauans refer to both political units by a single term, *beluu*. The most populous village is Oreor, actually a small island just south of Babeldaob, which for centuries has been the point of contact with foreign commercial, cultural, and political forces and which functioned as the District Center under the Trusteeship.

During the summer of 1979 the district of Ngeremlengui, like many other districts in Belau, was involved in a bitter political struggle prompted by the recently drafted national constitution. The original document, approved by the constitutional convention which met for four months in Oreor, was scheduled for final ratification in a public referendum on July 9. The draft constitution proudly proclaimed the political independence and territorial integrity of Belau and carefully balanced democratic principles with respect for traditional leaders and customs. Several provisions of the document, however, were directly inconsistent with the terms of the so-called Hilo Principles, previously adopted by the Political Status Commission negotiators, which defined the relationship of Free Association between Belau and the United States (Parmentier 1991). But the delegates to the convention refused to modify their draft and, confident that the public would overwhelmingly approve this historic declaration of Belauaness (*klbelau*), undertook a massive and costly effort in political education at the village level.

Trying to avoid jeopardizing the ongoing negotiations over Belau's Free Association status, members of the national legislature effectively voted to undercut the new constitution by repealing the enabling legislation of the already adjourned convention, arguing that the delegates had failed to draft a document consistent with the established principles of Free Association. The legislature's bill would effectively cancel the scheduled referendum and turn the constitution over to a specially appointed legislative redrafting committee. Thus, as July 9 approached two political factions were operative: the pro-constitution forces, led in Ngeremlengui by the two men who had been delegates to the convention, and the pro–Free Association (or pro-status) forces, led by the district's traditionally sanctioned chief, Ngirturong, and the district's elected representative to the legislature.

On the morning of July 7 people from Ngeremlengui assembled in Ngeremetengel village to meet with the United Nations Visiting Mission, a group of international observers sent to Belau to ensure that the electorate was informed and uncoerced and that there would be no irregularities in the election process. While waiting for the party to arrive by boat, villagers talked informally with their two convention delegates. An elder complimented them, saying that, having chosen two "children of Ngeremlengui" to represent the village in this important task, the people of Ngeremlengui would surely continue their support for the document they had "given birth to." The official meeting, which finally got under way in the early afternoon, was conducted in the normally polite style, with respect shown especially toward the foreign visitors. After a rather formal exchange of questions, the head of the visiting mission asked for a show of hands to see how many of those registered to vote had actually read the proposed constitution; only a few people raised their hands. As this meeting was drawing to a close, a second boat arrived carrying the district's high chief Ngirturong and its legislative representative, two individuals whose anti-constitution opinions were at variance with the general sentiment of the local people, who had recently become uncharacteristically vocal in their criticism of these two leaders.

Moments after the speedboat carrying the United Nations group disappeared down the mangrove channel, chief Ngirturong began to address the assembly, but the second-ranking chief, whose title is Ngiraklang, waved him off with the words: "Not enough ears," meaning that a third important titleholder, Ngirutelchii, had yet to join the meeting. He soon did, and Ngirturong began again, but this time three villagers interrupted him with a series of critical statements to the effect that Ngirturong and the legislative representative were trying to "kill" the very constitution which these delegates, "the children of Ngeremlengui," had given birth to, and that they had remained for too long in Oreor without returning to the villages to inform local people what was transpiring there. At one point a man actually shouted at the chief: "At every meeting I am sitting right here in the meeting house, but where are you?" Stung by this highly inappropriate attack from an untitled kinsman, the chief replied: "Are you daring to challenge my leadership? If so, let me remind you that *I* am Ngirturong, while you are the child of [a former] Ngirturong." Since titles normatively pass matrilineally, to be the "child of a chief" is to be removed from the direct line of power.

At this point I was totally shocked, for I had never seen such overt and pointed challenges to the authority of the chief, although I knew that there was widespread opposition to his political position. But what happened next made the preceding look tame. A middle-aged woman sitting at the end of the meeting house began to scream and stomp her feet violently on the floor. I barely managed to decipher what she kept repeating: "Ngirturong and Ngiraklang are not at Imiungs! Imiungs, Imiungs, Imiungs! I hate it, I hate it, I hate it!" This woman, I later learned, was completely unaware of her behavior and spoke the words of Uchererak (Foremost of the Year), the traditional god of Ngeremlengui. The import of these words was this: Ngirturong and Ngiraklang are the legitimate leaders at Imiungs (the poetic name for Imeiong), the capital of Ngeremlengui district, and yet the present titleholders are living and meeting in Ngeremetengel, a lower-ranking village in the district (see Parmentier 1986). Also, there is no sense talking about constitutions and treaties, for the government of Belau is not subject to democratic election but rather to the rule of traditional chiefs.

No one moved to restrain the possessed woman as she continued to scream and stomp for several minutes. Finally a lower-ranking titleholder from Imeiong shouted at Ngirturong: "Listen to her words, since they are indeed true." Ironically, the words of the god Uchererak were taken to be supportive of the local challenge to the chief, who was in favor of increasing Belau's dependence on

Western forms of political leadership and economic assistance. At this point the three ranking titleholders all slipped out of the meeting house, Ngirturong to his own house across the path, Ngiraklang to his nearby canoe shed, and Ngirutel-chii to another house in the village.

In the absence of his political ally Ngirturong, the legislator was now on his own, and the same vocal villagers started to bombard him with angry questions about his efforts to "kill" the draft constitution. His response was to claim meekly: "I did not write it, but now we legislators have to deal with it *and* with the Free Association agreement." Ngirturong returned shortly to his prescribed corner seat, where he sat quietly with his eyes staring blankly at the floor. During a lull in the political debate, he addressed a rhetorical question to the gathering: "What is the reason for this misbehavior?" The phrasing of this question and the chief's impatient tone of voice indicated to all that he did not consider the incident to be a valid communication from the god Uchererak (an impression confirmed in my subsequent discussions with him).

When Ngiraklang returned to the meeting house he said, "We should plead with the god to seek an appropriate person through whom to speak his words and beg him not to send his message through this woman or anyone else not in the proper role to receive these important words." He instructed the villagers that Imeiong's ninth-ranking house, Ngerungelang, held the title Chelid (God) and that the man holding this title is the proper spokesman (*kerong*) of the god (this house and the corresponding title have been vacant for some time). Then Ngirturong spoke directly to Ngiraklang: "Odisang [Japanese honorific], why don't *you* appoint a person yourself?" But Ngiraklang replied sharply, "No one can select the person to speak the words of the god; only *he* can seek out the proper person."

After about an hour, when many had had a chance to speak, various mechanisms of personal reconciliation began to operate. First, the woman who had been possessed by the god went over to ask Ngirturong for some betelnut, and they exchanged a few words in private. Ngirturong and the legislator then purchased two cases of soft drinks from the local store and distributed them as peace offerings (*tngakireng*) to the people still in the meeting house. Taking his cue from this gesture, the man who had been most vocal in his criticism of the chief thanked him for the drinks and said that everyone was once again "of one spirit" (*tarrengud*). He also tried to blunt the directness of his early criticism by putting it at a metalevel, saying that his real complaint had been the lack of communication between chief and village. The legislator, too, promised to keep in better touch with the villages.

Just as the meeting was about to end on this relatively peaceful note, one of the convention delegates (perhaps embrazened by the obvious support of the assembled villagers) put a blunt question to Ngirturong: "Before you return to

Oreor, we would like to hear you publicly state your opinion concerning the up-coming election." The chief hesitated and then repeated the question for Ngirak-lang, who had not heard the original query. Quickly, Ngiraklang came to the aid of his fellow chief by asking: "Who was it that asked Ngirturong this? I cannot approve of this *boy* asking Ngirturong to reveal his thoughts." Ngirturong then added that he would vote according to his personal opinion, but that he would never try to manipulate the village by using the weight of his title to back his position. Ngiraklang concluded this discussion by stating that it was silly to try to find out what the village would do before the election, since after the election is over everyone will know, and the chiefs and all the people will follow that decision.

These events of July 7, though obviously prompted by the current political crisis over the draft constitution, were also related to several long-standing sources of tension within the district. First, the district has long been a center of support for Modekngei (Let Us Go Forward Together), an indigenous yet syn-cretistic religious movement which preaches the self-sufficiency of Belau's natural environment and whose members worship certain gods from the traditional pan-theon (Aoyagi 1987). When this movement first developed during the Japanese colonial period, its leaders in the district decided to ignore Uchererak, the estab-lished god of Imeiong, in favor of other pan-Belauan dieties. The religious ten-sions between followers of Modekngei and members of various Christian groups (Protestant, Catholic, and Seventh Day Adventist) paralleled to some degree the district's political factions, since Modekngei people generally supported the orig-inal draft constitution and opposed those legislators who argued for closer polit-ical ties with the United States at the expense of local self-determination. Not ironically—given the well-established tendency for younger brothers and "off-spring of men" (*ulechell*) to seek nonchiefly avenues of power and reputation—in Ngeremlengui the Modekngei faction is led by individuals who are patrilaterally related to chief Ngirturong, who is not only Protestant but also an advocate of the pro-status position.

Second, the turmoil in the meeting house touched on the sensitive issue of relative village rank within the district. This problem has its roots in the fact that, while Imeiong is regarded as the capital of the district, the four highest-ranking or "cornerpost" titleholders of Imeiong (and thus the leaders of Ngeremlengui as a whole) moved to low-ranking Ngeremetengel shortly after World War II. Ngar-aimeiong, the council of titleholders which is the traditional governing body of the district, now meets in a Japanese-style meeting house in Ngeremetengel. The central square of Imeiong is overgrown with weeds; its two meeting houses were destroyed by typhoons decades ago and were never rebuilt. People still living in Imeiong, many of them related to the highest-ranking house owning the title Ngirturong, feel that their leaders have abandoned the legitimate locus of their rank. Finally, there is an institutional as well as personal tension between Ngirturong and Ngiraklang, the two leaders of the district. For many centuries the Ngiraklang title was first in rank, but in the late nineteenth century a Ngirturong titleholder had Ngiraklang assassinated and then usurped the leadership of Imeiong. Today, the incumbent Ngiraklang is considerably older and much more skilled in the "ways of politics" (*kelulau*) than Ngirturong, although he holds his title by virtue of weaker patrilateral ties (*ulechell*); Ngirturong, younger and far more involved in a Western life-style, is nonetheless a legitimate matrilineal (*ochell*) holder of the title. All three of these lines of tension, Modekngei/Christian, Imeiong/Ngeremetengel, and Ngirturong/Ngiraklang, became implicated in the political struggles of July 1979.

Ngiraklang's Speech to the Council

Toward the close of a lengthy meeting of the democratically elected Ngeremlengui municipal council a week later, Ngiraklang made several unsuccessful attempts to get the floor, but each time Ngirturong put him off, knowing that this second-ranking chief was likely to bring up the events of the previous week. Finally, Ngiraklang left his prescribed seat in the corner of the meeting house and moved closer to the center of the floor. From this vantage point he repeated his request, but this time to the elected magistrate, saying: "I have already asked Ngirturong for an opportunity to speak and it has not been granted, so now I am asking the magistrate for an opportunity to speak before the public." The magistrate had no option but to acknowledge this request from his social superior, and so Ngiraklang began an impassioned, stylistically brilliant speech directed primarily at those present who had been involved in the previous week's verbal fireworks. Ngiraklang had alerted me the night before that he intended to make a speech, so that I was ready with my taperecorder.

This speech focused not so much on what might appear to be the most important words spoken the week before, namely, the dramatic message of Uchererak delivered through the medium of the possessed woman, as on the highly irregular challenges from younger, untitled, and lower-ranking men made immediately prior to and after the possession incident. And in order to communicate what he felt to be the danger of these challenges to village leadership, Ngiraklang began by establishing a pointed analogy to events which took place in 1966, when the local men's club (*cheldebechel*) temporarily usurped the role of the chiefly council (*klobak*) by imposing a monetary fine on a young man and when the high chief (in fact, the mother's brother of the present titleholder) subsequently left the village in anger. This historical allusion clearly establishes Ngiraklang's reading of the danger of the present situation: that these public insults directed toward Ngirturong might have a result parallel to the events of 1966, namely, the departure of the chief from the village.

Later in the speech, events from 1934 are also referred to as marking the point at which the village god began a period of uninterrupted silence, broken only in 1979. There are, then, three relevant temporal contexts referred to in the speech: the time of the speech itself (July 14), the previous week's meeting with its embedded possession utterances (July 7), and certain parallel events and words from 1934 and 1966. As will be seen, part of the rhetorical force of the speech depends on the construction of a parallelism of "meaning" or "import" (*belkul*) among these various contexts and on the use of proverbial and normative expressions, which establish an overall authoritative, traditional aura.

My translation of Ngiraklang's July 14 speech to the municipal council follows. Numbered line divisions are based on pauses rather than on syntactic regularities; lettered divisions mark the thematic and formal segments to be analyzed below. In order to facilitate discussion I have underscored all segmentable metapragmatic portions of the speech, including verbs of speaking, quotative complementizers (some represented by *that* and others by *:*), direct and indirect quoted speech, references to verbal behavior, citations of proverbs, quasi-performative formulae, first- and second-person personal pronouns, and linguistically relevant deictical references to the parameters of the present moment (excluding personal names and spatial deixis). I enclose explanatory interpolations in brackets.

A

[1]   *My speech* is *like this:* when *I start speaking now*, I am going to *talk* of
        affairs from about 1966 up until the *present day*
        When *I speak like this*, those who want to *listen* should *listen*, and those
        who want to reflect should reflect, and after *you* have reflected *I*
        want *you* to *ask questions*; if some dislike what comes out, that is all
        right too
        Because *I* am going to *say* many *proverbs* concerning the village of
        Ngeremlengui, not about the [municipal] council and not about Ngarai-
        meiong [chiefly council]

B

        Ngeremlengui is like a canoe, and *I* have watched this canoe for almost
        seventy years
[5]   And as *I* observe *us* people living in Ngeremlengui, when this canoe cap-
        sizes there is not one of us who could right it, since no one is skilled
        in the technique of bringing a canoe back to the surface
        When *you* were building the school, *you*, Ngiraikelau, and *you*,
        Okerdeu, were working, and Tebelak over there and Ngirturong here

I was at my house, and when you assembled as Ngaratebelik [club] to build the school, there was a coconut tree log which was brought up to be used as the launching log; then Ngirturong departed and Ngiraklang departed

You know this

I am not *decorating my speech in saying that:* I watched this situation grow worse

[10]   How many trips did *I* make to that quonset hut *to speak* in order to bring *you* all together, in place of the absent Ngirturong?

What served as a sign of this for *me* is that when *you* were setting up the launching log, *you* acted like Ngaraimeiong and fined people like Tebelak and Ngiralulk and took a kldait-type valuable

That was a sign to *me that:* Ngaraimeiong had vanished, that Ngaratebelik had become the new Ngaraimeiong, but that was all right because Oingerang, the child of Ngirturong, was there, as well as Rechediterong, the one from Chol [village], who was the offspring of a woman from Klang [house]

Ngirturong ignored all this and remained patient, *knowing that:* Oingerang and Otaor were there

And *I* also rested easy *knowing that:* Remarii was there

[15]   But then *I* watched the situation turn even worse

And when *you* fined Ngiralulk, then Ngirutelchii, the father of Maidesil, should have paid the fine, right?

He *said, "I am not going to pay the fine"*

The *meaning* was *like this:*

He did not pay the fine on behalf of Ngiralulk, for *you* members of Ngaratebelik [club] had become Ngaraimeiong [council]

[20]   If only those of Ngaraimeiong had fined Ngiralulk, then it would have been a simple matter for Ngirutelchii Rechuld to pay his [son's] fine

I observed this situation become worse, and so *I* spent a kldait-type valuable to pay the fine of Ngiralulk and to quiet down the *situation*

Perhaps it did not exactly remedy the *situation*, but at least it smoothed it over for a while, and enabled *you* to return to work, and *you* finished the school and took payment for it, and *you* were of one spirit as *you* began to pave the road from Umad [channel] to Imeiong

What happened when *you* went to Imeiong? *You* were very unified and had even decided to clear the mangrove channel. What happened there?

Ngirturong departed and went to Oreor, and *you* members of Ngaratebelik disbanded

[25]   *These things I am listing, I do not list* them so *that:* they will necessarily become true

First *we* need to understand what happened from that time up, up, up, up until the *present day*

Well, if we do not know these things, then Ngeremlengui will detour from the path, and there is not one among *us* who is able to put it back on course

Absolutely not, and *I think that:* the canoe is overturned, and *I think that* the canoe is sunk and not one of us inside this meeting house is able to bring it back to the surface

This is one thing

C

[30] The day before *yesterday*, what happened then was the launching log for *something* concerning the god, right?

Be forewarned, *I* am going to *say words* which *you* will perhaps dislike

The day before *yesterday*, the eighth [sic] day of the month, what occurred in this very meeting house?

I believe that if it was really Uchererak who came down and *spoke his words* and that if *we* just remained with *closed mouths*, then *I know that:* Ngeremlengui has not detoured from the path

But when Uchererak came down and *spoke*, people *said, "Go ahead and speak your words! Go ahead and speak your words!"*

[35] What was the *meaning* of *this*?

Maybe *my tone of voice* is a bit severe concerning this *affair*; I am merely *clarifying*

When they all *said, "Go ahead and speak"*

What was the *meaning* of this *expression* for *we* people of Ngeremlengui or else for the people of Imeiong?

I think *that* the *meaning* is not at all good, since it is capable of pushing the village of Ngeremlengui off the path because no village can have two leaders in it

[40] And if *we invite* the god to come in, the god cannot be *interrogated* and cannot be subject to fining; rather, *we* can be fined or else be subject to *questioning*

D

I am trying to *explain this situation clearly*, and this does not have any *significance for me* personally, but it is extremely *significant for me* if *you* cause the village of Ngeremlengui to detour and take a different course, for this would be to ignore the *words* which came down here, which they *said* were the *words* of Uchererak

It would be ignoring them, just like taking up stones and throwing them at the village

This at least was *my* perception of what happened, Shiro; these are not *bad things to say*

I am just *reminding*, since should Ngeremlengui take a detour, then its spirit also detours, and if the spirit of Ngirturong detours, then Ngeremlengui detours and no one can bring it back

[45] And so *I ask you* who are here, is there one of *you* who can patch up the relationship between the god and Ngaraimeiong? (No) All right, then, and if the god comes down, *we* people are to be in charge of him

I also *remind you*, Chedelngod, and *you* people of Imeiong *that:* who in Imeiong is capable of *commanding* Uchererak?

Don't dislike what *I* am *saying*

Who in Imeiong *today* is capable of *commanding* Uchererak: *"Go ahead and speak your words to someone"*?

I really think there is no one

[50] No one at all

Uchererak is a god and is not to be *commanded*

Although in ancient times Ngaraimeiong could *claim* that Ngaraimeiong *commands* him, or else they could *ask* him for his *words*

And yet *today all of us here* have become *like this*, and *I speak these words* because *I* am worried about the village, about the spirit of the village

These things we are *talking* about *these days* [i.e., the constitutional debate] and in the future are certainly good things, and yet concerning these *affairs* which recently took place *I* strongly *remind you that:* when the spirit of Ngirturong detours, then *I* detour and the chiefs of Ngaraimeiong detour

[55] It is not the case that, should Ngirturong's thoughts be upset, *we* can steady the *affairs* of the village

Keep calm and think about the old people who still know about these *matters*

E

And so *I* am just *reminding*

I am *reminding you today*

If *I* had just *kept silent* and walked by, come the next meeting, then what?

[60] These *words* which *I* am *saying*, their *meaning* is this: *I* am not *scolding* and *I* am not angry; *my tone of voice* is severe toward *you* because *I* am *reminding* the village of Ngeremlengui

F

When *you* went to Imeiong to build the road this last time, Ngirturong
  fled and went to Oreor and stayed there for many months
Which man in Imeiong brought him back by means of an chelebucheb-
  type valuable, so that he came back carrying this chelebucheb?
This is a very difficult *thing* to accomplish
We do not know for sure: what was it that brought Ngirturong back to
  the village?
[65] Perhaps this was *just talk*
Whoever the person was who was skilled in these *techniques* brought
  Ngirturong back to the village, as if he had been playing around in
  Oreor, and none of the elders *complained, saying, "This person is
  coming here without having paid his entry money"*
Just *listen* to *these things I am saying* and discard them if *you* wish, since
  the world is growing different; but *I* really hate to be alive at almost
  eighty years old and *hear these strange words* which threaten to detour
  Ngeremlengui
If it detours after *I* am dead, then *I* would feel good because *I know
  that:* there is no one left in Ngeremlengui who is skilled at bringing a
  large canoe back to the surface, and no one is skilled at bringing a
  sailing canoe back to the surface, and no one is skilled at bringing a
  swift canoe back to the surface, and a war canoe is the most difficult
  of all to bring back to the surface, and Ngeremlengui is even more
  difficult to bring back to the surface than a war canoe
Let *us* remain calm in our spirit, for Belau has need of *us, knowing that:*
  Ngeremlengui still stands prepared
[70] But if *we* are going to *talk* about the *"poker and tongs"* of Ngeremlengui, then no one will have need of Ngeremlengui
Agreed

G

I know . . . the one *I have just mentioned* . . . *I* have known two deaths
  of Ngeremlengui, *like we say, "the death of the canoe which races
  with the goatfish"*
I know two [deaths]
And a person also caused them, not money
[75] And they didn't *think:* this person will take care of it so that it will work
  out fine and be all right
And now *you* are just *talking*, but *I* know what is wrong; and as *we say,
  "you are talking, so why don't you go do it?"*
And then *you* raise up *your* hands

I know, *I* really do not not know *this*

And it is a good thing to think about it

[80]   And if the likes of Uchererak comes again, *we* will all *keep silent*. No one knows *his words*

And whoever knows *his words* has become himself a god who carries Ngeremlengui and pushes it under the water

I do not not know the *meaning* of the departure of Uchererak from the village, so that he has been *silent* up until *today*

I know

In 1934 he became *silent*, and there was an opportunity for Ngirturong Sulial and for Kodeb from Chol

[85]   And Ngirturong tricked his daughter Dibech into marrying Kodeb, and he brought her to Ngerungelang [house], where they lived for many months

And there he spread this *message* of Modekngei and made Uchererak so that he was not necessarily evil, but just sleeping

It remained this way up, up, up until the eighth day of the month, although there may have been a few other times which *I* do not know about; but *I* did find out on the eighth of the month *that:* he was awaking and looking out, looking out at the village of Ngeremlengui to see if it was destroyed or not destroyed

At the very instant [the names] *"Ngiraklang and Ngirturong"* were *mentioned I* headed for the canoe shed and left the meeting house

[90]   *I* did not see her pace up and down and *I* did not see her pound on the floor

From *that moment these words* have weighed upon *my* heart because *I* know who the people were who *spoke*

They are like the "council" of Uchererak and *speak the words* of Uchererak toward the village of Ngeremlengui and to Ngaraimeiong

H

This is just a personal thought and not necessarily the *truth; I* am just speculating

When they *opened their mouths to speak* on the eighth of the month, was the *purpose to declare that:* they are the *messengers* of Uchererak and now are *speaking?*

[95]   If so, then it was just their opinion

But if it was their opinion, never think that again, because Ngeremlengui is not *"a snake with two tongues"* from ancient times up until *today,* and neither is it a green snake

Now I am *talking* to *you* in order to *remind you:* never do that again, because "*cold on the way out, hot on the way back,*" or else, "*words which go out uncrowded cannot fit back into our mouths*"

Those who *spoke* will *learn this: their words* were uncrowded going out, but when Ngirturong and *I* turn them around, they will not be able to eat them

Just like taking the ashes from a cigarette or from a fire and stuffing them into the mouth of a person .

[100] Let *us* remain calm and reflect *that:* the village still exists and so do the titleholders

And *this* is the *significance of saying that:* respect is vanishing from Ngeremlengui

And yet *you* know, Shiro, that respect is the foundation of the law of Belau, nothing else

It is not a material object, it is just *our* respect for titleholders and for any old person with a bald head

This foundation [Japanese term] is like the foundation [Belauan term] of the law of Belau

[105] And *today* as much as *we* try, respect almost vanished at that time and this is the reason that *I spoke up* so quickly

I

This is what has been on *my* mind from this morning up to now, and what *I have spoken you* can throw away and that would be fine, for *I* have become happy once more, now that *I have spoken* the bad thoughts in *my* heart about the village

My physical body has no *importance*; *I* am now eighty years old and *I* am nearing *my* final journey, or else *I* will soon just sit as a senile old man

I am just reminding you young people and *you* people with bright minds, and those who should *speak the words of the village, we* should think a bit

The words of the village which we speak also have a limit; *we* do not go around *saying things* without thinking

[110] *Now* perhaps Ngirturong is happy because the people who *spoke* to Ngirturong are younger patrilateral relatives of Ngirturong, and so he is happy, but *I* am a man of the public and *I* really hated *hearing this*

Now, Ngiraikelau, *my tone of voice in this speech* has been very severe, as *I proclaim:* never *speak* like that again to Ngirturong

Whether among the elders or with senior women, but never in a public meeting, *we* always go home to *say these bad words and make decisions together*

If *this* happens when *we* are assembled together, then *I* am very sorry for the public of Ngeremlengui and for the Ngirturong title and the Ngirutelchii title and the Ngiraklang title, all of which are about to vanish

The respect for these things is about to vanish and, they stand *today* like aging men who can no longer accomplish anything for Ngeremlengui, and *you* should *now* be prepared to steady the village of Ngeremlengui and the taro patches of Ngeremlengui, and to show honor toward old people

[115] Don't just stay away at school and then come back no longer caring for the village

J

I think that now my words are coming to a close

I just *say again that: I think* Ngirturong was shocked at *hearing these words*, but *I* hate that they were even *spoken*

And if *I* were to go to *speak* to Ngaraimeiong, *"Together we know who spoke, so let us summon them and ask them about it, and then fine them,"* then *you* would just take *us* to court

I think so

[120] Yet what *I* have *said* are *just words*, and maybe it will not turn out to be like *this*

Ngirturong is no longer so unhappy about the *words* which were *spoken*, and *I* feel *like*: *"biting the bitter fig fruit"* from the eighth day of the month up until *today*

And *now* what *I* had to *say has been said*, and *my* bad thought concerning the public of Ngeremlengui has gone, and *I* will forget it

They do not remain any longer, since the public of Ngeremlengui is not *my* possession; it is the possession of the village of Ngeremlengui, and *you* young people own it

And so, thank *you* very much

Ngiraikelau, one of the men involved in the vocal attack on the chief, then took the floor and in muted, contrite tones thanked Ngiraklang for teaching the village lessons (*llach*) which they had never heard so clearly articulated before. He assured him that, knowing these principles, they would never again speak this way in public. All the people assembled in the meeting house should be grateful, he continued, for what Ngiraklang had said and should be careful to avoid the same errors in speaking. Ngiraklang then took the floor to add a brief coda to his speech, suggesting that the people of Imeiong village should investigate the reason for Uchererak's sudden return to life. Since the god does not speak for no reason, it should be possible to discover some specific problem in one of the houses which was the cause of the god's anger. If the problem is not uncovered and rectified, there is no chance that Uchererak would not return to the village. Ngiraklang concluded this coda with his usual self-deprecating good humor, saying that his speech sounded like a "personal ghost" (*deleb*) talking.

The conversation continued for a few more minutes with mild laughter and other expressions of renewed solidarity. One man confessed that he was startled when the possessed woman started to speak because she was not exactly a stranger—that is, he is related to her! The tension generated by the speech was thus diffused and the municipal council meeting proceeded as if nothing had happened. What had happened?

Metapragmatic Elements in the Speech

This speech provides an excellent confirmation of Bakhtin's observation, noted above, that much of our talk involves speaking about the words of others or about language more generally. This dialogic apprehension of others' speech is certainly to be expected in this ethnographic case, since Ngiraklang is addressing a political crisis essentially involving language, both speech events and norms for speaking. The initial meeting of July 7 focused on various interpretations of the written draft constitution, itself the final bilingual codification of months of verbal debate among elected delegates to the constitutional convention held in Koror. The strictly political character of this meeting's discourse was interrupted by the message of Uchererak delivered by a woman through whom the god spoke; the god's utterance was taken to be a partisan critique of the speech (or absence of speech) of the district's chief. The immediate reactions to the possession incident focused more generally on problems of communication between leaders and villagers, with the chief claiming immunity from the verbal assaults of his lower-ranking relatives and with the second-ranking titleholder, Ngiraklang, defending the chief's right to ignore demands for the public expression of his opinion. And then the July 14 speech by Ngiraklang attacks the problem of divided leadership from a largely linguistic angle, arguing that the words of the god can only be useful if delivered through an appropriate spokesperson selected by the god but in accordance with traditional privileges of the village's ninth-ranking house, Ngerungelang. Also, he insists that younger relatives of a titleholder must refrain from airing domestic strife in a public context, since such public scolding (*ngeroel*) not only undermines the stature of the chief but also repudiates, by implication, the authority of all other titleholders.

This linguistic complexity of the surrounding situation is matched by the richness of reference to different contexts of language use in the speech itself. Ngiraklang not only makes reference to the various utterances and interactions from the previous week's meeting but also brings in instructive parallel words and deeds from 1966, as well as comments on timeless cultural rules of speaking. There are, thus, three classes of linguistic contexts involved here: (1) deictical or indexical self-reference to the language and contextual parameters of the ongoing speech itself, (2) reports of and reference to tokens of speech uttered in other contexts (e.g., 1966, 1934, and the previous week), and (3) reference to semantic and pragmatic types (proverbs, cultural routines, pragmatic rules, etc.), that is, speech forms which are normative or "traditional." A tabulation of references to these three classes is given below:

1. *References to ongoing speech event*

[1]	My speech is like this:
[1]	when I start speaking now
[1]	I am going to talk of affairs
[2]	when I speak like this
[2]	to ask questions
[3]	I am going to say many proverbs
[9]	I am not decorating my speech in saying that
[25]	These things I am listing, I do not list them
[36]	Maybe my tone of voice is a bit severe
[36]	I am merely clarifying
[41]	I am trying to explain
[43]	these are not bad things to say
[44]	I am just reminding
[45]	And so I ask you
[47]	Don't dislike what I am saying
[53]	and I speak these words
[54]	I strongly remind you
[57]	And so I am just reminding
[58]	I am reminding you today
[60]	These words which I am saying, their meaning is this
[60]	I am not scolding
[60]	my tone of voice is severe
[60]	I am reminding the village
[67]	these things I am saying
[72]	the one I have just mentioned
[97]	Now I am talking to you in order to remind you
[105]	the reason that I spoke up so quickly
[106]	what I have spoken
[108]	I am just reminding you
[111]	my tone of voice in this speech has been very severe
[111]	as I proclaim

[116]   now my words are coming to a close
[117]   I just say again
[120]   what I have said are just words
[122]   what I had to say has been said

2. *Reference to other speech events*

[1]   affairs from about 1966
[10]   to speak in order to bring you all together
[17]   He said, "I am not going to pay the fine"
[33]   and spoke his words
[33]   we just remained with closed mouths
[34]   Uchererak came down and spoke
[34]   people said, "Go ahead and speak your words!"
[37]   When they all said, "Go ahead and speak"
[38]   What was the meaning of this expression
[39]   I think that the meaning is not at all good
[41]   the words which came down here
[41]   which they said were the words of Uchererak
[48]   "Go ahead and speak your words to someone"
[54]   These things we are talking about these days
[59]   If I had just kept silent
[65]   Perhaps this was just talk
[66]   none of the elders complained
[66]   saying, "This person is coming here without having paid his entry money"
[67]   these strange words
[84]   In 1934 he became silent
[86]   he spread this message of Modekngei
[89]   [the names] "Ngiraklang and Ngirturong" were mentioned
[91]   these words have weighed upon my heart
[94]   When they opened their mouths to speak
[94]   was the purpose to declare that
[98]   Those who spoke
[117]   these words, but I hate that they were even spoken
[118]   to go to speak to Ngaraimeiong, "Together we know who spoke, so let
        us summon them and ask them about it, and then fine them"

3. *Reference to speech types*

[3]   many proverbs concerning the village
[40]   if we invite the god to come in
[40]   the god cannot be interrogated

[40]   we can be fined or else subject to questioning
[46]   who in Imeiong is capable of commanding Uchererak?
[48]   Who in Imeiong today is capable of commanding Uchererak
[51]   not to be commanded
[52]   Ngaraimeiong could claim
[52]   Ngaraimeiong commands him
[52]   or else they could ask him for his words
[70]   if we are going to talk about the "poker and tongs" of Ngeremlengui
[72]   like we say, "the death of the canoe which races with the goatfish"
[76]   as we say, "you are talking, so why don't you go do it?"
[80]   we will all keep silent
[80]   No one knows his words
[81]   whoever knows his words
[82]   he has been silent up until today
[84]   he became silent
[92]   speak the words of Uchererak
[94]   the messengers of Uchererak
[96]   Ngeremlengui is not "a snake with two tongues"
[97]   "cold on the way out, hot on the way back"
[97]   "words which go out uncrowded cannot fit back into our mouths"
[101]   the significance of saying that: respect is vanishing
[108]   speak the words of the village
[109]   words of the village
[109]   saying things without thinking
[111]   never speak like that again to Ngirturong
[112]   go home to say these bad words and make decisions together
[121]   "biting the bitter fig fruit"

Throughout the speech, the orator's strategy is to draw close attention to the unfolding meaning of the discourse and to the attributed parallelism between contemporary political events and events of 1966, so that the listeners will analogously attribute similar objectivity to the basically timeless or normative references to rules of speaking. The speaker builds up his rhetorical authority to pass judgment on contemporary violations of rules of speaking by demonstrating his ability to impose a coherent interpretation on historically distinct events. Historical omniscience, thus, creates an aura of decontextualized wisdom, which is formally supported by the numerous switches in temporal reference within the speech itself.

Beyond these multiple references to various contexts of speaking, the speech contains many examples of reference to what Silverstein (1993) calls "explicit metapragmatics," that is, specific lexical machinery for referring to the relationship between linguistic signals and their contexts of use. The most frequent meta-pragmatic form is *tekoi*, the unmarked noun for "word" or "talk" (as in 53, 60, 92, 98, 116, 117, 121). Much like the Latin *res*, *tekoi* can also combine language and action in the sense of "affair," "accomplished deed," or "situation" (as in 1, 21, 54, 55). Finally, *tekoi* can enter into more complex constructions, such as *di tekoi* "just talk" (65), in contrast to real accomplishment; *mo tekoi* "become true" (25, 93); *belkul a tekoi* "proverb" (3; literally the joint or elbow of speech); *tekoi el beluu* "words of the village" (108); and *mekngit el tekoi* "bad things to say" (112).

In the twenty-seven instances of use, Ngiraklang takes advantage of the un-marked quality of *tekoi* in order to contrast this word with a variety of more semantically restricted metapragmatic verbs labeling types of speech acts, such as *dmung* "say," *kallach* "make decisions together," *lmuk* "keep silent," *mededaes* "explain," *melekoi* "speak," *mellach* "admonish," *mengedecheduch* "speak for-mally," *mengerodel* "complain," *moilikoik* "talk carelessly," *oker* "ask ques-tions," *oldurech* "command," *oleker* "summon," *omasech* "enumerate," *omeke-takl* "clarify," *omeklatk* "remind," *ongeroel* "scold," *orrenges* "hear." This explicit labeling of speech acts allows the speaker to impose his own "analysis" on his own and others' language by categorizing before ("I am going to say words which you will perhaps dislike"), during ("Now I am talking to you in order to remind you"), and after ("I am not scolding") the discourse referred to.

An even more powerful way for the speaker to impose an interpretation on the ongoing discourse is the use of the metapragmatic term *belkul* "meaning." A Belauan equivalent to Peirce's semiotic concept of "interpretant," *belkul* can re-fer to the significance, implication, intended purpose, and accomplished effect of both speech and action. The text contains eleven instances of this direct form of metapragmatic glossing:

4. *Metapragmatic glosses*

[18]   The meaning was like this:
[35]   What was the meaning of this?
[38]   What was the meaning of this expression
[39]   I think that the meaning is not at all good
[41]   this does not have any significance for me personally
[41]   but it is extremely significant for me
[60]   These words which I am saying, their meaning is this:
[82]   I do not not know the meaning of the departure of Uchererak
[94]   was the purpose to declare that:
[101]   And this is the significance of saying that:
[107]   My physical body has no importance

The interaction of all these classes of metapragmatic forms can be observed in the speech's eleven instances of direct quotation, including five reports which represent contextually specific utterance tokens and six reports of culturally typi-fied proverbial expressions (*belkul a tekoi*).

5. Reports of utterance tokens

[17]   He said, "I am not going to pay the fine"

[34]   people said, "Go ahead and speak your words! Go ahead and speak your words!"

[37]   When they all said, "Go ahead and speak"

[66]   none of the elders complained, saying, "This person is coming here with-out having paid his entry money"

[118] if I were to go to speak to Ngaraimeiong, "Together we know who spoke, so let us summon them and ask them about it, and then fine them"

6. Reports of proverbs

[72]   like we say, "the death of the canoe which races with the goatfish"

[76]   and as we say, "you are talking, so why don't you go do it?"

[96]   because Ngeremlengui is not "a snake with two tongues"

[97]   because "cold on the way out, hot on the way back,"

[97]   or else, "words which go out uncrowded cannot fit back into our mouths"

[121] I feel like: "biting the bitter fig fruit"

Additionally, the multiple embeddedness of these passages is evident in the fact that three of the token reports (34, 37, and 118) contain speech about speech; similarly, four of the cited proverbs (76, 96, 97, and 97) are concerned with norms of speaking. Also, the importance of the speaker's constant monitoring of interpretation is seen in the fact that the first three token reports (17, 34, and 37) are all followed immediately by explicit discussion of their "meaning" (*bel-kul*). In contrast, the import of proverbs is in each case entirely presupposed. This pattern suggests that the rhetorical risk of directly reporting specific utterances is that the speaker surrenders the role of "analysis" in favor of the role of "trans-lation" (in Bakhtin's sense of these terms) whereas, in indirect quotation, gains in analysis are countered by loss of authoritative discourse. In Ngiraklang's speech, however, this danger is somewhat attenuated, since analysis of the speech tokens follows immediately in many cases.

But more is involved here than monitoring of interpretation, for each case of token report is actually an example of what I want to label "typifying reported speech," that is, reported speech that has the surface linguistic form of direct quotation but which does not in fact report discourse which ever occurred in the past. I was not present in the village in 1966, but it would be highly uncharacteristic for a titleholder to make the statement reported in [17], for these kinds of financial dealings are generally handled privately and silently. I was present in the context reported in [34] and [37] and no such words were spoken. The discourse represented in [66] is explicitly stated *not* to have occurred, and the speech reported in [118] is expressed in the future conditional.

Pragmatically, Ngiraklang is using his authority as a high-ranking titleholder and as an accepted expert on Belauan tradition and village history to typify rather than merely to report discourse, and to do so under the guise of transparent or iconic quotation forms. Rather than simply presupposing the existence of previous utterances, the linguistic form of which is represented, these examples of reported speech entirely create the utterances through the convention that direct quotation naturally mirrors some original event of speaking. As a result, what appears formally as the extreme case of "translation," that is, the accurate reproduction of a previous utterance, emerges as the most powerful mode of "analysis," since the speaker creates the utterance as well as imposes upon it a definitive interpretation (see Larson 1978:59). It is interesting, by contrast, that at no point in his speech does Ngiraklang dignify the words of Uchererak, which he claims not to have heard (or more accurately, which he intentionally avoided hearing by leaving the meeting house) with the historicizing mantle of his reporting discourse.

The function of citing traditional proverbs can be understood, finally, in terms of the speaker's need to legitimize his own position as an authoritative voice. The proverbs not only contribute explicitly toward fixing the global metapragmatic theme of the speech (see Seitel 1977:91) but also convey their presupposed naturalness (i.e., they are quoted exactly as prescribed) to the other creative examples of quoted speech. In other words, a speaker who can perfectly recite proverbs is judged to be likely to report other utterances with the same transparent objectivity.

Textual Pragmatics

Our analysis of the rhetorical devices of the speech is not exhausted by typologizing various instances of explicitly metapragmatic signals, with no concern for the temporal order and contextual linkages of the discourse. There is an important sense in which the linear or syntagmatic architecture of the text, that is, its "textuality," contributes an additional metapragmatic dimension to the speech's social effectiveness—and, in this case, to its ineffectiveness as well. In order to show how the text as performed constitutes what Peircean terminology

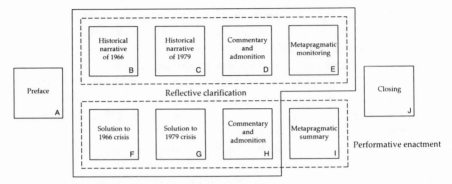

Figure 4.1. Textual organization of the speech

calls an "indexical icon," that is, a contextually anchored diagrammatic sign, by means of which the speaker intends to effect a change in the village's political situation, I have divided the speech into ten component segments (labeled A–J) on the basis of thematic and formal coherence and parallelism. Segments A and J bracket the entire speech event: the prefatory remarks in A indicate what the hearers can look forward to ("many proverbs concerning the village of Ngeremlengui"), and the concluding remarks in J express the speaker's changed personal feelings having uttered these words ("my bad thought concerning the village of Ngeremlengui has gone"). Within these framing brackets the speech consists of two parallel groups of segments, depicted in Figure 4.1.

In the first group, segments B and C narrate the history of events from 1966 and 1979, respectively; these two segments are clearly separated from each other by the textual marker in [29]: "This is one thing." Segments B and C have parallel internal organization, with an instance of reported speech (17 and 34) followed by discussion of the "meaning" of the quotation (18–20 and 35), and a summary of the points made in each segment (25–28 and 38–40). Following this extended historical narrative, segment D provides a more focused commentary on the significance of events described in C. The climax of D is [45], which is clearly an example of "chiefly admonition" (*mellach*) about rules of speaking: if a god descends to the village, authorized persons are in charge of prompting and interpreting the god's utterance. The next section, E, changes referential levels and monitors the meaning of the ongoing discourse thus far, by insisting that Ngiraklang's own speech is to be taken as "reminding" rather than as "scolding."

Exactly half-way through the speech (at line 61) Ngiraklang returns to the events of 1966 in segment F and to 1979 in segment G, but this time from the new perspective of discussing the agents of solution to each crisis. In F, Ngiraklang reminds everyone—indirectly, to be sure—that *he* was the one who manipulated the situation by means of a chelebucheb-type valuable. And segment G, marked off from the preceding segment by [71], "Agreed" (parallel to line 29 in the first group), returns to the events of the previous week. And this is then followed by segment H, which (parallel to segment D) concerns the "meaning" of the events described in G. Just as in D, in segment H a "chiefly admonition" is pronounced: that respect is vanishing from the village. Segment I (parallel to E) takes the whole of the present discourse as its object and announces the central metapragmatic theme of the oratory: don't ever scold the chief in public (111–13).

The apparent symmetry of the text's organization conceals an essential asymmetry, the clue to which is the presence of the string of proverbs in segment H. My analysis is that the quotation of proverbs in place of the quotation of token utterances (as in B and D) is intended to focus the aura of chiefly authority (discussed above) at this exact moment, that is, at the turning point (*belkul*) when the speech shifts from being a reflective clarification to being a performative political enactment. How this works out can be easily seen by looking once more at the overall thematic movement of the oratory, as represented in Figure 4.1.

Ngiraklang's speech is an effort by a high-ranking titleholder to solve a particular political crisis in the village by means of a verbal performance which, under the guise of being a gentle reminder ("I am merely reminding") or clarification ("I am just clarifying") of past events parallel to the present situation, actually intends to effect the solution through its utterance. The basis for this "pseudo-performative" force (Silverstein 1981b) is the syntagmatic construction of a proportion between, on the one hand, two events which seriously disturbed the political stability of the village and, on the other hand, two agents of resolution to these crises. The parallel events, what the speaker calls the "two deaths of Ngeremlengui," both have to do with devastating challenges to legitimate authority, essentially involving the temporary usurpation of the power of chiefly speech.

In 1966 untitled members of the local men's club, Ngaratebelik, imposed a fine on one of their members, a right reserved to sacred titled members of Ngaraimeiong chiefly council. The young man's father refused to pay the fine, the legitimate chiefs departed from the village, and the men's club disbanded—three events which left the village in shambles. In 1979, just one week prior to the time of the speech, the words of the god Uchererak, silent since 1934, were enthusiastically received by younger relatives of chief Ngirturong, whose pro-status political position was being challenged by lower-ranking villagers. Both of these events, according to Ngiraklang's explication, illustrate that the principal danger of a village with two voices of authority (the "snake with two tongues"), either two councils (Ngaratebelik and Ngaraimeiong) or two leaders (Uchererak and Ngirturong), is the potential departure of the legitimate titleholders. And, as he repeats, if the titleholders "detour," then the village itself "detours."

The speech completes the analogy by constructing, in the second half of the text, a parallel argument concerning the agents responsible for the solution to these crises. Without identifying himself by name, Ngiraklang draws upon the common historical knowledge of all present that it was his own skillful negotiation which made it possible for Ngirturong to return to the village in 1966. And it is the diagrammatic organization of the speech itself which supplies the missing fourth part of the proportion: as Ngiraklang cleverly repaired the political damage created by split authority in 1966, so his same skill, as abundantly evidenced in the rhetorical brilliance and traditional knowledge displayed in the proverbial citations contained in the speech itself (especially in H), will bring the present situation to a resolution. This resolution is not, however, merely referred to in the speech, but it is intended to be accomplished *by its very performance*. What appears at first to be a static diagram turns out to be a syntactically generated indexical icon with performative force designed to be the solution.

In attempting to remind the village of certain traditional norms of language use and to perform a resolution of certain political tensions exacerbated by recent violations of these rules, Ngiraklang obviously places great store not only in his own political weight but also in the power of speech in general to effect the goals sought. For some people in the village, however, the speech accomplished an unintended purpose—that of standing as a "historical marker" (*olangch*) (Parmentier 1987a:12) of the demise of chiefly authority and respect. Part of this reaction stems from the fact that, despite its "traditional" orientation, themes, and references, the speech itself constitutes a highly modern, idiosyncratic event. First of all, the speech followed no established genre for the chiefly use of language. Traditionally, meetings of assembled titleholders were carried out according to a system of relayed whispering (*kelulau*), in which messages passed silently from lower-ranking men to the four high-ranking titleholders, who communicated among themselves through two messengers. The titleholders remained seated while the messengers, heads bent low, passed up and down the floor of the meeting house. High-ranking chiefs had little need to persuade others of their views through public oratory, since their final decisions (*telbiil*) were not subject to questioning or even debate (cf. Comaroff 1975:145). In fact, passive silence was one of the hallmarks of presupposed chiefly authority; as one proverb puts it: "The dugong [sea cow] sleeps in deep water," that is, a chief hides himself from easy public scrutiny. So Ngiraklang's highly persuasive speech about the relevance of traditional rules of speaking belies its own message; or to put the point the other way around, to the degree that the speech was perceived as persuasive, it was so judged according to nontraditional criteria.

Second, the context of the speech contributed to a lessening of its political effectiveness. Ngiraklang was forced to ask permission from a democratically elected magistrate to get the floor, and his speech was basically an extended interruption of the meeting of the elected municipal council, a body representing exactly the sort of dual authority Ngiraklang criticizes so strongly. This second point relates to the analysis presented above according to which the speech as performed is an indexical icon, since part of the meaning of any indexical or pragmatic signal is determined by the presupposed elements in the context in which the signal appears. In this case the negative contribution from the context was strong to the degree that the speech anchored itself, both spatially and temporally, in that context.

PART III

Comparative Perspectives on Complex Semiotic Processes

5 | Tropical Semiotics

Levels of Semiosis

THE FIELD OF cultural semiotics, in its many manifestations, has increasingly addressed the methodological issue of how to analyze formally complex semiotic constructions, such as mythic narratives, ritual processes, and aesthetic objects, without reverting to the sterility of structuralism. Just because these kinds of cultural products appear to have a high degree of "textuality" is no reason to assume that texts can be analyzed without reference to the connection between the shape of their discursive forms and the conditions of their contextual enactment. For example, it is apparent from the cross-cultural study of ritual that there is often a relationship between the discourse—internal textuality of formulaic language (considered in terms of its formal complexity, internal segmentation, and prescriptive fixity) and the "performative" power released in its contextually anchored realizations. It is as a contribution to this area of semiotic research, what Silverstein (1976, 1981b, 1993) has labeled "metapragmatics," that the theory of "symbolic obviation" can be evaluated. Symbolic obviation is a semiotic concept developed by Roy Wagner in several books, including *Habu: The Innovation of Meaning in Daribi Religion* (1972), *Lethal Speech: Daribi Myth as Symbolic Obviation* (1978), *The Invention of Culture* (1981), *Asiwinarong: Ethos, Image, and Social Power among the Usen Barok of New Ireland* (1986), and *Symbols That Stand for Themselves* (1986). More recently, it has been given an important empirical application by James F. Weiner in *The Heart of the Pearl Shell: The Mythological Dimension of Foi Sociality* (1988), a superb ethnographic study of a Papua New Guinea people. The purpose of this chapter is to explicate the method of symbolic obviation, to point out a number of problems with its development in the writings of Wagner and Weiner, and to suggest a broader set of semiotic issues that are engaged by these studies.

Wagner and Weiner share the basic premise that semiotic phenomena should be divided into a least two hierarchical levels. The first level of meaningfulness (what they frequently call "semantic," "literal," or "structural") involves the distinction between one element functioning as a sign or "signifier" and a second element functioning as a referent, object, or "signified." At this first level, these functionally differentiated elements can be related (and can be interpreted as related) in several ways on the basis of the motivating ground or reason for the relationship. According to Peirce's well-known trichotomy, signs at this level can be iconic, that is, grounded in formal resemblance; indexical, that is, grounded in spatiotemporal contiguity; and symbolic, that is, grounded in arbitrary, conventional agreement (see Chapter 1). Symbols, though created only by the imputed ground between sign and object, are subject to speakers' "assumption of invariant referential value" (Wagner 1983:3) across contexts. The second level of meaningfulness, labeled tropic or metaphorical by Wagner, consists of the relationships among complete signs (regardless of the kind of internal motivation) which are contextually innovative changes introduced upon semantic units. As Ricoeur (1974b:99) explains:

> But the semantics of the word demonstrates very clearly that words have *actual* meanings only in a sentence and that lexical entities—words in the dictionary—have only potential meanings and for the sake of their potential uses in sentences. As concerns the metaphor itself, semantics demonstrates with the same strength that the metaphorical meaning of a word is nothing which may be found in a dictionary (in that sense we may continue to oppose the metaphorical sense to the literal sense, if we call literal sense *whatever* sense may occur among the partial meanings enumerated in the dictionary, and not a so-called original, or fundamental, or primitive, or proper meaning). If the metaphorical sense is more than the actualization of one of the potential meanings of a polysemic word (and all our words in common discourse are polysemic), it is necessary that this metaphorical use is only *contextual*; by that I mean a sense which emerges as the result of a certain contextual action. We are led in that way to oppose *contextual* changes of meaning to *lexical* changes, which concern the diachronistic aspect of language as code, system, or *langue*. Metaphor is such a *contextual* change of meaning.

In contrast to semantic units at the first level, tropic symbolizations engage a "moral content," that is, relate a particular metaphor to the broader "values and precepts of society" (Weiner 1988:124).

A clear example of semiosis at the first level would be the linguistic form *kara'o* signifying the "oil of the *Campnosperma brevipetiolata* tree" (Weiner 1988:63); semiosis at the second level would be the Foi cultural association of this *kara'o* oil with "male wealth" and the exchange of this symbolically rich material object for wives in affinal exchange rituals. The meaning of the exchange using this oil cannot be understood if all we know is the "literal" signification of the word *kara'o*. The full meaning involves ramifying cultural categorizations (wealth vs. nonwealth, male vs. female, oil wealth vs. pearl shell wealth) and metaphorical associations (the interior cavity of the *kara'o* tree and a woman's uterus [Weiner 1988:229]). No amount of knowledge about the Foi linguistic system at the first semiotic level would enable the analyst to grasp the intention of a young Foi man who, seeking a marriageable young woman, requests, "Do you know a white cockatoo feather you could give me?" (Weiner 1988:126). An important contrast, then, between the complementary elements brought together in semantic signification and the paired terms of a metaphor is that, in the latter, the terms are *simultaneously* different and similar: "women are marsupials" (Weiner 1988:124) and yet no man would marry a marsupial, except in myth. This is called the "reflexive" quality of metaphors, since these symbolic figures tend to merge the "vehicle" or signifying term and the "tenor" or signified term within a relatively self-contained expression, what Wagner terms "symbols that stand for themselves" (Wagner 1986b:6; Weiner 1988:124).

> The interchange between signification and metaphorization, wherein each draws upon the other, produces a situation in which meaning is a function of change as well as of formal signification and in which the creative aspect of change is metaphoric innovation. Any meaning that impinges upon, or "opposes," a central cultural tenet or proposition must take the form of an innovation upon it, a metaphoric expression involving the tenet itself, and in fact metaphorizing it. (Wagner 1972:168)

Wagner notes that literal symbolization tends to involve a maximal degree of separation between semiotic representation and its context of occurrence (that is, a tendency toward decontextualization), while figurative symbolization "assimilates" to the context (1977b:391).

It is helpful to compare the operation of single, isolated signs and multiple, interlocking signs at both the semantic and the tropic levels. It was Saussure's (1959:127–34) great discovery that, at the first level, signs relatively unconstrained by iconic or indexical motivation (what he labels "signs" and what Peirce labels "symbols") are free to generate complex linkages along two dimensions, the co-occurence of signs in the same construction (the "syntagmatic" chain) and the association of signs which can replace each other in a given environment (the "paradigmatic" chain). Individual phonic signs without motivation are created entirely by the "reciprocal delimitation" of their differential yet absolutely correlative planes; a linguistic "unit" is a conventional fusion of phonic and conceptual differences by the relational operation of language. But linguistic signs, viewed as the inextricable bond of signifier and signified, belong to higher-order regularities also determined by conventional rules of "syntagmatic solidarities" (word formation, morphological complexity, concatenation) and paradigmatic "opposition" (the reciprocal "summoning up" of concepts). Saussure went so far—too far, no doubt—as to argue that, in the realm of linguistic signs at least, signs viewed from the perspective of their position in syntagmatic and paradigmatic chains generate semiotic "value" which entirely replaces the isolated signification of individual signs—signification itself (denotational "naming," for example [Saussure 1954:68–69]) becoming an illusion perpetrated by the systematicity of the linguistic system. Not only is reference projected upon the world from systems of semiotic value, but that world takes on the orderliness generated from its semiotic model; in Wagner's terminology, when "words, pictures, diagrams, models" combine together they present a "consistent, collective ordering of things" (1977b:392).

Collectivizing and Differentiating Symbolization

At the tropic level, semiotic processes parallel to the paradigmatic and syntagmatic chains emerge when metaphorical signs are studied as cultural complexes. Whereas the systematicity of signifying systems becomes rigidified to the degree that their component signs are purely conventional, the flow of metaphors in culture guarantees the dynamism of their innovations. This is because tropes have the power to bring into articulation in certain contexts terms which have not been previously linked (Fernandez 1986:37) and because the resulting metaphoric equivalences constitute new, "nonconventional" layers of cultural meaning (Wagner 1972:6, 1981:43). Tropes, as Schwimmer (1983:124) points out in a more general discussion of images and metaphors in New Guinea, rely on the heritage of conventional symbols and meanings "but creative use of this set involves drawing on it in unexpected contexts and in response to inner prompting." An innovative trope manifests a fragmenting or "differentiating" symbolization in that, by refusing to adhere to the established order of cultural meanings, it "operates upon other signifiers to draw them into a new relation" (Wagner 1972:6):

> Since tropic usage sets one symbol (or denominate entity) into some relatively nonconventional relation to another such symbol (or entity), replacing the "nonarbitrariness" of conventional usage with some more specific motivation, it is obvious that a notion of simple (literal) reference no longer applies. The nonconventional relation introduces a new symbolization simultaneously with a "new" referent, *and the symbolization and its referent are identical.* We might say that a metaphor or other tropic usage assimilates symbol and referent into one expression, that a metaphor is a *symbol that stands for itself*—it is self-contained. Thus the symbolic effect of a tropic usage opposes or counteracts that of conventional usage in two ways: it assimilates that which it "symbolizes" within a distinct, unitary expression (collapsing the distinction between symbol and symbolized), and it differentiates that expression from other expressions (rather than articulating it with them). (Wagner 1978:25)

The opposition between fixed, ordered, and presupposed semiotic structures and innovative, open-ended, and creative semiotic structures which, at first, characterizes the distinction between the formal semantics of language and the play of tropic symbols can also be seen in the operation of tropes themselves. That is, metaphors generated in one context that are then repeated across contexts become regularized and thus "decay" (Wagner 1972:6) into what appears to be a "conventionalized" lexical formality. (I place this word within quotation marks to call attention to its figurative usage in this context, a problem that will be considered below.) These automatized, habitual symbolic expressions, what Wagner calls "collectivizing symbolization," in turn, tend to congeal into generalized interlocking patterns such as social ideologies (Wagner 1972:170), technical rules, mathematic equations, rationalized juridical interpretations (Bourdieu 1987), and norms of personal demeanor (Wagner 1978:22, 1981:42). Collectivizing symbolization, being "obsessed with the artifice of order" and attempting to transparently mirror the natural world through some format of representational rigor, necessarily renders the presence of serious cultural polysemy as mere "connotation" (Wagner 1972:23).

Collectivizing and differentiating modes of symbolization can be contrasted, further, by the ways signs refer to contextual phenomena: while the former presuppose a separation between symbol and referent, the latter work to erase this distinction in favor of metaphorical self-referentiality by identifying disparate experiences as similar or homologous. At the collectivizing pole, "symbols themselves are thus *contrasted* with their referents, they form an ideal "set" or "family" among themselves, one that must necessarily separate and distinguish itself from the phenomenal world" (Wagner 1972:22). At the differentiating pole, "the tension and contrast between symbol and symbolized collapse, and we may speak of such a construction as a "symbol" that stands for itself. The unique experiences, people, objects, and places of everyday life all correspond, in those features that render them distinct, to this mode of symbolization—as "'symbols,' they stand for themselves" (Wagner 1981:43). And, again parallel to the referential projection precipitated by the linguistic system, these centered, organized, or integrated patterns promote the objectification or reification of the objects they denote.

Unfortunately, in explicating Wagner's semiotic model Weiner (1988:6) introduces a degree of confusion by modifying the definition of the central concepts:

> The crucial characteristic of a trope is that it is a relationship between two elements that are simultaneously similar and dissimilar. The symbolic operation that focuses on the similarity between elements in a tropic ("trope-ic") equation can be termed *collectivizing* symbolization, in Wagner's scheme, while the converse operation that takes the differences as the focus of intent can be labeled as *differentiating* symbolization.

Part of the difficulty, I think, is that Weiner is relying on a different set of connotations of the terms "collective" and "differentiating"; by "collective" he wants to suggest the moral force of the Durkheimian social collectivity, as in his discussion of "collectively defined status" (Weiner 1988:10)—whereas Wagner's usage plays on the connotation of collation or collection of symbols—and by "differentiating" he wants to imply a series of contrasts or complementaries in social role relations, that is, "social differentiation" (Weiner 1988:9)—whereas Wagner's usage relies more on the sense of "making different" or fragmenting some standarized semantic relations. Wagner himself sometimes speaks of collectivizing symbols as deriving from the "collectivity" (1986a:175) and even reverses the definitions at several points, such as in his discussion of "collectivizing acts . . . that recharge the symbols of their ordinary differentiating existence" (1981:118). Despite this definitional confusion, the key point is clear: the opposition between convention and innovation parallels the distinction between collectivizing symbolization and differentiating symbolization; indeed, innovation is the "sign" of differentiation (Wagner 1981:43; Weiner 1988:143).

Convention and Innateness

At this point it becomes essential to begin disambiguating several contradictory senses of the term "convention" that appear in the Wagner and Weiner texts. Two usages have already been noted. In the strict Peircean sense, "conventional" labels a semiotic ground linking sign and object such that the sign would not stand for the object it does without some further sign, its "interpretant," representing it to be so related. Thus, a conventional sign (a Peircean "symbol") is maximally unmotivated, since it requires neither kind of "natural" linkage, namely, iconicity or indexicality. The important point to keep in mind about Peircean conventional signs is that they are inherently semiotic, since apart from the triadic process of semiosis the sign and the object would not even exist as functionally related entities (see Chapter 1). I will represent this sense of convention as convention-P (for Peirce). Clearly, conventions-P can belong to the first level of semiosis, for example, many linguistic signs. As Wagner (1986b:8) notes:

> The conventions—rules, syntax, lexicon—of language stand in a reciprocal relation to that which can be, and is, said in the language. As we speak by working transformations upon those conventions, *figuring* our meanings through them, so the set of conventions can be seen as the metaphor of all that could be said in this way.

Tropes such as metaphors and other figurative expressions are not, strictly speaking, conventional-P because, in establishing the mutual transformation of vehicle and tenor, their motivation lies in rich layers of cultural association, "analogic construction" (Wagner 1986b:30), and "recursive implication" (Wagner 1986b:126) rather than in grammatical regularities. But note that even the most highly innovative metaphor relies for its striking effect on conventional-P signs, namely, the linguistic components (Wagner 1978:25).

The second sense of convention that we have encountered refers to the habitual, typical, taken-for-granted, literal, or normative quality of cultural symbolization—what I will call convention-N (for normative). Conventions-N include not only nonfigurative semantic meaning but also, and more importantly, the "dead" or "standard" (Weiner 1986:125) tropes whose innovative fragmentation has given way to tired or "counterinnovative" (Wagner 1981:44) repetition.[1] Wagner is referring to convention-N when he describes the dialectical relation between conventional and differentiating symbolism (1981:44). And it is in this sense that he speaks of "linguistic conventions of Daribi narrative form" (Wagner 1978:38) or "the conventional opening of a Daribi story" (Wagner 1978:45), and when Weiner talks about "conventional social roles" (1988:130) or of women and marsupials as "two conventionally contrasted elements" (1988:124). And it is in this sense of convention-N that Wagner can say that, just as tropic usages metaphorize literal meanings (conventions-P), "so conventional[-N] nonarbitrariness often threatens to displace the tropic variety" (1978:25). The seemingly contradictory formulation of the seemingly contradictory phrase "conventional nonarbitrariness" (recall that arbitrariness is a characteristic of conventions-P) refers to the standardization or habituation of social rules. As it turns out, both tropes and conventions-N are "motivated," although in different ways: tropes are motivated because, as signs at the second level of semiosis, they creatively assert fresh associations; conventions-N are motivated because they code the self-evident force of cultural traditions.

Since both Wagner and Weiner (1988:138–39) regularly conflate convention-P and convention-N, it is often difficult to figure out—other than figuratively—what a given sentence means. In particular, their arguments frequently slip between the hierarchical opposition of semantic and metaphorical signs (the former being conventional-P) and the contextual opposition between standardized cultural images (convention-N) and innovative, differentiating tropes, as, for example, when Weiner (1988:12) writes: "Meaning, as I argue, results when the elements of conventional[-P] syntagmatic orders are inserted into nonconventional[-N] contexts. The resulting figurative or metaphorical expressions define at once both the particularizing nature of metaphor and its dependence upon conventional[-P] semantic or syntagmatic references for its innovative impact." Certain passages in Wagner (1978:54) seem actually calculated to obscure the distinction between convention-P and convention-N:

> Unlike our [Western] literature, [Daribi] myth belongs to an ideological regime in which the conventional aspect of symbolization (the semantic mode) is believed to be innate or immanent in man. This means that the conventions that pertain to the narrative medium are perceived as "given," a kind of implicit moral appropriateness appearing spontaneously within an activity whose appropriateness is itself self-evident.

In this passage, Wagner skips between talking about the semiotic character of language ("the semantic mode," clearly convention-P) and about a particular cultural interpretation of typical or habitual genre rules (clearly convention-N) "believed to be innate or immanent in man"—which they most obviously are not in the least.

The critical point to observe in this relative distinction is that it is based on a cultural "interpretive distinction" (Wagner 1981:51), that is, an indigenous theory *of* semiosis employed in contexts of social action. Both Wagner and Weiner consider the possibility that, in some societies, the taken-for-grantedness of conventions-N results in their being regarded as not produced by individual intention or cultural artifice (i.e., as *not* convention-P) but rather as "innate," "given," or "self-evident" in the cosmos, the environment, or human nature (Wagner 1977b). The rhetorical thrust of this argument seems to be to relativize the classical opposition between *thesei* and *physei*, that is, between phenomena in the realm of human responsibility or cultural artifice and phenomena that are viewed as products of the natural order. For example, while from the neutral stance of comparative cultural semiotics a codified legal system can be assumed to be the historical product of cultural intention, for people subjected to it this same legal system, especially if its totalizing moral authority is acutely felt, is likely to be interpreted as a force of nature, a product of divine will, or a deduction from principles of human nature. This, in turn, opens up the possibility that there could be a systematic inversion in the "characteristic mode of symbolic construction" (Wagner 1978:29) between tribal societies like the Daribi and the Foi of New Guinea and Western industrialized societies:

> The core of any and every set of cultural conventions is a simple distinction as to what kind of contexts, the nonconventionalized ones or those of convention itself, are to be deliberately articulated in the course of human action, and what kind of contexts are to be counterinvented as "motivation" under the conventional mask of "the given" or "the innate." Of course, for any given set of conventions, be it that of a tribe, community, "culture," or social class, there are only two possibilities: a people who deliberately differentiate as the form of their action will invariably counterinvent a motivating collectivity as "innate," and a people who deliberately collectivize will counterinvent a motivating differentiation in this way. As contrasting modes of thought, perception, and action, there is all the difference in the world between these two. (Wagner 1981:51)

In New Guinea, tropic symbolizations are understood to belong to the realm of human artifice and responsibility, while conventional-N regularities of society ("rules, laws, traditions") are seen as part of the "innate" flow of the order of nature (Wagner 1978:27). This point is needlessly blurred when Weiner asserts that, for the Foi, "differentiation *is* convention" (1988:10); what he means, I guess, is that Foi innovative, tropic symbolizations are acknowledged to be humanly produced, whereas norms of collective conduct appear to be part of the natural order of things, that is, as being a set of "innate conventional distinctions" (1988:139).

In the West, in contrast, forms of collectivizing symbolization are considered the product of cultural construction opposed to the innate, given tendencies of individual personalities, and differentiating symbolization is relegated to the world of aesthetic ("artists, writers, musicians"), subcultural ("black Americans"), and fictional countercultures ("Hollywood scriptwriters") (Weiner 1988:10):

> In such a [Western] milieu, rules are the focus of conscious human articulation, since they are designed to regulate and systematize an inherently chaotic and differentiated cosmos. Our view of social artifice basically derives from such early social philosophers as Locke: society is the systematic application of constraints upon the inherent willfulness of the self-contained individual. The meaning of all social and cultural forms—including myth—is thus above all else referrable to their function in maintaining societal order. Convention in this worldview thus emerges as a result of progressive acts of collectivizing symbolization, focusing on the artifically imposed similarities among elements and statuses to arrive at the occupational, educational, and geographical specializations (to name a few) that comprise our social categories and the system of laws, written and unwritten, that govern their relationship to each other. In such a system, the differences that are also a part of the metaphor of social identity are seen as innate or inherent; and indeed, the morality of convention lies in the fact that it is seen to accommodate and control such difference. (Weiner 1988:7–8)

This typological contrast implies a corresponding difference in cultural theories of the self, that is, the "point to which conception, action, and response are attributed" (Wagner 1977a:147). If in the West the self, whether as "ego" or "personality," is considered to be entirely personal, for tribal peoples the self is the product of social mediations involving other people and objects of exchange. Conversely, social conventions such as language and morality are differentially evaluated. In tribal societies they are thought to be "discovered" within the person, who is believed to be a "homuncular simulacrum of a cultural 'humanity'" (Wagner 1977a:147), whereas in the West the individual's task is to become socialized into conventional norms existing outside the person.

My own reaction to this global typology of cultures is that it should not be taken too seriously, since the characterization of Western cultures at least seems grossly mistaken and since the semiotic process of the "naturalization" convention can be identified in both tribal and industrialized societies (Silverstein 1987b:5; see Chapter 8). Certainly many scholars have documented for Western culture a pervasive tendency to turn historically derived "structural conditions" into "individual inevitability" (MacKinnon 1987:306) and a corresponding deontological effort to justify the practices and institutions of the status quo as good by revealing them as natural (Kitcher 1985:245). It was the great contribution of John Locke to locate in the "state of nature" the essential building block of liberalism, private property. Rather than seeing, with Weiner, convention as the artificial attempt to harmonize innate differences, convention can also be viewed as the propensity to impose systematic differentiations or discriminations on the basis of assumed given similarities among people. And rather than treating, with Weiner, social conventions as imposing constraints on individual wills, the natural order can be considered as setting constraints on the possibilities of the social system, or social systems can be calculated to be the deductive consequence of individual decision making or utility maximization. The difficulties involved in Wagner's global typology are so severe that, at one point, Wagner himself reverses the terms of the argument by stating that the "order, structure, or system" of social contract is regarded in Western social thinking as being "innate" (1986a:176).

Despite these reservations, I believe that a more interesting ethnographic project can be salvaged: to describe the semiotic constructs of a single culture in terms of (1) the dialectical hierarchization of the levels of semantic and tropic semiosis and (2) the contextual play of conventional-N ("collectivizing") vs. innovating ("differentiating") symbolic forms at the second level of semiosis. And this is precisely the ambitious task that Weiner has set for himself in *The Heart of the Pearl Shell.*

Obviational Exchange

Fundamental to Foi conceptualization of their social life are two interlocking postulates. First, the Foi believe that male and female spheres are complementary, continuous, and contrapuntal (Weiner 1988:90), so that consanguineal lineality is the prerogative of men yet requires the "natural" generative powers of women. As a result, "the responsibility of men . . . is continually to transform the sexual productivity of their own females into the artifice of male patrilineality" (Weiner 1988:90). Second, the impasse of this conjuncture of nature and artifice requires the mediation of objects of value that, in social exchanges, simultanously objectify and metaphorize "male" and "female" domains. Exchanges are tropic because they set in motion a series of analogies between conventional-N images of social differentiation. For example, the wife-taking group's act of presenting "male" valuables to the wife-giving group, who give both a female and "female" items, invokes the standard images of the forces of male/female complementarity which the Foi see as pervading human and cosmic realms. (Unfortunately, Weiner's diagram [1988:140] reverses the symbolism of this analogy by lining up "male and female" with "wife-givers and wife-takers.") The ritual alignment of the domain of intersexual differentiation and the domain of affinal opposition is itself a trope, not only because the "female" wife-givers are in fact men but also because the "male" valuables *and* meat they receive from the wife-takers invert the reciprocal exchange of the valuables *for* meat in nonaffinal contexts (i.e., *aname kobora* exchanges of "female" pork and "male" pearl shells). Next, the presentation of pigs by wife-takers when the first child is born in turn "shifts" the conventional-N meanings belonging to the standardized image of affines. Whereas affines are supposed to be normatively differentiated, they have become related through a child; the wife-givers are now the child's matrilaterals. Finally, the status of cross-cousins in the next generation becomes ambiguous, since it uneasily combines two previous idioms of exchange, the sharing consanguinity of "brothers" and the oppositional stance of affines (Weiner 1988:145); their exchanges act out the most inclusive metaphor: "affines are consanguines" (Weiner 1988:286).

Weiner uses Wagner's term "obviation" (Wagner 1978:31–33) to describe the complex discursive process whereby, first, innovative symbolic meaning is created out of the raw materials of conventional-N associations and, second, the motivation for the original association is either exposed or rationalized. Obviation is a "processual form of the trope" (Wagner 1988:xi) that tacks back and forth between conventional-N symbolism, where sign and meaning tend toward functional separation, and tropic dislocation, where the first symbolization is unified in the mutuality of metaphor. Although Wagner and Weiner illustrate obviation with ritual and narrative examples taken from their respective Papua New Guinea ethnographic cases, the model is not intended to be a local genre rule nor an emic mode of indigenous interpretation. Presumably, however, part of the meaningfulness of cultural constructions for the people who produce them depends on an implicit recognition of semiotically well-formed instances (cf. Hanson and Hanson 1981, 1983:191). What is special about obviational symbolism is that the sequence of tropes in a ritual or in a myth achieves a degree of closure whereby the last metaphor returns to the origin point of the discourse:

> As this continues, the effects of the tropic assimilations become cumulative; eventually the distinction between the modalities, recast into ever more liminal form, is eroded away, and the initial construction, pushed to the point of paradox, collapses into its modal opposite. The metaphorizing of one element or episode by another leads, progressively and cumulatively, to the metaphorizing of one modality by the other. The effect suggests the closing of the traditional hermeneutical circle, for, in the final metaphorization, the reflexive component of construction, normally "out of awareness," becomes apparent *as a consequence of the construction.* (Wagner 1978:32–33)

For example, the multitiered analogy set up between sexuality, affinity, and consanguinity is an emergent rather than a static series of substitutions. At every point in the ritual sequence when one trope "metaphorizes" the previous one, that previous metaphor is "rendered apparent" or "obvious" (hence "obviation"). Contrary to Weiner's claim (1988:143) that obviation is a semiotic process working *between* the hierarchical levels of conventional-P semantic meaning and metaphors or tropes, the examples he gives clearly demonstrate that obviation operates entirely within the second level of semiosis as the process by which innovative usages fragment, deflect, and "differentiate" conventional-N symbols.

Why is exchange such a productive arena for tropic obviation? Exchange is a collective social activity involving, on the one hand, individuals and social groups and, on the other hand, symbolically charged mediational objects (food, wealth items, persons). These activities are organized so that paradigmatic or categorical oppositions (male vs. female, wife-givers vs. wife-takers) are realized in syntagmatic interactional contexts. And, more importantly, the syntagms can be viewed as "forms of discourse" (Weiner 1988:149) that set up sequential substitutions which constitute equivalences without denying differential values. They do this in two senses: (1) equivalences between objects given for each other (e.g., valuables for wives) or in replacement for each other (e.g., pearl shells for *kara'o* oil) and (2) equivalences between analogous exchange scenarios (e.g., intersexual and affinal).[2] This is, of course, an elaboration of Jakobson's (1987) famous principle of poetic projection: in poetry, syntagms are broken up into parallel linguistic segments and create an artificial "projection" of equivalence, usually restricted to the paradigmatic axis of conventional-P semanticity, into the syntagmatic axis. Poetry tropically turns language upon itself, since any and all of its conventional-P features can be the effective source of parallelism. In Foi exchange, "the artifice of sociality" (Weiner 1988:139) is created in and by the playing out of an asymmetrical series of transactions in which various media invoking conventionally-N defined values are rendered contextually equivalent. Social roles, categories, and groups are, thus, "differentiated" (Wagner 1974:111) through exchange, a process Weiner describes as "the tropic creation of the Foi moral universe" (1988:149).

Like the fleeting character of poetic equivalence, Foi affinity is an inherently contextual relationship, since a man and his wife's brother, opposed foci of the bridewealth transactions that created his marriage, join together in contributing bridewealth for his male children and share the wealth brought in as a result of the marriages of his female children. Yet Foi exchanges are subject to the same potential for "dying" into stale repetition that can be the fate of even the most creative poetic metaphors. That is, ritual reenactments necessarily encourage the "collectivizing" tendency of symbolization (Wagner 1978:29). Fortunately, Foi exchange, considered as an independent semiotic modality, can also become the metaphorical tenor for a further innovative semiotic vehicle, storytelling.

Tropes and Narrative

The "heart" of Weiner's ethnography is the analysis of Foi *tuni* "moral stories," which display substitutional sequences parallel to those described for exchange rituals. Weiner and the earlier ethnographer of the region, Francis Edgar Williams, both note a functional differentiation between two genres of Foi narratives, namely, amusing stories told for recreational purposes and cultic myths associated with magical spells. Williams (1977:302–3) divides Foi narratives into *tuni* and *hetagho*. The former are short tales involving nameless characters and unspecified locales; they are told by both men and women in various social contexts and are without magical significance. The latter are "true myths" dealing with "ancient events of fundamental importance and consequently possess a religious as well as magical meaning" (Williams 1977:303); although these myths involve named characters associated with cultic roles, these names are suppressed in performance. This division suggests a connection between the ideology of texts and the pragmatics of performance such that greater contextual specificity, including restriction on utterance (secrecy, name suppression), situational appropriateness (cultic contexts), and contiguity with other discursive forms (magical spells) correlates with the higher degree of collectivizing symbolization of "true myths." In contrast, Foi *tuni* (corresponding to Daribi *namu po* "moral tales" studied by Wagner) are acknowledged to be artificial constructions rather than cosmologically important myths. The Foi stories typically involve fanciful plots, imaginary characters (giants, ogresses), magical transformations, and colorful reversals of conventional morality (Weiner 1988:150).

Whether because the contemporary Foi prefer to keep those myths associated with magical spells secret or because the cultic situation has declined in importance, Weiner's data consist primarily of the recreational stories.[3] Weiner uses one story, "The Hornbill Husband," as a methodological demonstration (although the particular procedures applied in this case are not, in their entirety, repeated elsewhere in the book).[4] Fundamental to the method is the determination of a sequence of thematic substitutions or transformations that (1) move the plot along its "actional" path and (2) invoke unspoken cultural presuppositions. No principled criteria are adopted for identifying these tropical substitutions, which can involve two actions, characters, values, or categories within the text whose relationship can be metaphorical equivalence (A equals B), transformation (A into B), negation (A into not-A), substitution (A replaced by B), or transaction (A for B, B for A) (cf. Todorov 1971:39). In addition, substitutions are identified in which the second term exists only as an extra-textual presupposition. The substitutions are selected with an eye toward placing them in an interlocking pattern such that they alternate between those involving relatively conventional-N, collectively constituted cultural associations (called, following Wagner

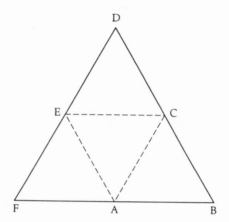

Figure 5.1. Obviational sequence

[1978:48], the "facilitating modality"), and those involving relatively innovating, differentiating acts of individual characters (called the "motivating modality").

Careful examination of these substitutions should reveal one in particular which marks the point where the plot returns to some tropic variant of the opening scene or situation—this point is hopefully about halfway through the story. The substitutions of this "first obviational sequence" (from the opening to the return point) are then arranged together in such a way as to reveal two triangular structures, an external triangle summarizing the first half of the plot (A through F) and an internal triangle created by joining together the facilitating substitutional points (ACE). The apices of the external plot triangle (BDF) mark the motivating substitutional points; an easy way to remember this is to think of the angular points BDF as twisting or turning the plot along (Figure 5.1).

Note that these embedded triangles (ACE and BDF) are not a direct schematization of the plot's sequence of functions, as in Propp's (1968, 1984) method, nor are they opposed columns of paradigmatic relations oblivious to the linearity of the story, as in Lévi-Strauss's (1967, 1976) method (Meletinski 1984:61). Rather, they are analytic models designed to reveal ways in which the tale is constituted by the "mutual mediation" (Wagner 1978:177) of collectivizing and differentiating symbolizations. Like the poles of any metaphor, these two dimensions of symbolism "can be taken as whole metaphors themselves" (Weiner 1988:165). According to Wagner (1978:48), the method's originator:

> The diagram is not intended to represent self-evident or empirically discoverable motifs or segments of the text; it is *not* presented as an inductive summary of the plot, a *hypothesis* regarding the mythmaker's intentions. It is, rather, a deductive construction depicting the implications and interrelationships of a set of events that are themselves relations (substitutions). The substitutions that I identify with this schema may be more or less obviously featured in the text,

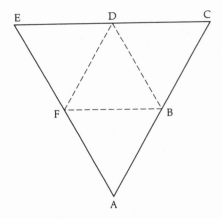

Figure 5.2. Inverted obviational sequence

yet the important thing is not the (literal) closeness of "fit," but the rapport that the interpretation finally achieves with the sense of the tale—the degree to which the interrelationships make sense.

Weiner's demonstration proceeds, next, by showing how the second half of the story "The Hornbill Husband" inverts the first half. This inverted structure begins with the narrative's return at F, but since this point is found to inaugurate a systematic inversion of the entire A-F plot, its initial correspondence is not, as might be expected, with A but rather with D (the point of maximal differentiation from A on the external triangle). Starting with the inversion of D, the substitutions in the second half of the story follow the first-half plot point for point but in the opposite direction: D to A and continuing around to E. As the systematic inversion of the first triangles, the second half of the story can be modeled as in Figure 5.2. The resulting embedded triangles reverse the identification of facilitating modality and motivating modality: the inversion of motivating D is facilitating D-inverted, the inversion of facilitating C is motivating C-inverted, and so on.

An effective way to evaluate the method of obviational analysis is to consider Weiner's (1988:158–61) own interpretation of "The Hornbill Husband" and then to suggest problems with the analysis based on actual ethnographic data.

The Hornbill Husband

Once there lived a young woman. She was working in her garden one day when a *ka buru* [female ogress] approached her and said, "Sister, my *hagenamo* leaves are ready to pick and I want to gather them. But since I am too old to climb up the tree and pick them, I have come to ask you to help me." The young woman agreed and they left. When they approached the *hagenamo* tree, the *ka buru* said to the young woman, "Remove all your clothing and leave it at the base of the tree here; take my clothing instead before you climb up." The young woman did so and climbed up the tree. While she was in the top branches picking leaves, she heard the *ka buru* whispering to herself below. "What is she saying?" the young woman wondered and called out to the *ka buru.* "No, it is only that some biting ants have stung me," the older woman replied. Then the young woman heard the sound of the tree trunk being struck repeatedly. "Now what is she doing?" she wondered. The *ka buru* called out to her, "I am going to marry your husband. You will stay here and die." And with that, the trunk of the *hagenamo* tree elongated greatly and the branches spread out in all directions and the young woman was marooned in the top of the tree. She looked down at the ground now far below her and thought, "How shall I leave this place now?" and she cried. That night she slept. In the morning she awoke and found that someone had built a fireplace and a small house. In this house she lived. At night while she slept, someone had fetched firewood and with this she made a fire.

She lived in this manner in the little house in the *hagenamo* treetop and presently she became pregnant. She continued to live in this manner, and then she bore a son. She gave birth to this child in a small confinement hut that someone had built for her. The unseen provider also began to bring food for the small infant boy as well as the mother. When the child grew up to be a toddler, one night the woman merely pretended to be asleep. Waiting there in the dark, a man arrived and held the child. The woman quickly arose and grabbed the man's wrist. He said to the woman, "Release me," but she refused. Finally, the man said to her, "The *ka buru* who trapped you here is married to your husband. But here near this tree where you live, they will soon come to cut down a sago palm. You must make a length of *hagenamo* rope and tie one end onto the middle of the sago frond. In this manner, you may pull yourself and your child onto the top of the palm. When they come to cut down the palm, you can then jump off and return to the ground." The woman did as the man instructed her, and with the aid of the rope she and her child pulled themselves onto the sago palm.

The *ka buru* and her husband arrived to set up the sago-processing equipment. While the *ka buru* erected the washing trough, the man began to chop down the palm. When it fell, he went toward the top to remove the fronds and gave a cry of surprise when he saw his other wife sitting there with a child. The *ka buru* heard his exclamation and called out to him, "What is it?" "No," he replied. "Some wasps have stung me." The *ka buru* asked suspiciously, "You haven't found another woman perhaps?" The man meanwhile looked at his long-abandoned wife and was filled with shame. He brought her over to where the *ka buru* was making sago and the two women continued working together. They all returned when the task was done and lived together.

The two women began making a garden together, but the *ka buru* would constantly shift the boundary marker between her ground and the younger co-wife's ground, making her own bigger. The younger woman repeatedly moved the marker back to its proper place and the two eventually fought. The husband discovered their quarrel and blaming the younger wife, hit her on the head with a stick, drawing blood. The young woman became very disconsolate and remembered the words of her treetop husband: "While you live with your husband on the earth, I will be around. If he mistreats you, call out to me, I will be flying in the sky above." For he was really a hornbill and his name was Ayayawego or Yiakamuna. Now the young woman called out to him, "Ayayawego, Yiakamuna, come fetch me!" There she waited and she heard the cry of the hornbill. It approached and grabbed the woman by her hair and pulled her up along with her child. They then returned to their treetop home. The overwrought husband cried, "Come back, wife!" But in vain. At the same time, the *ka buru* turned into a cassowary and crying "hoahoa," she departed. That is all.

Any mature Foi person hearing a recitation of this story would bring to the act of interpretation a series of collective understandings, expressions, categorizations, and metaphors which do not need to be explicitly stated in the narrative. In the case at hand, these presuppositions might include: (1) the principle that providing nourishment for a child is an essential part of being a parent, (2) the metaphor of calling co-wives "sisters" and the norm that, despite inevitable tensions, they are supposed to cooperate in supporting their husband, (3) the rule that collecting leaves of the *hagenamo* tree is a task for female labor, while production of sago requires the intersexual cooperation of a marital couple, (4) the knowledge of other folktales saying that, originally, the hornbill hawk lived on land and the cassowary in the sky, until the two exchanged positions, and (5) the metaphorical labeling of the hornbill and the cassowary as "cross-cousins." Given these assumptions, the story is obviously a commentary on the "difficulties of polygyny and its resolution through the separate marriages of women" (Weiner 1988:163).

Weiner's formal analysis can be condensed in the following list of substitutions (some of which I have expressed differently for clarity):

A: solitary female labor in the garden to collaborative female labor gathering edible *hagenamo* leaves
B: wife puts on ogress's clothing
C: through treachery, ogress replaces wife, who moves from ground to treetop
D: terrestrial female treachery replaced by arboreal male nurturance
E: wife, who ascended on *hagenamo* tree, descends on sago palm
F: terrestrial husband replaces arboreal husband; female cooperation replaces rivalry

Substitution F returns the plot to the original situation, which has been significantly transformed: whereas at the beginning the ogress, though calling the young woman 'sister,' tries to steal her husband, at F the two women find themselves in the relation of co-wives.

Although up to this point only half of the story has been segmented, it is possible to subject the method to a provisional evaluation by seeing if these substitutions fulfill the requirement that they alternate between the conventional, collective, facilitating modality and the innovative, individual, motivating modality. What is immediately striking is that two highly particular, clever, even magical acts in the story, the ogress's stranding the woman up in the tree in order to steal her husband (C) and the arboreal male's clever plan to repay this trickery by having the woman descend by the very sago palm the ogress and her new husband are cutting down (E), are placed in the faciliting modality. Considering the fact that these two acts are performed by the two metaphorical personae in the story (the ogress is a cassowary and the arboreal male is a hornbill), this labeling is even more puzzling. Furthermore, the narrative itself provides an important clue that these are the operant, parallel magical moments: after each event, the person being duped by the trickery thinks he or she hears something being said (perhaps a magical spell?) and each time is reassured (falsely) that nothing is amiss: "Some biting ants have stung me" and "Some wasps have stung me" (cf. R. Bauman 1986:97). What is equally strange is that the two substitutions which best mirror conventional norms of Foi sociality, the provisioning of the woman by her arboreal husband who builds a fire, a house, and a birth hut and nurtures the woman's child (D) and the return to cooperative labor by co-wives (F), are both listed as motivating modalities. These problems should be sufficient to raise suspicions, especially in light of Wagner's principle, cited above, that an interpretation must have rapport with the sense of the tale.

Nevertheless, Weiner (1988:165) claims that his identification of the two classes of substitutions is proper: "The facilitating modality represented by substitutions ACE detail the transformations in the relationship between the two women, while the motivating modality represented by substitutions BDF detail their competitive relationship to husbands, impelling their assumption of a co-wife relationship." Again, serious problems arise. First, it is not clear what these two sets of conditions have to do with the relationship between conventional and innovating dimensions of symbolization, which are by definition the criteria for identifying the facilitating and motivating modalities. Second, if anything serves as a metaphor for the transformation in the relationship between the wife and the ogress it is the act of switching clothing (B), but this is listed in the opposite modality; and if anything serves as a metaphor for the competitive rivalry these two women have in relationship to the man it is the ogress's stealing the woman's husband (C), which is also listed in the opposite modality.

The next phase of Weiner's analysis involves the demonstration that the second half of the plot forms an inverted triangle in which facilitating and motivating modalities are subject to point-by-point reversals:

D-inverted: rejoins husband (obviating bond with arboreal husband)
C-inverted: co-wives cooperate gardening (obviating treacherous collecting tree leaves)

B-inverted: ogress appropriates land (obviating exchange of clothing as personal identities)

A-inverted: fighting between co-wives (obviating solidary cooperation)

F-inverted: young woman calls hornbill in sky (obviating return to terrestrial husband)

E-inverted: rescued to arboreal home (obviating descent to terrestrial home)

Although it is not part of the formal substitutional analysis, Weiner points out that the end of the story is to be interpreted as effecting not only the change of the ogress into a cassowary (explicit in the narrative) but also the change of the young woman into a hornbill (not expressed in the narrative). These obvious metaphorical transformations are not, however, the crucial points in Weiner's account, which insists that the second half of the tale involves the transformation of the marital destinies of the two women, whereas the first half involves the transformation of the relationship between the women from cooperative "quasi-sororal identification" to rivals and finally to (temporarily) cooperative co-wives. I have not been able to determine how the substitutions in the second half are examples of inversions of the facilitating/motivational modalities of the first half. But more important—and a point not clearly articulated by Weiner—it is evident that these latter substitutions have a different semiotic status than the substitutions in the first half. In the first half, the two poles of each of the substitutions (A through F) are established at the point of the substitution itself (e.g., changing clothing, moving from treetop to ground, etc.); in the second half, the two poles of the substitution exist in different halves of the narrative. That is, it is not so much that the substitutions in the second half of the story (D-inverted through E-inverted) are formal inversions of counterpart substitutions in the first half; rather, the second-half points supply one pole of a discourse–internal trope, the other pole being a point in the first half of the narrative. In this way, the narrative turns back upon itself in order to harness enough rhetorical energy to accomplish the magical transformations described and implied at the end.

This observation does match the sense of the text, which clearly begins an asymmetrical repetition at the moment when the co-wives go out gardening together (recall that the story opens with the solitary young woman on her way to garden). This suggests that the second group of substitutions does not start inverting at D, as Weiner claims; rather, it recapitulates the narrative from the beginning in a series of obvious parallelisms:

First Half	Second Half
solitary female gardening	co-wives gardening
trickery of ogress	scheming of co-wife
ogress hits tree so woman will die	husband hits wife, drawing blood

ogress calls to woman: "I am going to marry your husband"	woman calls to future husband: "come rescue me"
woman and child descend by rope to sago palm	woman and child ascend to treetop by hair
woman living as hornbill returns to be human spouse	co-wife transformed into casso-wary
husband has two wives	husband has no wives

This pattern of inverted parallelisms can be found in many of the *tuni* presented in *The Heart of the Pearl Shell,* and it is unfortunate that Weiner's emphasis on the alternation of facilitating and motivating modalities hides this structure.

The moral lessons of the story seem clear: if in myth ogresses turn out to be co-wives, in real life co-wives tend to be ogresses; if in myth cassowaries nurture a woman and her child up in the trees, in real life husbands better be out hunting cassowaries to feed their families; if in myth a man can try to be married to creatures as symbolically opposed as a hornbill and a cassowary, in real life a man married to such contraries is likely to end up with no wives at all—just like in the myth!

Foi Cultural Semiotics

By standing back from these criticisms of the details of Wagner's obviational method it is still possible to appreciate at a more general level Weiner's interpretation of the genius of *tuni* in relation to other semiotic constructions of Foi culture, including magical spells (*kusa*) and exchange rituals. Magical spells are fixed metaphorical formulae the utterance of which transfers power from language itself to some object or activity. Williams's (1977:246) characterization is remarkable given the fact that it was written in the early 1940s, prior to the spread of semiotic techniques into anthropology:

> It is plain, then, that the spell in essence consists in a statement, a setting forth, of the hoped-for result as if it were sure to happen; but in so far as this is a plain statement it seems very doubtful if anyone would be prepared to call it magic. It is in a certain round-aboutness that the spell finds its characteristic magical value. The component factors in the situation are represented by symbols—in the manual rite by natural symbols or symbolic actions; in the spell by verbal symbols, substitutive words. It would be a thesis worth propounding that magic in this verbal guise was simply metaphor with a purpose. The symbol used is something which the magic-maker desires to emulate, to copy, to reproduce in action or being; it is a substitute on a large scale, or in some more potent sense, for the actuality of the moment. He wishes things to turn out that way, so he imagines, makes believe that they do.

For example, prior to leaving his house to hunt marsupials, a hunter pronounces a spell over red leaves used in this activity (Weiner 1988:130):

I am chewing the leg, the tail of the dark marsupial
I am chewing the leg, the tail of the *igini* cassowary
I am chewing the leg, the tail of tree kangaroo
I am chewing the leg, [long list of desired species]

Perhaps because the closing line is omitted, this spell does not illustrate the asymmetry found in other Foi spells (Silverstein 1981b). Williams (1977:325, n. 21) provides an excellent example, the spell associated with the important myth of the origin of pearl shell valuables. In order to magically acquire pearl shells, the chanter recites:

furubu tree I desire (in my liver)
konjuguri tree I desire
fogabu bird I desire
ware bird I desire
aba bird I desire
fifi tree I desire
tugu tree I desire
Kobira Piwi I desire

The repetition of conjoined classes of objects (trees and birds) sharing the red quality thought to resemble the highly prized color of pearl shells culminates in the utterance of the unique, secret name of the mythic character responsible for the introduction of these valuables.

Spells are privately owned, purchased as commodities, and retain a fixed linguistic form; though clearly tropic, they are instances of collectivizing symbolization. Weiner (1988:13) points out a systematic opposition between magical spells and mythic tales (though the force of the comparison is dulled by awkward wording):

> The relation between myths [*read* magical spells] and their associated magic spells [*read* myths] is a good example of the relative distinction between collectivizing and differentiating modes of symbolization, and hence between semantic (structural) and tropic (obviational) analysis. . . . While both rest on the force of tropic construction for their effectiveness, myth and magic occupy opposed discursive contexts. Myths are above all else public narration; the longhouse is the most common and perhaps only socially approved setting for their telling. A magic spell, on the other hand, is individual property, and spoken to no other person, except in the act of its transfer for payment, like any other valuable. . . . The magic spell focuses on the deliberate articulation of a similarity; it is a collectivizing trope, stressing the resemblances between the two elements that form the point of transfer of a specific capacity or power. One might say that magic is the Foi's own form of structural analysis, drawing similarities between putatively distinct domains, articulating metaphor in its collectivizing mode and, in addition, having the function of transferring or focusing power between those domains. The myth, by contrast, achieves its

moral force by differentiating a sequence of tropes from a conventional image of ordinary social discourse, revealing the conventional nature of this image itself, indeed, recreating it by a particular innovation or individual perspective on convention.

Thus, magical spells, though secretly held, rely on collectively shared conventions for their effectiveness; myths, on the other hand, though publicly recited, are creative products of individual inventiveness. This is one place where the danger of Weiner's conflation of "collectivizing" symbolization and Durkheimian "collectivity" manifests itself: spells are "collectivizing" as semiotic forms yet privately held as cultural objects, while myths are "differentiating" semiotic forms yet collectively shared cultural objects.

Furthermore, whereas magical spells generate sets of metaphorical equivalences, myths are free to differentiate cultural conventions by placing into fresh, tropic juxtaposition Foi roles and categories that, in social life, would forever remain contradictory, paradoxical, or incompatible; and in doing so myths "present such contradictions in terms of images not given by the conventions of normative social process and language" (Weiner 1988:287). The tales do not offer "solutions" so much as suggest the field of "play": narrative flow can accomplish in a moment of storytelling what social exchanges spend generations working out (e.g., the creation of agnatic lineality out of female reproductive power) and can place in the same syntagmatic context oppositions which are normally kept contextually separate (e.g., *aname kobora* [pork/shell] exchanges and affinal exchanges). Finally, this freedom of compositional innovation is matched by a freedom *from* contextual entailment (Silverstein 1992): whereas spells are uttered only when magic power is being delivered or when the spells as objects are being purchased, tales are told in the most neutral social setting possible, in the after-dinner relaxation of the longhouse. Moral tales are, as Weiner correctly argues, obviational devices because they simultaneously metaphorize cultural norms and render these same norms apparent.

Wagner and Weiner use the dialectical distinction between collectivizing, conventional-N symbolization and differentiating, tropic symbolization in three contexts: (1) as a global typological opposition between Western societies and tribal cultures such as the Daribi and the Foi (implying a reversal in the valuation of "artificial" and "innate" cultural forms), (2) as a contrast between the closure and the openness of local semiotic constructs (the distinction between Foi magical spells and moral tales), and (3) as alternative poles in sequential metaphorical substitutions within the texts of a discursive genre (the motivating and facilitating modalities of social exchanges and stories).[5] I have voiced doubts about the value of the global typology argument and the sequential alternation argument; the former seems to be a naive variant of the theoretically vacuous "great divide" model of the world's cultures (Goody 1977), and the latter does not seem adequate either to the narrative data themselves or to the indigenous interpretive models (Foster 1989:154). I am, however, intrigued by the middle hypothesis that, within a given culture, semiotic constructs can be placed along a continuum in terms of certain form-function correspondences. This analytical focus could highlight the connections between the obviational method and other semiotic proposals, such as Bakhtin's (1981) contrast between monoglossic poetry and heteroglossic novels in European literature and his analysis (1968) of dialogically linked layers of the petrified clerical culture and the carnivalesque universe of popular laughter in the late Middle Ages,[6] Turner's (1969) descriptions of structural and anti-structural moments in Ndembu social life, and Boon's (1982, 1984:199) reflections on monastic and ludic or parodic strains in Balinese cultural symbolism.

Finally, Wagner and Weiner both provide an interesting challenge to the by-now normal assumption that the powers-that-be in a society legitimize their power by increasing the systematicity of the symbolic order, often to the degree that its very artificiality is forgotten, especially by those who cannot break out of the regimenting authority of a dominant worldview. As Bourdieu (1979:80) puts it:

> The different classes and class fractions are engaged in a specifically symbolic struggle to impose the definition of the social world that is most consistent with their interests; the field of ideological positions reproduces the field of social positions, in a transfigured form. They may pursue this struggle either directly, in the symbolic conflicts of daily life, or vicariously, through the struggle between the specialists of symbolic production (full-time producers), for the monopoly of legitimate symbolic violence, i.e., the power to impose (and even inculcate) instruments of knowledge and expression (taxonomies) of social reality, which are arbitrary but not recognized as such.

Figurative symbolization, on the other hand, remains the one arena of cultural opposition, a possibility for authentic countercultural or revolutionary alterity by which subordinate voices can be heard in the diverse languages of inversion, humor, parody, and criticism. But Wagner and Weiner hint at another possibility: societies in which "the revelation of social power must necessarily involve the nullification, or obviation, of conventional social meanings" (Wagner 1986a:217). Semiotic creativity, according to this idea, is not primarily the refuge of antistructural social categories (the mystics, matrilaterals, and mummers of Turnerian comparative symbology); rather, it is the power to recontextualize or refigure existing cultural categories so that the force of cosmic or sexual energy is constantly channeled into the "flow" of social relations. This is not to deny that metaphoric innovation often takes the form of aesthetic vision in which the artists "invoke and compel the power that 'new' meanings represent through the creative displacement of 'given' meanings" (Wagner 1972:171). It is the recognition that such creativity lies at the very heart and not at the margins of "sociality." In some societies, then, power might be best viewed as the harnessing of forces through innovative semiotic tropes rather than as the manipulation of cultural conventions by differentiated social hierarchies (J. F. MacCannell 1985:452; Wagner 1983:4).

6 | The Semiotic Regimentation of Social Life

Social Action and Semiotic Text

RECENT INTERDISCIPLINARY WORK in the social sciences and humanities employing semiotic concepts and methods, *Social Semiotics as Praxis* by Paul J. Thibault (1991) being an exemplary case, has benefited greatly from the realization that the analysis of culturally constituted sign systems is doubly grounded in contexts of social action. First, many kinds of semiosis engage indexical modes of meaningfulness and, consequently, the work of analysis requires discovering contextual parameters that are involved either on an ad hoc basis or as a matter of systematic regularity. Since these indexical parameters themselves partake of the concrete realities of space, time, and matter, and since the token occurrence of indexical sign types requires physically manifested, temporally experienceable sign vehicles, the operation of indexicals permits no absolute disjunction between meaningful and material worlds. As Thibault (1991:7) puts it: "Thus, textual productions, their contextualizations, and the social agent/discursive subject relations these produce are always immanent in some patterned transactions of matter, energy, and information." This position, called "neomaterialism" by Thibault, does not at all imply that the systematicity of cultural sign systems is determined by a reflectionist representation of nonsemiotic referents—though such a logic of referential correspondence does characterize certain *ethno*semiotic perspectives, such as the religious worldview of the Christian Middle Ages and the "copy theory" in modern Western epistemology. The point is simply that indexicality consists of the semiotic contextualization of the "prediscursive" world.

Second, semiotic analyses and subsequent abstract theorizing are forms of social action and, as such, not only employ linguistic codes of expression but also are subject to institutional constraints as in any "disciplinary" discourse:

> Theory must become part of praxis and praxis part of theory. Critical social semiotics must articulate its own relations to and functions in the meaning making practices of which it is a part. . . . All theories, however, inevitably take part in the play of praxis, enacting either the stabilizing social discourse through which the system of disjunctions is maintained or the potentially destabilizing discourses that resist and potentially alter these. (Thibault 1991:243–44)

Thibault captures these two axes of contextualization in the title phrase "social semiotics as praxis," which implies a sensitivity both to the pragmatic character of social codes and to institutional embeddedness of modes of theoretical reflection.

Parallel to this complementarity of real-space/time contextualization and institutional contextualization is a second realization witnessed in recent semiotic scholarship, namely, that the distinction of levels between object language and metalanguage pertains not just in obvious cases where, for example, a relatively detached theoretical discourse refers to the operation of signs in social contexts but also in the realm of social action, much of which, as Bakhtin (1981:338, 1986:103) and Geertz (1973:15) tirelessly observe, involves "talk about talk" or "interpretations of interpretations" (see Chapter 4). No semiotic analysis can claim to be adequate without recognition of these multiple levels of semiosis, whether intertextual or hermeneutical, as part of the explanation of semiotic theory. While, as Taylor (1985:117) so forcefully argues, it would be a gross error merely to accept *as* a full analytical account the metasemiotic expressions of a text or an action, this meta-level potential must always be itself accounted for in a systematic rather than in an ad hoc fashion. The existence of metasemiotic understanding in the social collectivity is never a matter of complete agreement by social actors, since the ability to create accepted meta-level discourse is a key to the power of dominant versus "muted" groups (Ardener 1975:22; Goldschläger 1982:13). And the "semiosphere," to use Lotman's term, of a given culture or cultural era can also be characterized by the relative degree of metasemiotic strength in the center or core of the tradition:

> As a result, in the centre of the cultural space, sections of the semiosphere aspiring to the level of self-description become rigidly organized and self-regulating. But at the same time they lose dynamism and having once exhausted their reserve of indeterminancy they became inflexible and incapable of further development. On the periphery—and the further one goes from the centre, the more noticeable this becomes—the relationship between semiotic practice and the norms imposed on it becomes ever more strained. Texts generated in accordance with these norms hang in the air, without any real semiotic context; while organic creations, born of the actual semiotic milieu, come into conflict with the artificial norms. (Lotman 1990:134)

Not all texts or actions, however, contain in themselves the stipulated rules for interpreting meanings, so the metasemiotic level needs to be, additionally, sought in general ideological assumptions, historically transmitted in each culture, that transcend particular events or utterances. As Thibault (1991:233–34) observes:

> Texts do not tell us how to read them, nor are meanings simply contained "in" texts, waiting for the reader to extract them during a purportedly asocial reading process. Textual meanings are made in and through specific socially and historically contingent meaning making practices, which enact specific systems

of foregrounded meaning relations. Meaning making practices construct and index both local and global relations of equivalence, contrast, generality, and specificity in the partial hierarchies of thematic and actional resources in the social semiotic.

Few would take exception to these two general points, but Thibault goes further in specifying several more axioms that should meet with equally enthusiastic approval. As enacted social practices, cultural semiosis usually takes place neither in the condition of an isolated sign (along the axis of semantic meaningfulness Saussure [1959:114] called "signification") nor in the condition of a fully enacted code, the completeness of which is only a matter of potentiality and the coherence of which a matter of virtuality. Rather, action and discourse occur in realizations of "texts," a term which refers to middle-order semiotic forms, between signs and codes. From a semiotic point of view, texts are type-level discursive regularities, in whatever medium of expression (contra Harris 1984), the meanings of which involve conventions of organization beyond that of their component signs (see Hanks 1989). Texts, when contextually realized, encounter each other in social life, which can thus be seen as an intertextual field—not only because texts refer to each other but also because materially embodied texts are items of exchange, negotiation, and valuation. And texts are products of social actors in nonrandom ways, such that a correlation exists between the social positions of actors and the discursive fields of intertextuality.

Next, like Foucault (1978:97, 1980), Bourdieu (1984), and others, Thibault stresses the close connection between social action as the realization of positioned texts and local power relations, in its many dimensions. I think it is useful to further conceptualize semiotic power along distinct dimensions of semiosis. At the level of codes, power involves the delimitation of potentially meaningful utterances and the correlated degrees of awareness, misperception, and projection channeled by these form-function regularities. As Jakobson (1985) points out, the grammatical codes of language condition what *must* be conveyed, not what can be conveyed. This accounts for the Whorfian dimension of "semiotic mediation" (Mertz and Parmentier 1985). At the level of texts as organized discursive types, power resides in the conventional understandings that control genre production, in the institutional strictures that regulate the occurrence or nonoccurrence of text tokens in particular contexts, and in the valuation of prototypical or exemplary text-types in specific discursive fields. Textuality is the key to understanding the creative or performative power of certain utterances and actions such as ritual and oratory where the degree of formal organization foregrounds the collective origination of the semiotic complex (Valeri 1990:255).

Beyond the levels of code and text, power can be further analyzed in terms of two kinds of metasemiotic "regimentation," to use a term introduced by Silverstein (1981c:4, 1987a, 1992) to label the semiotic process of stipulating, controlling, or defining the contextual, indexical, or pragmatic dimension of sign function in "discursive texts" by means of the construction of a relatively fixed or coherent "interactional text." Although Silverstein intends the term to refer primarily to linguistic phenomena, he suggests that it can be extended to describe the normative constraints on ˌsocial behavior and understanding deriving from sociopolitical forces. The first deals with varieties of institutionally enforced metasemiotic, including "metapragmatic" (Silverstein 1976), discourses that regulate the range of acceptable interpretants of specific segments of social semiosis. The enforced closure of the play of interpretants can be accomplished by explicit metasemiotic framing ("the meaning of X is Y") or by constructing an implicit yet systematic representational world that silences subaltern "voices." The second is ideological regimentation, that is, metasemiotic discourse that creates a general, relatively decontextualized atmosphere of perception, knowledge, and expectation about semiosis. Whereas institutional regimentation controls the interpretability of specific discursive forms in context, ideological regimentation operates to create a presupposed cultural theory of semiosis.

While all four of these ways that semiosis is inflected with power are discussed by Thibault, though under different labels and with different theoretical aims, his book offers few empirical examples that would illuminate them in terms of the comparative study of social and historical processes. In his analyses of passages from Nabokov's novels, Thibault privileges the realization of power relations in the realm of literary intertextuality, whereas a semiotically inclined ethnographer would focus more on patterns of social activity and collective experience. I propose here to offer three related studies drawn from my current research, each illustrating a different dimension of semiotic regimentation. The cases have been arranged in a continuum, moving from the semiotic dimension of explicit type-level textuality, to the implicit text-internal metasemiotic power of sign complexes, to the ideological projection of fully metasemiotic discourse. In the following sections I discuss, first, the way ritual action and language in many societies foreground the conventionality of systems of textual signfiers; second, the way historical museums communicate to tourists about history but also about how to interpret the historical signs contained within; and third, how legal discourse about commercial advertising skews popular assumptions about the general communicative function of advertising messages.

Context and Type in Ritual Performativity

My first example concerns the phenomenon of ritual, which in many cultural traditions functions to change social relationships, convey divine powers, cure diseases, or coerce natural forces. The argument will be that the high degree of presupposed textuality of ritual forms is the key to this contextual power, a position that can best be explained by using as a foil Tambiah's influential essay, "A Performative Approach to Ritual." Fundamental to Tambiah's argument is his delineation of the "dual aspects of rituals as performances" (1985b:124). On the one hand, rituals exhibit "invariant and stereotyped sequences," while on the other hand, their efficacy depends on socially anchored "variable features." He describes ritual's "duplex existence" in terms of its being "an entity that symbolically and/or iconically represents the cosmos and at the same time indexically legitimates and realizes social hierarchies" (1985b:155). I want to investigate further this dualism of formalization and contextualization from an explicitly semiotic point of view in order to explore the fundamental question of the source of ritual power.

Rather than speak of "dualism," I prefer to think of these two dimensions as a paradox, namely, that while the action and language of ritual often appear highly structured and conventional, the powerful efficacy released by ritual is narrowly channeled or "situationally patterned" (Turner 1977:207; cf. Wheelock 1982). Rappaport (1980:187) expresses this paradox as the reflexive relationship between order and performance: "By participating in a ritual, the performer becomes part of an order which is utterly dependent for its very existence upon instances, such as his, of its performance."

Tambiah, along with almost everyone else who has written about the nature of ritual, notices several cross-cultural features of ritual action, including segmentation (clear division into sequential parts), hierarchical organization (multiple levels of embedded structures), and stereotypy (careful prescription on exact repetition). We can condense these properties by saying that rituals have structural properties, that is, they are cultural constructions with a high degree of textuality. Ritual acts are not just patterned, they are "among the most perfectly recurrent social events" (Rappaport 1992:14).

Of course, many cultural phenomena showing complex semiotic organization are structured. The architecture of a building, with four front pillars on the first level, three pillars at the second level, two on the third level, and a single cupola on top shows a triangular organization that is its syntagmatic structure. But rituals are not just structured; they are "hyperstructured" in that these cultural forms literally call out: behold the structure![1] Compare this triangular architectural form with the Beaubourg museum in Paris, where the architect took elements from the infrastructure—pipes, wiring, and other mechanical features—and put them on the outside of the building visible to the public, thus reversing the "container" and the "contained" (Baudrillard 1982:3–5). There is no way to look at this building without thinking: the "deep structure" and the "surface structure" have been inverted, and, thus, to reflect on the nature of architectural form. Poetry, as Mukařovský (1977b) and Jakobson (1987) demonstrate, is another example of a hyperstructured semiotic phenomenon. In contrast to decorative or elegant language often found in political oratory, persuasive advertising, and fictional prose, the language of poetry, with its rhythmic pattern, metrical verse structure, sound alliteration, and metaphorical sequence, calls attention to the "structure of the linguistic sign" (Mukařovský 1977b):68). Just as great architecture is really about architectural design, great poetry, according to these two theorists, is about the structure of language. In a parallel fashion, ritual can be interpreted as hyperstructured *social* action, in which segmentation, hierarchy, and stereotypy are not just contingent aspects of performance but are the means of calling attention to the structuredness of action.

The second aspect of ritual which generates the paradox noted above is that rituals are context specific. Rituals are often assigned to very restricted temporal intervals: calendrical or seasonal rites that take place at the passing of the New Year, or when the Pleiades rise at sunset, or when the Tigris and the Euphrates overflow their banks. In addition, rituals are prescribed for certain places: on the altar within the central chamber of Ezekiel's imaginary temple (J. Z. Smith 1987:62–63), over the "domestic fire" burning in the northeast corner of the house where Vedic texts say invisible spirits dwell (B. Smith 1980), or along the sightlines of megalithic stones pointing to sunrise at the equinox. Ritual rules also define the social roles allowed to participate in or take on assigned responsibilities for the performance, and specify the prior conditioning required for all participants. Only initiates knowledgeable of the sacred myth and purified by bathing can march along the Sacred Way from Athens to Eleusis to participate in the "mysteries," where the main priest, torchbearer, and herald come from specific aristocratic families (Burkert 1987:37). For the Baruya of Papua New Guinea, the master of male initiation ceremonies, the controller of powerful ritual sacra, must come from the founding clan, also named Baruya, which represents the society as a whole (Godelier 1986). Mayan shamans cure their patients by maintaining verbal deictic linkage with them throughout the ritual discourse (Hanks 1990:240). But the word "contextual" can also be taken in a performative sense, that rituals change or modify things *in context*. A college student approved to undergo the rite of fraternal initiation cannot stay in the library; a couple about to get married must appear in person before a minister or magistrate and witnesses must sign a document testifying to their physical presence; a Catholic priest delivers a blessing upon those in attendance and, in fact, only upon those within the arc of the cruciform hand gesture. The effectiveness of ritual does not usually extend beyond the spatial and temporal contexts of the occurrence of the actions, and when it does the extension is carried by some material vehicle—water, stones, relics—endowed *at* the event with durative sacred powers.

So the paradoxical dimensions of ritual are, first, excessive formality and, second, contextual anchoring. At first glance these seem to be strange if not contradictory things to put together, since the formal pattern of ritual action, like the formal pattern of architecture and poetry, might suggest that rituals are relatively *decontextualized* in several related senses. First, ritual appears decontextualized in being "distantiated" from the intentions of participants, as in the medieval doctrine of *opus operatum* ("the work accomplished") which guarantees the efficacy of the sacraments apart from the spiritual standing or intentional state of the officiant or recipients or as in the operation of the Hawaiian temple rituals in which the authority of ritual officials derives from the superior authority of the ritual text (Valeri 1985:342). This implies that the meaning of a ritual is recoverable across the variability of particular contextual enactments.

Second, ritual is decontextualized in being "decentered," that is, freed from the limitations of contextual specification and reference. Highly conventional, rule-governed performances can transcend contextual reference and be interpreted as referring to general rather than particular contexts. In many cases the denial of referential specificity enables rituals to concentrate on reference to eternal or universal truths, in much the same way that, as Mukařovský´ (1977a:84) argued, the aesthetic function of a work of art is freed from particular denotational value. There is a sense in which the hyperstructure of ritual can be appreciated outside the actual context of occurrence because it displays a completely self-contained conventional shape. At the recent consecration of the first female bishop of the Episcopal Church, the ceremony was taken out of the Boston cathedral (which is, after all, the proper "seat" of the bishop) and put into a civic building in order to handle the crowds and media. This is one of the most highly structured ritual performances in the Episcopal Church, and one in which the indexical or contextual features are highly evident—especially the focal act of "laying on hands" that physically guarantees the historical chain of contiguity from St. Peter to the present. But this ritual could be decentered and moved to a nonreligious environment precisely because of its power to overcome the limitations of a particular context. So this sense of decontextualization is evident in the character of ritual to survive radical spatial dislocation.

Third, ritual is decontextualized by encouraging a phenomenological "bracketing" of the surrounding social world and by creating a coherent world within the ritual sphere. In ritual time and space, mundane concerns are suppressed and the universe for assigning truth-value is marked off as a "separate, self-contained world ruled exclusively by the comprehensive and exhaustive order of the ritual" (Heesterman 1985:3). By replacing everyday social logic with a special set of equivalences, rituals can make symbolic assertions which cannot be held up against the standards of mundane norms and goals—despite the fact that rituals may function specifically to legitimate real political power (Kertzer 1988:51). Alexander (1986) argues that part of the dynamic of the Watergate hearings was that Congress constructed the event as a ritual rather than as a purely political process, thus bracketing the question of personal motives, partisan strategies, and historical details.

Fourth, ritual is decontextualized in being "self-referential." In other words, the hyperstructured components of ritual form a network of mutual implication (each part in the sequence is linked to previous and subsequent parts) and internal metareference (rules for ritual action, like liturgical rubrics, become part of the structure of the ritual). The self-referentiality of ritual is also manifest in the taxonomic relationship among different ritual sequences: a particular ritual is taken to be a subspecies of a more general category (a minor sacrament vs. a major sacrament) or else in systematic opposition to parallel ritual actions within the same culture (male initiation vs. female initiation in Baruya; Luakini vs. Makahiki rites in Hawaii) or to analogous rites in contradictory traditions (Hebrew sacrifice vs. Canaanite sacrifice).

In semiotic terms, then, all these dimensions combine so that the prescribed series of actions in ritual is understood as a "type" rather than a "token," that is, a system of general conventional regularities rather than a sequence of concrete, realized instances. No one doubts that rituals occur as token instances; but their hyperstructural self-reference leads participants to look beyond the "eventness" of ritual action and to concentrate on their formal textuality. In the terms of the paradox: on the one hand, the power of ritual requires contextual enactment at the token level; four dimensions of this situational anchoring were specified: temporal sequence, spatial location, prescribed participant roles, and contextual effectiveness. On the other hand, the focus on form or structure implies a decontextualized view of ritual in which a token performance demands that it be viewed as a type of social action. This decontextualization was seen to be the result of a combination of factors, including distantiation, decentering, bracketing, and self-referentiality. I want to suggest that this is an empirical paradox, and the trick is not to try to mediate it or avoid it but rather to see what the paradox signals about the nature of rituals in many societies.

I think that the organization of Tambiah's argument does not make sufficiently clear how his theoretical approach solves the initial paradox of the "duplex" character of ritual. He is trying to account for ritual effectiveness in context, as in the Austinian sense of the word "performative." And then he says that rituals must be performed, that is, they must be instantiated as tokens or replicas of general types of action. And then he observes that rituals have indexical sign features, as opposed to sign phenomena which do not require any contextual knowledge. So the three features are effective power, tokenness, indexicality. But it seems that he has put the most difficult thing to explain, namely, effective power, as the first step in the argument, using tokenness and indexicality as supplementary components of effectiveness. But if the question is asked: how are rituals effective in context? then the features of tokenness and indexicality are not in themselves sufficient to account for the power of ritual. We need to add another feature, the notion of hyperstructure discussed above. Now, Tambiah does in fact talk about hyperstructure, but he does not precisely show the theoretical importance of it. The socially effective power of ritual performances in context cannot be accounted for without noting the semiotic contribution of the highly structured, conventional, rule-governed character of ritual action.

As noted above, rituals are events in which the component signs are highly indexical. But where does effective power come from? When the king of Babylon comes out from the *akitu* building on the tenth day of the New Year festival to marry his royal bride, they dress up like the god Marduk and the cosmic bride (Black 1981). Their earthly marriage is an instance of a divine prototype or model, and their human fertility is iconically understood as cosmic generativity. The marriage ritual is collective, that is, involving the whole society (as we know from Durkheim, there is power emanating from the very sociality of ritual events), but the presence of lots of people and the contextual anchoring of the event cannot, in themselves, account for the power. Hyperstructure is the key to this, since ritual actions are not just conventional, they are so conventionalized that they highlight or call attention to the rules, that is, to the pattern, model, or semiotic type which the ritual action instantiates. And it is the cosmological or transcendent grounding of these cultural prototypes that is the ultimate source of the power of ritual to "offer a glimpse of a higher order of things" (Babcock 1978:293). As Eliade (1954) repeatedly stresses, an earthly marriage is an instance of a divine marriage; a liturgical performance is an instance of a divine sacrifice; a New Year rite is an instance of a cosmogonic event (Pallis 1926:247); the dismemberment of raw flesh of sacrificial victims is a repetition of the paradigmatic event when the infant Dionysus was torn to pieces (O'Flaherty 1988:106). (But Eliade sometimes forgets to stress equally the other side of ritual: power residing in cosmology cannot be realized as socially effective other than in context-specific events.) The Mambi of East Timor believe that the efficacy of ritual depends on the continued and invariant observance of patterns of symbolic action started by the ancestors, whose role as the source of the "original archetype" (Traube 1986:163) provides the motivation for their being invoked in ritual chants: "My mother did not pass on some different thing/My father did not hand down some altered thing/I follow in the footprint/I know the grass track" (cf. Parmentier 1987a:132–35).

But it is an illusion to think that the power comes *de novo* out of the moment of performance, despite the fact that participants in ritual events might feel that this power emerges at that moment (cf. Boyer 1990:79–90). A moment's event is simply a token, but a ritual event is a token which is an instance of a general regularity, that is, a Peircean "replica" that brings *into* context the legitimized authority, divine precedent, or mythological charter behind ritual action. One of the results of ritual repetition is that the token quality of the action is lifted out of the category of "sinsign," that is, a token sign without a corresponding generative type, to be grasped as a replica, which is created by *cultural* rather than natural semiosis. In this way, ritual performance signals not just cultural conventions but conventionality itself (Rappaport 1979:194). And this, then, is the function of the hyperstructure of ritual processes, since rituals call attention to the existence of cultural templates or predictive "blueprints" (Tambiah

1985a:51) derived from supernatural or transcendental sources existing beyond the moment of performance (Bell 1992:206–7). So ritual does occur at the level of event, but these events are realizations of general patterns (cf. Kuipers 1990:161–62).

We can now return to reexamine the nature of linguistic performatives from this new perspective. Why does "I promise" have social power? It can create something new because it is a replica which instantiates at one moment in time a general cultural type, a rule-governed social routine called "promising." People know that this routine is being instantiated because of the peculiar semiotic properties of language use in the event: the word uttered is transparent to the lexical label for the operant routine: "I promise" and "promise" (Silverstein 1977). For someone merely to say "Yes, I think I'll do it" is not to produce a socially valid promise. This is exactly parallel to the earlier case of the king of Babylon's marriage. Going through the ritual is just like saying "I promise": the marriage is transparently iconic with its divine template. That is why the participants dress up like gods and earlier in the ritual sequence actually recite word for word— note the transparency or iconicity—the text of *Enuma elish*, the epic of the creation of the gods, the formation of the cosmos, and the institution of the Babylonian state. Actual recitation is a way of calling into this political context the same kinds of supernatural power that, at the beginning of time, effected the cosmogony and of reinforcing the analogy between political stratification and cosmological hierarchy (Kuhrt 1987:37).

In conclusion, the initial paradox, that rituals are characterized by two seemingly incompatible aspects, extreme formal patterning and contextual anchoring, is easily resolved by the semiotic perspective which sees ritual in many societies as the contextual anchoring of hyper-conventional forms, forms which have regimenting power due to their association with original or transcendent cultural types: it is Marduk, not the king, whose marriage is being celebrated.

Institutional Regimentation of Touristic Experience

In ritual, semiotic types of social action are made manifest as tokens and dwell among us; their tokens are not ad hoc events but exemplary replicas which transparently reveal the cosmological model. The high degree of organization of the signs creates in the experience of participants in ritual performance a sense that the entire event or discourse is a single text. But what about experiences in which the coherence and systematicity of signs and their meanings are not the product of entextualization in a clearly evident sign complex but rather are produced in syntagmatically less formal ways? My second example suggests that some contexts of social life contain strong metamessages delimiting the range of possible interpretations, but which do so indirectly, implicitly, or inductively. The regimentation found in these contexts is all the more powerful because social actors are not confronted with explicit metasemiotic forms (as will be the case in the final example).

An important dimension of the ethnographic study of history as a cultural system is the analysis of locally deployed semiotic mechanisms which regiment peoples' understanding and experience of the past. These mechanisms, including, for example, textual forms, visual images, behavioral rules, consumption goods, ritual processions, architectural monuments, and museum exhibitions, are instruments of the historicizing institutions of a society. A particularly powerful example of the regimentation of historical consciousness in the United States is Colonial Williamsburg in Virginia, where I carried out a brief period of fieldwork in 1987.[2]

A methodological principle of the research was to experience the restored city as much as possible as a typical tourist would. I did not establish contacts with local scholarly authorities, I did not inspect archival records not publicly available, and I did not engage in formal interviews with either tourists or staff. During my stay, however, I attempted to visit as many exhibition buildings as possible, and at each location I took notes on the communication between interpretive staff and tourists, photographed informational signs, and collected pamphlets, guide books, official publications, local newspapers, and maps. In approaching the research I kept in mind the point made by Dean MacCannell (1976:110), that "the first contact a sightseer has with a sight is not with the sight itself but with some representation thereof." I certainly did not experience the "glazed" look Mark Leone observed on the faces of visitors during his research, and I would disagree with his harsh statement that "despite the site's motto about the future learning from the past, very few facts, no social context, and nothing we would think of as historical interpretation are normally taken away" (1981b:13). The visitors I watched were engaged if not overwhelmed, inquisitive, and observant.

Colonial Williamsburg is a reconstruction of the eighteenth-century capital of Virginia when the city functioned as an administrative center, housing the Capitol, the Governor's Palace, a military garrison, courthouse and jail, and the residences of prominent members of the Tidewater planter class and over a thousand slaves. Because Williamsburg was devoid of significant industry or trade and because it was isolated from the principal urban centers of the period, it was an exceptional if not unique colonial city:

> Virginia practiced only a few basic crafts and had virtually no industries aside from tobacco producing and processing for market and such a rare endeavor as iron making. Heavy importation of luxury items not made on the self-sustaining plantations or in the town shops was universal. That Williamsburg in colonial times was a far cry from Boston, Philadelphia, or New York cannot but impress the thoughtful visitor, even though the point is not stressed in the interpretation. (Cotter 1970:420)

But the "smallness of [its] world" did not hinder its eagerness to "receive the latest fashions, to be in touch with the polite world, and to enjoy the benefits of a cultured high society" (Isaac 1982:235). After the administrative functions moved further inland to Richmond in 1780, the city continued to be the location of the College of William and Mary and of the Public Hospital for the insane.

The contemporary tourist site is the result of financial contributions of John D. Rockefeller, Jr. Starting in 1926, Rockefeller arranged for the purchase of land, the removal of nineteenth- and twentieth-century structures, and the construction or reconstruction of eighteenth-century buildings. Modern buildings were added to accommodate the tourist crowd, such as the Abby Aldrich Rockefeller Folk Art Center, the DeWitt Wallace Decorative Arts Gallery (self-proclaimed as "one of the foremost collections of English and American decorative arts of the 17th, 18th, and early 19th centuries" [Cooper cited in Leone 1987:4]), the "award-winning" Williamsburg Inn, the Williamsburg Lodge, Conference Center, and Auditorium, and various retail stores, including one for Colonial Williamsburg furniture reproductions. In short, Colonial Williamsburg offers a "total historical environment" (Fortier 1979:252), if not a "total social order" (Wallace 1986a:148).

Today, Colonial Williamsburg is an enormously popular tourist destination, hosting over a million visitors per year; and it is an equally important educational and historical institution, with an operating budget of over $75 million. Its hotels, restaurants, golf course, and meeting rooms make it suitable for all sorts of corporate, educational, and political conferences (such as the Summit of Industrialized Nations in 1983). Its prominence is reflected in the names of the men serving as the Board of Directors, which included in 1985 the Chairman of the Board of AT&T, the Senior Vice-President of IBM, the President of the Rockefeller Brothers Fund, the Librarian of Congress, the Secretary of Education, an Associate Justice of the Supreme Court, the President of the University of Virginia, the C.E.O. of New York Life Insurance Company, the C.E.O. of Brooks Brothers, and David Brinkley of ABC News.

The thesis I want to argue is that Colonial Williamsburg's overt educational and recreational functions mask a powerful covert function of reproducing and legitimizing a system of social distinctions in contemporary American society, and that this is accomplished by the promotion of an ideology of scientific transparency that anchors present distinctions in the colonial past. From the moment a tourist enters the Visitor Center on the outskirts of the Historic Area and views the thirty-five-minute docudrama orientation film *Williamsburg—The Story of a Patriot*, Colonial Williamsburg proclaims itself to be a story of freedom and democracy and presents the tourist experience as a "journey through history." The reconstruction is said to represent not just a remarkably important colonial city but the very birthplace of the "idea of America." This idea is formally described in terms of the "Five Cornerstones of Freedom": integrity of the individual, responsible leadership, self-government, individual liberties, and equality of opportunity. The tourist is continually reminded that eighteenth-century Williamsburg was a perfect example of the harmonious mingling of different social classes: the British aristocracy, the local planter elite, the "middling sort" of hard-working farmers and craftspersons, and the slaves—Indians, as we shall see, occupy an utterly outcaste position. And those members of the community who found themselves at the lower end of this hierarchy were, at least, engaged in the process of "becoming Americans." There is, thus, an explicitly constructed identity between the "melting pot" process of modern multiethnic America and an original coexistence of social differences under the aura of democratic ideals. And while at Colonial Williamsburg visitors are encouraged to use the experience as a means to "rededicate" themselves to these transhistorical verities.

What the tourist's experience of this "living museum" consists of is, however, quite different from the official orienting ideology. The pervasive message of the discourse, images, interpretive signs, and overall site organization taken as an implicit semiotic text is that of rigid social "distinction" (Bourdieu 1984). Not only do the costumed interpreters repeat the hierarchy of aristocracy, planters, craftsmen, and slaves, but even finer distinctions are drawn within each of these categories: for example, between masters, journeymen, and apprentices, or between skilled and unskilled slave labor. This lesson is communicated largely through the interpretation of material objects. Furniture is divided into fine, imported items and rough, locally produced items; houses are evaluated in terms of the presence or absence of multipurpose rooms; patterns of activity are separated into leisure (such as "politics") and labor (such as craft production); different terms of address are used to set off "ladies" and "gentlemen" from the rest of the populace; and distinct styles of clothing mark fine gradations in the social ladder (gentlemen's shoes are designed to be too tight to actually walk in). This system of distinction, though rigid, did not prohibit middle-ranking persons from hoping to climb up the social ladder: I attended an evening performance of "Keeping the Best Company," described as a dramatization of the "clothing, manners, and diversions of the gentry of eighteenth-century Virginia to which the middling class aspired."

At the Gaol we were told that "upper class" people received bail; debtors, middle-class women, and the insane were confined in not-so-uncomfortable spartan rooms ("the only place in Williamsburg with indoor plumbing"), while criminals from the lower classes—that is, real criminals—were bound in miserable cells. The tourist's experience is that these last are the stereotypical or focal criminals, although the guide did note that, in eighteenth-century Williamsburg, most criminal cases involved the propertied classes. After leading us through these various gradations of incarceration, the interpreter commented that, luckily, "today, times have changed," meaning that horrid conditions and arbitrary justice no longer characterize our penal system; a man next to me disagreed, muttering, "It's a better system than we have now."

Only after visiting a range of different exhibitions did I begin to realize that, in addition to the pervasiveness of the enscription of difference at the level of manifest content, there was a subtler regimenting mechanism at work at the "phenomenological" level of touristic experience. The exhibition sites can be loosely arranged in a hierarchy of regimentation, using several intersecting variables, including financial outlay for admission, relative restriction of visiting hours, difficulty of access, rigidity of interpretative program, and comprehensiveness of textual material provided. This phenomenological hierarchy corresponds to the position on the hierarchy of eighteenth-century society instantiated at each exhibition.

The streets and lawns of the Historic Area are open to the walking public at all hours of the day and night and require no admission fee. One can, for this minimal level of engagement, see the outsides of buildings, enjoy the gardens, and mingle with other tourists. Having traveled all the way to Colonial Williamsburg, however, few will fail to purchase one of three general admission passes: the Basic Admission, the more expensive—though tainted with a loyalist label—Royal Governor's Pass, and the still more expensive valid-for-a-year Patriot's Pass. The Basic Admission allows one to see the orientation film at the Visitor Center, to visit various everyday sites such as the Blacksmith, the Wigmaker, the Gunsmith, and the Wheelwright, and to tour the (democratically inexpensive) Capitol building; the Royal Governor's Pass is good for all these plus entry to the Governor's Palace and the Wallace Gallery; but only equipped with the Patriot's Pass can you enter Carter's Grove Plantation or the Rockefeller mansion, Bassett Hall. Additional special admission tickets are required for special programs, films, musical concerts, theatrical productions, lectures, seminars, and other activities. Tourists with either limited time or specific interests can also enter some of the more popular exhibits such as the Governor's Palace and Carter's Grove Plantation by purchasing a Separate Ticket. There is, I understand, an additional Museum Ticket, designed for those visitors who want nothing of historical reconstruction and desire only to see the formal galleries and the Rockefeller homestead, itself housing a private collection of American folk art. Like the fine gradations in eighteenth-century fashion, the ticketing system at Colonial Williamsburg requires careful study and practice.

The hierarchical regimentation of touristic experience can also be seen in the regulations stipulating visiting hours and reservation requirements. The orientation film is shown continuously and tickets may be obtained moments before a showing. Most of the craft buildings are open all day, though every other day—requiring the diligent tourist to spend more than one day in local hotels, restaurants, and shops—without reservation and without the presence of a special interpreter other than the craftsperson working the exhibition. Tourists are free to wander around, talk with the craftspersons, and stay for as long or as little as they want. Domestic houses are staffed by costumed interpreters who informally assemble a small group of tourists and guide the group around the house and grounds; their discourse is conversational rather than scripted, and they do not act the role of eighteenth-century persons. The one-hour Patriot Tour requires advance reservations to join a group of about twenty people, all wearing distinctive badges, who are led around the city on foot and in bus by one tour guide, whose monotone recitation varies little from group to group.

In contrast, lines form outside the Capitol and there is no possibily of visiting this site without delay or apart from a numerically limited group. Visitors are accompanied at all times by an interpretive guide who engages in scripted conversations with costumed actors playing eighteenth-century roles. The Governor's Palace is much like the Capitol, except that the lines are longer and the entry ticket is more expensive; a separate guide pamphlet is distributed indicating the significance of every room, describing the experience the tourist is supposed to have, and justifying the imaginative "living interpretation" of the reconstruction—a touchy point since the original building was destroyed in 1781 and all researchers had to go on was an image on a copper plate found in the Bodleian Library at Oxford.

Still higher on the scale of regimentation and distinction is Carter's Grove Plantation, located on the James River about eight miles from the city. To get there one must have a private car or hire a limo. The Country Road itself, described and mapped in a separate pamphlet, is designed as a touristic experience: "You have set off on a drive that will take you through the woodlands, ravines, meadows, and marshlands that compose a landscape typical of tidewater Virginia." The journey is not only through space and time, but also through social class, since at the end stands the plantation, whose masters, like the flora along the road, emerged naturally from the scenery. As the official guide brochure states:

> The Country Road has brought you from prehistory through the first years of European settlement and into the eighteenth century. By the middle of that century a class of wealthy planters appeared in Virginia. Because they had sufficient capital to invest in vast acreage and many slaves, the biggest planters profited greatly by producing tobacco.

Carter's Grove Plantation is like Colonial Williamsburg in miniature. A lavishly illustrated orientation display welcomes the traveler at the Reception Center, where I watched interpreters-in-training preparing for a competence exam by transcribing the information in the display windows—an excellent example of the circularity of the habitus—and where a brief film provides the overview of the experience about to be experienced. This heavy interpretation contrasts with the poverty of information provided on the short path leading to the mansion. Here, we are told, is the future site of the slaves' quarters currently being reconstructed as a one-room shelter; slaves shared a single room because "they had no need for privacy." The poverty of the people and the poverty of the information are mutually justified by the exigencies of scientific reconstruction: "little documentation is available to indicate what objects slaves actually owned."[3] This sign echoes a comment made in 1972 by the museum's resident audiovisual expert, that while filming "Music of Williamsburg," "it was desired to depict the burying of a field slave, but to the astonishment of the film makers not a single scrap of information was available on method, emotion, practice, and music (if any) [!] of black burials. The sequence had to be abandoned" (Smith 1972:7). And across the path stands a small sign pointing into the woods where the hunting-gathering Indians roamed. The Indians, we are informed, put up strong resistance to the early English settlers, and if their assaults had been as successful elsewhere as here "the course of American history might well have been changed." This was not to be, and the Indians, "weakened by disease, were no match for the English"—as if their eventual destruction was, in the end, their fault. Throughout this site, the language of description systematically uses ergative verbs for the victors ("a planter class emerges") and transitive verbs for the victims (who "burned" houses, "killed" settlers, and "embraced" Christianity).

Partial validation of my hypothesis about social distinction came when, just prior to my departure from Colonial Williamsburg, I attempted to visit Bassett Hall, now a museum but formerly the residence of the Rockefeller family. Though armed with my Patriot's Pass, I discovered that admission is very limited and that a potential visitor must register ahead of time (in a large volume looking like a guest-book) for an "appointment." In contrast to other exhibit sites, which permit those without proper passes to stroll the grounds, Bassett Hall's 585-acre tract is restricted to pass-holders. Unfortunately I did not have time to wait for my appointment and went away only with the comfort of authenticity, knowing that the house has been kept in exactly the same shape as when the Rockefellers lived there in 1956–60. At the top of the hierarchy of regimenting historical interpretation stands the home of the Rockefellers, the very agents responsible for the preservation and reconstruction of the surrounding eighteenth-century city. Although their residence dates only thirty-five years into the past and although their national economic power originates only in the late nineteenth century, the Rockefellers have managed to place themselves at the apex of a hierarchy of distinction anchored at the very birth and birthplace of the democratic ideal.

Wallace (1986b:170) is certainly correct in claiming that both Rockefeller and Henry Ford (at the reconstruction of Greenfield Village near Detroit) "sought partly to celebrate their newly won preeminence and partly to construct a retrospective lineage for themselves by buying their way into the American past." The power of social distinction in the present is thus projected into the colonial past and rendered part of our cultural heritage worth preserving and perpetuating. As Leone (1981a:309) notes with reference to the museum at Shakertown in Kentucky: "Naturalizing the present by imposing some part of it on the past is, as all historiographers know, inevitable and unavoidable."[4]

Two brief observations need to be made in closing, though each requires more extensive examination than is possible here. First, I believe that the scientific or educational function of Colonial Williamsburg is one of the principal ways it legitimizes its reproduction of social distinction. A motto repeated by interpreters is that Colonial Williamsburg is constantly changing, for "the more we learn the more things change" as the exhibitions draw closer and closer to an accurate depiction of the past. Indications of serious scholarly activity abound, including ongoing archaeological excavations, research publications for sale, an impressive schedule of academic conferences, and periodic announcements of important "discoveries." As Cotter (1970:422), a professional archaeologist, observes:

> The backbone of the physical restoration, reconstruction, and interpretation here is Colonial Williamsburg's remarkable research facilities. An enormous corpus of microfilm, usefully indexed, and excellent library resources, together with curatorial and archaeological expertise fortified with many thousands of artifacts and hundreds of thousands of fragmentary objects from the earth—all provide the researcher with incomparable components of the historical scene.

Colonial Williamsburg's interpretive program is strong to the degree that it is motivated by what I would call the goal of historical transparency, that is, for the authority of the site to appear to the tourist as flowing naturally from the scientific accuracy of the reconstruction and from the scholarly validity of the interpretation *without* the processes of reconstruction and interpretation's revealing any signs of regimented "semiotic mediation" (Culler 1981:134–37). This evidence of academic creditials, coupled with the metasemiotic rhetoric insisting on the realism of the reconstruction, combine to create what Barthes (1986:139) labels the "reality effect," that is, the function of any historicizing sign "whose sole pertinent feature is precisely to signify that the event represented has *really* taken place." Or, as Handler (1986:4) puts it, "in modern society, the temple of authenticity is the museum."

Second, the message of Colonial Williamsburg is not only communicated to tourists while at the city or taken back to the classroom by schoolchildren who visit on fieldtrips, but it is also for sale in the form of commodities at various retail stores.[5] The tourist is encouraged to take advantage of these free-market shopping opportunities, since all the stores are "ticket not required" sites. Williamsburg Reproductions, claiming to be authentic replicas of period furniture and thus embodying the aura of history so carefully constructed by Colonial Williamsburg, are sold in fifty-nine stores throughout the country. Small signs on each piece of furniture resemble the signs on the pieces on display in the various reconstructed buildings except that "do not touch" is replaced by a price tag and an order number. In Colonial Williamsburg's annual report for 1982, the proud claim is made that

> Colonial Williamsburg has enhanced a wide public awareness of the value of good design which, in turn, has had a profound effect on the general level of taste. A distinguished editor of a prestigious house furnishings magazine has suggested that the Williamsburg Reproduction program has been the greatest single influence on elevating American taste and teaching appreciation of the lasting values of fine craftsmanship and design.

The reproduction of distinction is disseminated through the commoditization of historical reproduction.

Ideological Regimentation in Advertising

Colonial Williamsburg does not put forth a decontextualized ideology about "history" in general. Its interlocking signs work to structure possible interpretations of the site for visitors at the site itself; its semiotic regimentation is, in other words, indexically anchored. This final section, in contrast, deals with a set of independent signs (commercial advertisements) that, together, rely on a pervasive ideology about communication and referentiality.

It is a commonplace for analysts of contemporary American culture to point out the powerful impact of advertising on the development of a "culture of consumption," characterized by the shift from production to consumption as the basis for socially recognized values and as the source of artificial or symbolic needs unrelated to relatively more objective use-values (Lears 1983; Leiss, Kline, and Jhally 1990:281–84). What is less clear, however, is precisely *how* advertising succeeds in this manipulation of consciousness, that is, how the pragmatic functions of advertising as a system of communication are achieved. My argument here is that the functional effectiveness of advertisements cannot be understood apart from its "semiotic ideology," a term modeled after the notion of "linguistic ideology" formulated by Silverstein (1979), namely, a culturally determined, historically grounded set of interpretive standards for understanding linguistic and, by extension, visual communication. In other words, messages of any sort are received in the context of explicit understandings and implicit assumptions of a general nature about how various communicative signals function. And these understandings and assumptions are themselves products of social institutions which, for example, regulate communicative usages, impose canons of interpretation, and codify the principles of communicative ideology. To make an argument parallel to Silverstein's (1985a) paper on gender categories and Mertz and Weissbourd's (1985) work on legal ideology, I argue that modern consumers' understanding of particular ads is significantly skewed by the effects of a regimented view of the general nature of commercial speech and, further, that this official ideology is so far from being an accurate account of the forms and functions of advertising messages that their manipulative potential derives at least in part from consumers' enforced misunderstanding.

I then hypothesize that the senders of advertising messages, namely, the agencies representing various commercial interests, are fully aware of this disjunction between the communicative character of advertising and the available interpretive standards and have, in fact, structured their commercial messages to maximally exploit this gap. The overall pragmatic function of advertising becomes a result of the combination of its communicative character (e.g., the ways language is employed, the role of visual images, and the presentation of value-laden symbols) and the surrounding standards that reinforce consumers' interpretive standards (e.g., assumptions about whether or not ads are to be believed, awareness of the "official" informational function of commercial speech, and tacit knowledge of existing governmental regulations). The basis for the argument consists of a study of the legal and regulatory decisions dealing with commercial speech, a review of empirical research done by others on the impact of certain deceptive forms of advertising on consumer beliefs, and continuing analysis of linguistic and visual forms of contemporary advertising on television and in magazines.

English and American jurisprudence has for centuries recognized a distinction between factual representations of commercial products subject to rules of warranty and misrepresentation and statements of personal opinion or exaggerations of product qualities considered typical of "seller's talk" (Preston 1975). This second category of statements, called "puffery," falls within the tradition of *caveat emptor:* the buyer is expected to know that sellers are wont to exaggerate and state opinions for which they are not to be held literally accountable. Consumers in the nineteenth century were expected to distrust commercial sellers and to exercise "that caution and attention which all prudent men ought to observe in making their contracts" (*Seixas and Seixas v. Wood*, 2 Cai. R [N.Y.] 48, 54 [1804], cited in Pridgen and Preston 1980:639). Sellers could even deliberately design such "puffs," since, as a Massachusetts court ruled in 1853, "it always having been understood, the world over, that such statements are to be distrusted."

The exclusion of these exaggerations and opinions from the category of actual misrepresentation thus rests on the explicit understanding that puffs are conventional linguistic routines involving the following features: a statement uttered in the context of commercial persuasion that, though it may appear formally to be a claim capable of verification, is regarded by all reasonable persons as functionally irrelevant to the process of rational market decisions. For example, a salesperson representing a soap manufacturer says, "This soap is made of the purest ingredients available anywhere in the world." The buyer's expected interpretation of this claim, under the legal doctrine of puffery, is to discount it as the expected inflation by an interested party, rather than to expend energy evaluating the truth-value of the expressed proposition.

Courts originally drew the line between puffery and misrepresentation by distinguishing statements that, on the one hand, magnify the advantages or qualities a product in fact has to some degree from statements that, on the other hand, invent or falsely assert the existence of qualities which the product does not demonstratively possess. This distinction suggests that the legal understanding of this type of communicative routine was that the product description's being patently inflated or personally slanted functions itself as an obvious indexical sign—a warning, in fact—of the biased attitude of the seller. In other words, exaggerated predication signals the motivated intentionality characteristic of sellers and alerts buyers to take a skeptical attitude. The expressed opinion or exaggeration is the clue for buyers to know that they are dealing with puffery rather than purported factual claims, despite the well-formed propositionality of the utterance; and the presupposed context of the persuasive sales talk signals the applicability of the rule of interpretation which constructs the proper functional assignment of such opinions and exaggerations as mere puffery.

What emerges from these initial observations is the existence of two levels of linguistic competence, the first level involving the mastery of referential or propositional codes and the second level involving a shared metasemiotic standard or rule of interpretation: in contexts of commercial persuasion, predicative exaggerations index the inflated opinion of seller rather than the qualities of the object being referred to. The legal term "puffery" is, then, an officially regimented "ethnometapragmatic" (Silverstein 1976) label, that is, a meta-level description of the complex pragmatics of advertising as contextually understood commercial speech.

So for an utterance to be a puff it must provide, through a combination of presupposed context ("sales") and creative indexicality ("exaggeration") a second-level message: "take this as a puff." Combined with a general skeptical attitude toward salespersons characteristic of the *caveat emptor* era, this metamessage at least partially guarantees that consumers will properly disambiguate the formal/functional skewing of acts of puffery. The legal recognition of this power to disambiguate is documented, for example, in *Berman v. Woods* (33 Ark. 351 [1881]), where the Court stated:

> As for the glowing representations with regard to the merits of their [printing] press, made by the plaintiffs in their [advertising] circulars, they are the usual artifices of enterprise and competition. If false or exaggerated, they are reprehensible, in strict morals, but the law supposes that the prudent people should estimate them at their usual worth. It is folly to rely upon them when made by unknown dealers, and they do not amount to warranties of every sale which

they induce. Purchasers should either examine for themselves or seek the advice of competent and reliable persons who may be indifferent.

Shortly after this decision a New York court stipulated that advertising claims that have the status of warranties must meet several conditions: (a) they must not be merely expressions of opinion but clear and positive affirmations, (b) they must be made for the purpose of assuring the buyer of the truth of the fact affirmed, and (c) they must be received and relied upon by the buyers as to induce them to make the purchase (*League Cycle Co. v. Abrahams*, 1899). As is evident from these two late nineteenth-century decisions, the presumption was that commercial speech was normatively opinionated puffery, unless contrary metapragmatic signals were present *and* understood. "Puffery," thus, differs from false representation in that the former involves "the mere exaggeration of the qualities [an] article has," while the latter "assigns to the article qualities which it does not possess" (*United States v. New South Farm and Home Co.*, 241 U.S. 64 [1916], cited in Grady and Feinman 1983:406).

When the history of puffery is traced into the contemporary period of the "culture of consumption" we find a curious reversal in the relationship between the legal regulations and corresponding interpretive standards shared by consumers and the actual formal structure of advertisements. I think that the increased federal regulation of advertising and the transformed character of language use in commercials have combined to destroy the metapragmatic consensus which was, in an earlier period, the best protection from sales fraud. Essentially, what happens is that legal institutions such as the Supreme Court, district courts, and regulatory agencies create a new set of assumptions about commercial speech: that it is at heart informational, ideally truthful, and subject to verification, and that the institutionalization of these assumptions contributes to the construction of an ideology of reference which not only irons out the multifunctionality of advertising language but which also imposes a false set of interpretive standards about advertising in general. From a functional point of view, in contrast, advertising is persuasive speech, that is, discourse designed to get the consumer to change an attitude toward a product or to strengthen an awareness of a company or brand label in the hope that purchasing behavior will be modified accordingly. In other words, while the tradition of *caveat emptor* constitutes a general background warning that commercial speech is basically persuasive, the modern regulatory environment assumes, falsely, that commercial speech is primarily referential, contributing valuable information essential to rational markets.

Unfortunately, in spite of this institutionalized shift in the surrounding ideology, the actual commercial function of ads has remained constant, namely, persuasion. The role of puffery has correspondingly reversed: from being regarded as the socially expected norm for commercial speech, puffs have come to be considered a small, forgivable remnant from an earlier irrational tradition. In fact, however, the frequency of puff claims remains high, and the *absence* of informational language becomes a notable feature of many types of ads, especially as visual images gradually replace the representation of language in mass media advertising (Richards and Zakia 1981).

The net result of the formal continuity of puffs in advertising and the growing ideology of reference is an increased tendency for consumers to interpret puffs according to clues as to their propositional form rather than according to formerly interpretable indexical cues. The regulated referentiality assigned to a portion of the ad is, then, transferred to expressions of puffery, attributing to them analogically the factuality previously dismissed by all reasonable people. And it is this transference that provides the ultimate haven for commercial advertisers, since their claims contained under the guise of puffs are not subject to either prohibition as misleading representation or the requirement of factual substantiation—and yet they are widely believed to be informational. Rather than protect consumers by fostering an accurate understanding of the form and function of advertising, the courts and regulatory agencies in fact contribute to the endemic metapragmatic opacity essential for effective commercial persuasion.

The recent history of legal consideration of commercial advertising involves two seemingly contradictory movements, first, the increasingly vigorous regulation of ads by the FTC and, second, the recognition by the Supreme Court of First Amendment protection for commercial speech. I say "seemingly contradictory" because, in the end, these two tendencies work together to promulgate the ideology of reference noted above. The FTC's actions between its inception in 1914 and 1938 were confined to regulating ads which violated Section 5 of the FTC Act, which states: "Unfair methods of competition in commerce are hereby declared unlawful." This wording, which applies almost wholly to the problem of antitrust violations, implies that misrepresentation in ads would hinder free competition, since false information regarding one product would necessarily harm other products in the same class. The authors of the original bill establishing the FTC explicitly identified its function as parallel to that of the Interstate Commerce Commission and viewed the new regulatory agency as a means of overcoming problems in enforcing the Sherman Antitrust Act. Although the original wording of the act did not mention deceptive advertising, the first cases to come before the agency were cases involving deception of consumers: for example, the labeling of goods containing less than 10% wool as "woolen" was ruled as deceptive and thus an act of unfair trade, since it diverted business from firms whose advertising did not falsely represent their product.

The FTC orders were, however, subject to judicial review. In *Ostermoor & Company v. Federal Trade Commission* (16 F2d 962 [1927]), the U.S. Circuit Court of Appeals annulled an FTC cease and desist order against a manufacturer of mattresses, whose ads constituted unfair competition. The FTC had decided that pictorial representation of the increased thickness of cotton filling freed of restraint as 35 inches or more, when in fact the expansion was closer to 3 to 6 inches, constituted a violation of Section 5, since it implied "a resiliency or elasticity far beyond the fact." The Court agreed with a dissenting FTC commissioner that "the slightest pictorial exaggeration of the qualities of an article cannot be deemed to be either a misrepresentation or an unfair method of competition." In fact, the Court ruled that the exaggeration fell within the "time-honored custom of at least merely slight puffing" in that the visual representation was clearly not intended by the manufacturer to be literally "descriptive" but merely "fanciful."

This case is instructive for it illuminates two of the legal criteria for the puffery exemption, first, that if the fanciful exaggeration is directed at some quality or property then the quality or property must be something which the product does in fact have to some degree (here, having the tendency to expand when released) and, second, there must be an absence of contrary signals within the ad itself which might suggest that the puff representation is to be interpreted as literally descriptive (say, by the use of an accurate measuring rod or the citation of "scientific" testimony). In other words, a legitimate puff cannot creatively predicate a nonexistent quality to some product and cannot communicate a false metapragmatic message that the puff is a factual claim.

The puffery defense was not admitted in *Fairyfoot Products Co. v. FTC* (80 F2d 684 [1935]), a case in which this second criterion of being "not calculated to deceive" was clearly violated. Advertisements for a bunion plaster claimed that the product dissolved bunions, stopped pain, and provided instant relief, and then created a powerful context of facticity by mentioning the approval of physicians and doctors. The petitioner argued that the exaggeration in the ads was within the realm of puffery and, where not, the ads were "largely justified by the facts." But the Court ruled:

> That the petitioner's plaster has virtue may, for the purposes hereof, be conceded. Indeed, it would be quite unreasonable to assume that one putting out a purported remedy for an affliction would not employ some ingredients or means calculated to benefit some cases at some stage. But this would not justify such sweeping claims as the condemned items of this advertising matter disclose, which were evidently intended to induce in the public mind the belief that here was an absolute and unfailing panacea for bunions of all kinds and degrees. Just where lies the line between "puffing," which is not unlawful and unwarranted, and misleading representations in advertising, is often very difficult of assertainment. But in our judgment this case does not present such embarrassment, since the advertising here condemned is well beyond any "puffing" indulgence.

The addition of the phrase "unfair or deceptive acts or practices" in the Wheeler-Lee amendment of 1938 made explicit the FTC's power to protect individual consumers to the same degree as its mandate to insure free competition among commercial interests. In a sequence of cases after 1938 puffery continued to be be defined as "an expression of opinion not made as a representation of fact" (*Gulf Oil*, 150 F2d 106 [1945]), which "it is . . . hard to imagine anyone reading it could have understood it as more than puffing" (*Moretrench*, 127 F2d 792 [1942]). Excluded from this category were all direct false representations that assign to products "benefits or virtues they do not possess," or that are made for the purpose of deceiving prospective purchasers (*Steelco*, 187 F2d 693 [1951]). Accepted were ads stating, for example, that a motor oil additive would enable a car to operate an "amazing distance" without oil (*Kidder*, 117 F2d 892 [1941]), or that a vitamin-candy was an "easy" method for weight reduction (*Carlay*, 153 F2d 493 [1946]), or that Ipana toothpaste will "beautify the smile and brighten and whiten the teeth" (*Bristol-Myers Co.*, 46 FTC 162). In this last case the FTC stated: "The Commission was of the opinion that the reference to beautification of the smile was mere puffery, unlikely, because of its generality and widely variant meanings, to deceive anyone factually."

Although most of these cases focused on the fine line between exaggerated opinion and false factual representation, several hinged on the question of the simultaneous metapragmatic message. In *Pfizer* (81 FTC 23 [1972]), for example, the makers of a sunburn cream argued that their product claims (e.g., "actually anesthetizes nerves" and "relieves pain fast"), while looking like factual, even medical claims, were merely puffs, since the metamessage included, among other things, "the frivolous nature of the dialogue," "the use of a bikinied model," and the general "aura of sexiness." Together, the company insisted, these constituted a "total setting of the ad" which provided a clear interpretive signal that statements in the linguistic form of verifiable medical claims should be understood as mere puffery. The FTC, on the other hand, ruled that this context was counteracted by the use of "scientific overtones," implying that the product claims were substantiated by "well-controlled scientific studies" (the mention of "doctors" and the adverb "actually") and that the ads were more than "harmless hyperbole."

Cross-cutting the increasing regulatory activity of the FTC were two Supreme Court rulings of 1975 and 1976 which transformed the constitutional context of advertising regulation by extending limited First Amendment protection to commercial speech. Previously, in 1942 the Supreme Court held in *Valentine v. Chrestensen* (316 U.S. 52) that an ordinance prohibiting the distribution of handbills containing on one side commercial advertising and on the other side noncommercial messages of political protest was not in violation of the First Amendment. The constitutional protection of speech is based on the communication of information and opinion necessary to the free flow of ideas in a democracy. The political message on the handbill, the Court ruled, was added with the intent to evade the prohibition of the city ordinance. The Court, citing no historical prededent, stated in conclusion:

> This Court has unequivocally held that the streets are proper places for the exercise of the freedom of communicating information and disseminating opinion and that, though the states and municipalities may appropriately regulate the privilege in the public interest, they may not unduly burden or prescribe its employment in these public thoroughfares. We are equally clear that the Constitution imposes no such restraint on government as respects purely commercial advertising. (Cited in Rome and Roberts 1985:19)

Commercial speech, in this view, is a form of business activity whose goal is the generation of profit rather than the exchange of ideas.

In 1975, however, this sharp differentiation between protected and unprotected speech was eradicated when the Court ruled in *Bigelow v. Virginia* (421 U.S. 809) that advertising geared to commercial interest "is not stripped of First Amendment protection merely because it appears in that form." This case involved an advertisement in a Virginia newspaper for the Woman's Pavillion of New York City, an organization for the placement of women desiring abortions. Since abortions, though legal in New York, were illegal in Virginia, the Supreme Court of Virginia ruled that the ad was in violation of state law. In overturning the state's decision, the Supreme Court noted the handbill, though proposing a commercial transaction, also contained "factual material of clear 'public interest.'" The Court did not, however, prohibit "reasonable regulation" of advertising, since commercial speech is after all a business activity and as such subject to regulation that serves a legitimate public interest. Rather, the intent of the Court was to recognize the complex nature of commercial speech as being simultaneously the expression of a business interest and the communication of valuable information. As Justice Blackmun put it: "The relationship of speech to the marketplace of products or of services does not make it valueless in the marketplace of ideas."

Both the Supreme Court and the FTC, I think, contribute to the same ideology that stresses the informational or referential function of advertising. Now, to be sure, both bodies well understand that advertising is a form of persuasive, that is, biased, communication, but the social effect of their decisions is to reinforce an interpretive standard according to which advertising, so far as the public interest and constitutional protection is concerned, is informational. This standard is at the basis of the Supreme Court's extension of First Amendment protection—since advertising is protected only to the degree that it is factual, that is, non-deceptive, in a truth-functional sense—as well as the FTC's decisions—since the agency's mandate is to be sure that consumers can rely on the information communicated in making market decisions.

The next important step in this regimentation of the referential function of language was the Supreme Court's ruling in 1976 in *Virginia State Board of Pharmacy v. Virginia Citizens Consumer Council, Inc.* (425 U.S. 748) that *purely* commercial advertisements enjoy some degree of constitutional protection. This case involved the advertising of prescription drug prices. At issue are no cultural, political, or philosophical ideas, nor any "generalized observations about commercial matters." Rather, the only "idea" these ads communicate is the purely commercial "I will sell you the X prescription drug at the Y price." In justifying overturning the previous state decision, the Court stated clearly the principle that "society also may have a strong interest in the free flow of commercial information." The decision then continues to make explicit the grounds for this reification of information:

> Moreover, there is another consideration that suggests that no line between publicly "interesting" or "important" commercial advertising and the opposite kind could ever be drawn. Advertising, however tasteless and excessive it sometimes may seem, is nonetheless dissemination of information as to who is producing and selling what product, for what reason, and at what price. So long as we preserve a predominantly free enterprise economy, the allocation of our resources in large measure will be made through numerous private economic decisions. It is a matter of public interest that those decisions, in the aggregate, be intelligent and well informed. To this end, the free flow of commercial information is indispensable. And if it is indispensable to the proper allocation of resources in a free enterprise, it is also indispensable to the formation of intelligent opinions as to how that system ought to be regulated or altered. Therefore, even if the First Amendment were thought to be primarily an instrument to enlighten public decision making in a democracy, we could not say that the free flow of information does not serve that goal. (*Virginia*, 425 U.S. 748 [1976] 765)

So First Amendment protection and FTC regulations work together to ensure the free flow of information that can be useful to citizens in that quintessentially rational forum, the marketplace, for the purpose of making available to them a dominant embodiment of social value, namely, commodities. The Court in 1976 was actually legitimizing a widespread view of advertising's role in a consumer-oriented society, a view which signals the end of the *caveat emptor* tradition's recognition of the rhetorical nature of advertising. As the FTC's Commissioner stated as early as 1973:

> My view of advertising is of course strongly influenced by my view of business in general. Just as I think well of the man who has the skill, energy, and imagination to *produce* something needed and desired by his fellow human beings, so I also think well of the one who has the skill, energy, and imagination to *sell* it for him. If production is useful and honorable, then distribution—including advertising—is entitled to the same honorable place in our esteem. The purpose of advertising, as I understand it, is to provide *information* to potential

buyers—to tell consumers that a certain product exists, that it has certain properties, that it sells for a certain price, that it can be bought at certain times and places, and so forth. This information, in turn, has profound effects on the workings of our economic system. (Thompson 82 FTC 76 [1973])

This understanding of advertising was condensed into a metapragmatic formula in 1980 when the Supreme Court wrote: "First Amendment's concern for commercial speech is based on the informational function of advertising" (*Central Hudson Gas & Electric Corp. v. Public Service Commission*, 447 U.S. 557). In fact, in drawing a contrast between protected speech and speech proposing a commercial transaction the Court reasoned that commercial speech was "more easily verifiable" than political commentary (Schmidt and Burns 1988:1288). In other words, constitutional protection extends to commercial speech to the degree that it is verifiably truthful. That corporations can now find First Amendment protection in their efforts at commercial persuasion is surely one sign of the dominance of corporate interests. But this has been interpreted, additionally, as marking the culmination of a lengthy trend toward the homologization of speech and commodities, whereby speech is conceived of as not merely about the flow of commercial goods but as itself an objectified value (Tushnet 1982).

I have sketched the development of an institutionalized ideology of commercial speech which contributes to the interpretive standards of consumers and which channels the production of ads themselves. Ironically but predictably, these two effects operate in opposite directions: at the same time that consumers are taught to rely on the informational function of advertising, the ads produced in this regulatory atmosphere increasingly avoid factual claims of properties, price, and availability. Taking advantage of the general referential ideology and faced with new stringent requirements such as prior substantiation and affirmative disclosure, ad agencies turn to persuasion based on visual imagery, emotional appeal, testimonials of the rich and famous, life-style ads, and other sophisticated (and protected) forms of puffery (Schmidt and Burns 1988:1293). And the consumer, believing both that it is illegal to make false representations and that ads in general communicate useful information, is caught with weakened metapragmatic defenses based on "healthy skepticism" (Preston 1989:66) against these new forms of advertising. Nothing, then, could guarantee a better climate for advertising than the failure of regulation to touch puffery and almost all aspects of visual communication coupled with the social acceptance of the interpretive rule that advertising is informational.

Several contemporary researchers have provided experimental documentation of the fact that consumers do interpret puff claims as if they were informational claims relevant to making consumption decisions. In a sense, of course, such empirical research is a redundant restating of the obvious, since if puffery is not widely successful in influencing consumer decision making it would have long ago ceased being part of the advertiser's rhetorical tool kit. In a study by

Rotfeld and Rotzoll (1980) the effects of five nationally distributed commercials were examined through questionnaires designed to ascertain what claims were communicated and whether claims independently judged to be puffs were believed. These researchers found that on average 39.6% of puffery claims were believed, and on average 11.4% of claims implied by puffs were also believed. For example 43% of the survey respondents believed the puff that St. Joseph's aspirin is "fast and gentle"; 62% believed that Kaopectate is "a lot of relief"; and 69% believed that Head & Shoulders shampoo "lathers nice." The conclusion drawn from this study was that the present legal definition of puffery as advertising messages not stating any factual claims is contradicted by empirical research. Rotfeld and Rotzoll do not argue, however, as I do here, that the consumer's contextually specific understanding is, in part, the result of an ideology of commercial speech as being, as a rule, referential.

A second study conducted by Shimp (1978) focused on "incomplete comparative" statements, such as "Mennen E goes on warmer and drier." Although courts have been stricter in ruling against such open-ended comparisons as allowable puffery, favoring to allow more obviously inflated claims in the superior degree ("the best," "the freshest," etc.), many comparatives do appear in commercials. Shimp found that consumers tend to believe that open-ended comparatives make claims, since they filled in the missing term themselves, as, for example, "Mennen E goes on warmer and drier than a lot of other spray deodorants." In this survey, 60% agreed that the ad claim was directly stated, and 38% believed that the claim was intended but not directly stated. This type of language is especially effective since it engages the consumer as the unwitting partner in *propositional* construction.

Other experiments support the general contention that puffs are interpreted as true statements. Surveys by Bruskin Associates (cited in Rotfeld and Preston 1981) found that people judged the statement in an Alcoa ad, "Today, aluminum is something else," to be completely true (47%), or partly true (36%). Similarly, the statement in a Hallmark ad, "When you care to send the very best," was rated as completely true by 62% of those surveyed, and the Kodak ad, "Kodak makes your pictures count," was judged completely true by 60%. In an experiment conducted by Rotfeld and Rotzoll (1981) consumers were presented with commercial advertisements containing factual claims ("helps control dandruff") and puffs ("makes hair look terrific"), the distinction having been previously determined by an independent group of legally trained "labelers." The respondents did not find that the fact and fact-implied claims possessed greater credibility than the puffs and puff-implied claims. As these researchers conclude: "What does emerge is that puffery does not possess an inherent and distinct inability to be believed" (Rotfeld and Rotzoll 1981:102).

Experiments have shown that ads containing puffs are more likely to catch consumers' attention, that puffs which communicated little information did so with high levels of confidence, and that puffs contributed to an overall higher evaluation of products in comparison with ads without puffs. Oliver (1979:14) summarizes these and other empirical studies of the effects of puffery:

> Specifically, the studies show that if ambiguous words or symbols of a super-lative or inflated nature are used to describe a product, people either perceive the implied content to be accurate (thus increasing the certainty of the be-liefs . . .), demonstrate a tendency to increase attribute levels or the evaluations of these same attribute levels, infer a greater number of highly rated attributes (inflating the favorable attribute set size), or rate the product higher than if an accurate description had been used (so that one's overall attitude or subsequent purchase intention is overrated).

These results suggest that advertisers can use puffs to cause a product to be over-appraised relative to the objective qualities the product has. This, in turn, pro-vides a clue to the mechanism by which ads inculcate symbolic values not found in products independent from their ads: that this creativity is largely accomplished through puffery.

I have argued that three legal trends converge to destroy consumers' semiotic acuity in interpreting ads: (1) the puffery exception in the post–*caveat emptor* period, (2) the FTC's regulation of false and deceptive messages, and (3) the Supreme Court's extension of constitutional protection to commercial speech. Each of these trends in its own way reinforces the notion that commercial speech is informational, a notion shared by both sides of the debate over regulation. Voices in favor of government regulation stress the need for scrutiny to keep the mes-sages truthful, while voices against regulation argue that regulations (such as a ban on all cigarette ads) constitute, in the words of an ACLU legal director, "pa-ternalistic manipulation of the individual through governmental control of infor-mation . . . covertly manipulating that choice by controlling the flow of informa-tion about it" (cited in Lowenstein 1988:1222). What both sides of the debate overlook is that advertising as efficacious language succeeds in part by misdirect-ing consumers' attention away from awareness of persuasion by postulation of an ideology of reference and by constructing messages that appear to be propo-sitional, as "indicatives without sentences" (Baudrillard 1990:94).

There are two additional recent tendencies which must be noted briefly in conclusion. The first involves attempts to expand the regulatory aura to non-informational or "symbolic" dimensions of advertising. Some legal scholars have concluded that courts, legislatures, and regulatory agencies should reverse the contemporary move toward recognizing First Amendment protection for com-mercial speech and increase the degree of consumer protection by looking into not just factually false claims but the "symbolic" features of advertising as well. These critics realize that continued reliance on the assumption that advertising is informational guarantees that only a small part of the total communicative range of ads will be addressed. While the regulators at the FTC obviously view their regulatory activity as protecting consumers from false or deceptive advertise-ments, thereby increasing confidence in the informational side of commercial speech, they would surely reject my claim here that the regulative environment works to disarm consumers through a false semiotic ideology. In fact, the Com-mission demonstrated, in a 1978 ruling, a real concern that "the viewer's critical faculties of classification and differentiation are drowned in patterns of imagery and symbols" (cited in Richards and Zakia 1981:115; see Zakia 1986). The important point to note is that this concern with "critical faculties" was voiced in the context of potentially deceptive visual representations and not in the con-text of language-based "informational" messages. But bringing symbolic images under the purview of the FTC is only another way of putting the consumer in a situation of false confidence that, now, even visual symbols are being inspected for accuracy. This, then, would parallel the legal arguments made by corporate interests that even "persuasion" in advertising is indirectly informational, because ads promote entry of superior products into the market, enhance competition by lowering prices, or stimulate product innovation (Fred S. McChesney cited in Lowenstein 1988:1232). Should consumers ever become persuaded that the sub-tle, symbolic, or connotative meanings of commercials have been approved by regulators, then an additional piece of armor will have disappeared from their already diminished interpretive arsenal.

The second recent trend is that some advertisers are increasingly rejecting the rhetoric of puffed exaggeration and the image-mongering of symbolic asso-ciation in favor of ad messages which refer directly and explicitly to advertising as a communicative form and function. The 1990s may well be a new era in the history of the metapragmatics of advertising. If in the first period consumers ex-pected the hard sell of puffery and protected themselves by *caveat emptor*, and in the second period the assumption of referentiality promoted by governmental institutions disarmed consumers faced with extensive verbal and visual nonref-erentiality, the third period can be identified as the age of the "meta-ad," that is, ads about advertising. Meta-ads, I suggest, signal a renewed effort on the part of advertisers to positively recapture their power to institute a generalized semi-otic regime for interpreting their ads.[6] Instead of passively assuming that consum-ers are metapragmatically naive, meta-ads build into their overt signals, for ex-ample, reference to previous ads for the same product, the behavioral effectiveness of ads, the truth value (or deception) of ad messages, the formal or poetic features of ads, the act of experiencing ads, the the technical process of broadcasting ads, and the institutional history of advertising as an industry.

In an ad for the American Express card, a man taking a shower is robbed while the television in the background shows Karl Malden warning viewers to carry traveler's checks. In an IBM ad, a portable movie screen shows commer-cials from the past ten years; a rose is tossed from the image on the screen into the space of the present ad. An ad for the RCA camcorder shows the camcorder making an ad for itself. A woman carefully reads the label on a bottle of Kraft-Free dressing and fervently affirms its truth value. Joe Isuzu makes repeated ridiculous claims about the price and quality of his cars, intentionally generating an image of the classic huckster whose puffery is never to be believed. (As if in dialogue with this ad, Lee Iacocca warns that "if Chrysler isn't a performance car, then I'm Joe Isuzu.") Bo Jackson, dressed as a singer, walks off the stage claiming "I'm an athlete, not an actor," and then passes through the television screen showing the commercial for Nike shoes. An ad for McDonalds "fast-forwards" itself to "get to the good part." John Cleese informs the viewer that "those smart people at Magnavox have asked me to tell you about all these highly intelligent [electronics] products in just fifteen seconds." A car phone installed inside the Lexus automobile is set to automatically dial the Lexus sales office, which answers "thank you for calling Lexus." Candace Bergen tells a couple watching her image on their television not to use the mute button of the remote. In what might be the ultimate non-ad, a farmer comes into a salesroom to look at John Deere tractors and leaves without buying a new tractor, though he is wearing a new cap with the company logo. Since meta-ads are all truthfully "about" advertising (in the sense that all metapragmatic utterances are inherently semantic), the viewer is led by this positively supplied set of interpretants to overlook the persuasive function being accomplished simultaneously. For as Boorstin (1961:213) prophetically wrote over thirty years ago: "Advertising fogs our daily lives less from its peculiar lies than from its peculiar truths."

PART IV

Social Theory and Social Action

7 | Comparison, Pragmatics, and Interpretation

> There exists a very strong, but one-sided and thus untrustworthy, idea that in order better to understand a foreign culture, one must enter into it, forgetting one's own, and view the world through the eyes of this foreign culture. This idea, as I said, is one-sided. Of course, a certain entry as a living being into a foreign culture, the possibility of seeing the world through its eyes, is a necessary part of the process of understanding it; but if this were the only aspect of this understanding, it would merely be duplication and would not entail anything new or enriching. *Creative understanding* does not renounce itself, its own place in time, its own culture; and it forgets nothing. In order to understand, it is immensely important for the person who understands to be *located outside* the object of his or her creative understanding—in time, in space, in culture.
>
> —Mikhail M. Bakhtin (1986:6–7)

Models and Strategies of Comparison

A NOTABLE FEATURE OF contemporary intellectual discourse in the "human sciences" is the flowering of the comparative perspective in both disciplinary and interdisciplinary domains.[1] The emergence of publications, journals, and conferences in fields such as comparative politics, comparative literature, comparative philosophy, comparative history, and comparative sociology, building on earlier endeavors such as comparative mythology and comparative philology, necessarily raises reflexive theoretical and methodological issues about the nature of the comparative enterprise. The multidisciplinary conferences "Religions in Culture and History" held at The Divinity School, University of Chicago, and the corresponding essays and books published in the *Toward a Comparative Philosophy of Religions* series raise a critical question for all these comparative activities: is the current trend toward comparative studies the fulfillment of the ultimate Western hegemony in which scholarly discourse becomes a powerful regimenting metalanguage, or is it a sign of global, multicultural, dialogic conversation and empathetic understanding that mirror the cultural heteroglossia of the modern world (Gadamer 1979; Schwimmer 1983:126)?[2] While these extreme poles of regimentation and dialogue are rarely manifested this boldly, they remain asymptotic options, each with serious implications for empirical work in the comparative vein.

Despite the apparent newness of much comparative discourse, it would be an error to assume that comparison itself has no historical lineage. In fact, some form of comparative thinking can be located in almost any intellectual milieu, especially if the assertion of noncomparability is taken as a negative modality of comparison. Today, forms of comparison are typically distinguished by the absence or presence of historical connectedness: similar phenomena that are remote in space and time can be compared by a logic of analogy or parallelism, whereas phenomena that are known to share a developmental source or to have been in contextual interrelationship can be analyzed genealogically or historically (Marc Bloch 1967:47; Gould 1989:213). This clear-cut distinction between analogy and genealogy does not, however, fully characterize previous models of comparative discourse.

It is easy to forget that for millennia the dominant mode of cross-cultural understanding, whether dealing with religion or any other cultural phenomena, was ethnocentrism, that is, the view that other societies can be placed on a continuum of familiar to strange, calculating out from one's immediate neighbors to the most remote peoples. Herodotus, commenting on the customs of Persia, notes that ethnocentrism frequently correlates with an assumption of moral superiority:

> Most of all they [Persians] hold in honor themselves, then those who dwell next to themselves, and then those next to *them*, and so on, so that there is a progression in honor in relation to the distance. They hold least in honor those whose habitation is furthest from their own. This is because they think themselves to be the best of mankind in everything and that others have a hold on virtue in proportion to their nearness; those that live furthest away are the most base. (Herodotus 1987:96)

Herodotus himself, on the other hand, was quick to locate the source of much of Greek culture, especially its religion, in "barbarian" traditions of Persia and Egypt, proposing thereby a model of borrowing and diffusion that angered Greek chauvinists such as Plutarch, who complained, "not only is he [Herodotus] anxious to establish an Egyptian and a Phoenician Herakles; he says that our own Herakles was born after the other two, and he wants to remove him from Greece and make a foreigner out of him" (Plutarch, *De Herodoti Malignitate*, quoted in Bernal 1987:113).

In medieval Arabic culture strictly linear ethnocentrism was modified by a systematic ecological determinism according to which societies were located in zones starting just above the equator (Al-Azmeh 1992). Those peoples enjoying the temperate climes of the middle zones (China, Arabia, India, etc.) are most favored, while those existing at the southern and northern extremes are victims of distemper—lethargy for black-skinned Africans and indolence for pale-skinned Slavs. According to Al-Azmeh, the rigor of application of this deterministic model of cross-cultural typology was itself conditioned by the Arab evaluation of the societies to be understood:

> It was a social judgement which ultimately determined the degree to which credence would be given to geographical determinism, and this determinism was applied mercilessly only in the construction of sheer barbarism, which was not merely a distemper with varying degree of severity, but fully a disnature. (Al-Azmeh 1992:8)

The inherent difficulties of comparative understanding were well articulated by Jean-Jacques Rousseau, who, despite Lévi-Strauss's (1976:33) pronouncement of his being the "founder of the science of man," warned that the period of European exploration would not likely yield reliable knowledge of other cultures because of the ethnocentric blinders of the observers:

> I am persuaded that we have come to know no other men except Europeans; moreover it appears from the ridiculous prejudices, which have not died out even among men of letters, that every author produces under the pompous name of the study of man nothing much more than a study of the men of his own country. . . . One does not open a book of voyages without finding descriptions of characters and customs, but one is altogether amazed to find that these authors who describe so many things tell us only what all of them knew already, and have only learned how to see at the other end of the world what they would have been able to see without leaving their own street, and that the real features which distinguish nations, and which strike eyes made to see them, have almost always escaped their notice. (Rousseau 1984:159)

Rousseau did not, however, give up on comparison, for he thought that it would be possible to replace the biased vision of these "sailors, merchants, soldiers, and missionaries" (Rousseau 1984:159) with a true scientific study of other cultures that would yield increased self-knowledge. His own reflections on the origins of inequality, for instance, performed a shocking inversion of the more usual ethnocentrism by arguing that the degree of human inequality radically increases with civilization and that individuals eager for the institutional benefits of progress in fact "all ran toward their chains believing that they were securing their liberty" (Rousseau 1984:122; see J. F. MacCannell 1981).

With the expansion of European colonialism and its supporting ideological matrix of evolutionism in the nineteenth century, comparison of cultures frequently involved the paradoxical principles of differential development and genetic explanation. According to the first, societies pass through a sequence of stages of evolutionary progress ("savagery," "barbarism," and "civilization," in the terms of several key writers) culminating in the scientific rationalism of modern European culture; according to the second, inexplicable phenomena later in time are accounted for by uncovering their rational origins at an earlier point in time. The paradox arises because instances of failed progress, whether in spatially distant "primitive" societies or in local irrational superstitions or residual social inequalities, are problematic "survivals" or "remnants" of modernity's historical trajectory. Our knowledge of the past, thus, depends on the contemporary persistence of societies and customs that once had coherent meaning (Stocking 1987:230). Whereas in the late eighteenth century Johann Gottfried Herder (1988:75) could argue that "remnants of the old, true folk poetry" of Europe ought to be collected before they vanish with the "daily advance of our so-called culture," nineteenth-century evolutionists were more likely to urge that such survivals should, in the spirit of enlightened rationalism, be either reformed or eradicated. Applied as a general principle of comparison, then, the doctrine of survivals stipulates that

> the fragmentary and disjointed nature of certain customs—their poor integration into a people's way of life, and the nonsensical nature of people's rationales for them—is itself one of the telltale signs that they are a survival from earlier times when they formed a more nearly seamless part of the web of life. In the West, it is this same fragmentary nature of certain customs that is taken as justifying the comparativist in arranging them serially across cultures: the less a custom appears to be integrated into life, that is, the less intelligible it is per se (or to those who now practice it), the more legitimate becomes the writer's assimilation of it into a list of similar customs practiced around the world. (Campany 1990:16)

I have mentioned linear ethnocentrism, self-critical reflexivity, and evolutionary survivals as three models for comparison that permeate cross-cultural understanding with moral evaluations. In much contemporary discourse, in contrast, such blatant evaluative stances are out of favor, as comparativists attempt to ground their work in more principled research strategies, perhaps reflecting the fact that scholarship takes place in a (post)modern world characterized more by the collage of what Clifford Geertz (1986:114) calls "clashing sensibilities in inevadable contact" than by automomous cultural isolates. Although I will not attempt to give a comprehensive listing here, several prominent strategies—typology, reconstruction, hermeneutics, and reductionism—need to be briefly characterized.[3]

Comparison by typology involves generating a set of analytical parameters, the values of which enable the analyst to locate different cultural systems on one or more continua of difference. As comparative work proceeds both the values and the parameters are modified, refined, and expanded as additional data are gathered. Anthropologists are particularly prone to dichotomize the societies they study into poles such as hot and cold, classificatory and instrumental, egalitarian and hierarchical, Aristotelian and Heraclitean, and group and grid; similarly, comparative philosophers still struggle with the simplistic opposition developed by Hegel of Western subjectivism and Oriental universalism (Hegel

1987:572). Clyde Kluckhohn (1960:137–39) provides a more sophisticated account of the typological strategy:

> Such enquiry, exposing the principles of cultural structure, would take us some distance toward ranging cultures in an orderly way as to their respective similarities and differences. It would also help us to isolate wherein rests the distinctiveness of each particular culture at a given time level—the "without-which-not" of that culture. . . . For typological models of structure and process we need to abstract from immediately visible "reality," disengaging the accidental by including in the models only those aspects of the observable that are relevant to the model being constructed.

Typologies can also be constructed by specifying the implicational relations among a set of variables, such that one variable presupposes a second variable but not vice versa: for example, *do ut des* ("give in order to receive") ritualism and macrocosm-microcosm cosmology (Heimann 1957) or "denaturalized" philosophical discourse and the assertion of universal truth claims (Griffiths 1990:80). All empirical cases are consistent with the direction of the implication but the posited universal regularity does not predict the presence of the variables in specific cases. A third kind of typology, in addition to those based on dichotomization and implicational relations, is semiotic typology, which organizes cultural data in terms of some "master trope," such as metonomy or metaphor, textuality or rules, prescriptive or performative, and signifier or signified (Jameson 1979:68). The logical danger here is that the analyst must locate the comparative enterprise itself in one of the hypothesized typological spaces, which implies that comparison is just another trope (Rochberg-Halton 1985:410).[4]

The most famous exponent of the comparative method of reconstruction in religious studies is Georges Dumézil. Without underestimating the situational creativity and intercultural borrowings from outside the Indo-European heritage, Dumézil postulates the persistence of "common underlying structures" (Littleton 1974:173) throughout the Indo-European world, from Vedic India to Celtic Ireland, particularly the representation in cosmology and history of deities, powers, and social formations belonging to three distinct functions, "magical sovereinty," "warrior power," and "peaceful fecundity" (Dumézil 1988:121). Dumézil asserts that

> the comparative study of the most ancient documents from India, Iran, Rome, Scandinavia, and Ireland has allowed us to give [Indo-European civilization] a content and to recognize a great number of facts about civilization, and especially religion, which were common to these diverse societies or at least to several of them. . . . It seems hardly imaginable that chance should have twice created this vast structure, especially in view of the fact that other Indo-European peoples have homologous accounts. The simplest and humblest explanation is to admit that the Romans, as well as the Scandinavians, received this scenario from a common earlier tradition and that they simply modernized its

details, adapting them to their own "geography," "history," and customs and introducing the names of countries, peoples, and heroes suggested by actuality. (Dumézil 1970, I:63–73)

According to this method, comparison is made possible by the recognition of similarities among traditions known to have been genetically related. The specifics of local variation from the reconstructed prototype cannot, however, be explained without invoking additional arguments of a sociological or historical nature (Lincoln 1991:123). In clever hands, of course, similarities to an imputed prototype can be used to hypothesize historical connection, as in Carlo Ginzburg's attempt to trace, following the principle that "isomorphism establishes identity" (1991:18), early modern ecstatic beliefs and practices to an origin in the nomadic shamanism of Scandinavian and Siberian paleolithic peoples.

Reflective hermeneutics, especially as defined and practiced by the philosopher Paul Ricoeur, is an important recent development in comparative scholarship in the humanities and social sciences. By modifying the classic "hermeneutical circle" from being a part-to-whole relationship *within* the domain of understanding to the reciprocal dialectic *between* textual explanation (i.e., linguistics) and textual understanding, Ricoeur's method of interpretation appropriates the texts of temporally distant cultures in the service of self-understanding (Ricoeur 1976, 1991:118).[5] Through interpretation, people living in a scientific worldview are able to recapture a lost dimension of human understanding, the mythico-symbolic world of archaic cultures (Ricoeur 1967:350–52):

> No interpreter in fact will ever come close to what his text says if he does not live in the aura of the meaning that is sought. And yet it is only by understanding that we can believe. The second immediacy, the second naïveté that we are after, is accessible only in hermeneutics; we can believe only by interpreting. This is the "modern" modality of belief in symbols; expression of modernity's distress and cure for this distress. . . . But thanks to this hermeneutic circle, I can today still communicate with the Sacred by explicating the preunderstanding which animates the interpretation. Hermeneutics, child of "modernity," is one of the ways in which this "modernity" overcomes its own forgetfulness of the Sacred. (Ricoeur 1974a:298)

Of course, the modern effort to think through primordial symbols, metaphors, and allegories entails a demythologization in which critical objectivity resists an equal dialogue with the "alien" text, since this earlier text contains only a pre-theoretical level of interpretation. This kind of comparative enterprise can easily become self-serving, especially if the myths of other cultures are studied not with the intent of grasping their meaning and function in their original context but rather for personal needs of acquiring pearls of ancient wisdom (O'Flaherty 1986:226).

Various works of comparison, finally, are based on kinds of reductionism, that is, on the finding of extra-systematic factors that account for the underlying patterns of similarity of cultural phenomena. These factors can be located, for example, in ecological variables, biological constraints, sociobiological adaptations, imputed facts of human nature, or the structure of the human mind, but all of these arguments share the limitation of treating variation as both random and epiphenomenal.

Comparative Philosophy of Religion as a Discipline

This account of three early patterns and four more recent strategies of comparison provides a methodological backdrop for examining the potentials and problems of the newly constituted discipline of the comparative philosophy of religion. The papers presented in the conference series offer three differentially weighted ways that this new discipline can be operationalized. For some, the discipline is the comparative *philosophy* of religions, that is, the strictly philosophical study, grounded in a comparative perspective, of the phenomena of religion. While this perspective takes a relatively narrow view of the analytical discourse required, it allows a broad acceptance of the range of phenomena to be considered "religion." And, according to this perspective, the motive for comparison lies primarily with the philosophically oriented analyst, rather than within the realm of religion. For others, the discipline is the *comparative* [study of] philosophies of religions; this implies a well-delimited object of the investigation, namely, texts (or discourses, in the case of nonliterate cultures) created by philosophers of religion (including esoteric specialists and ritual elders), yet allows for considerable flexibility in the analytical methods used, including history, ethnography, and philology. Finally, for several participants the discipline can be characterized as the comparative philosophies *of religions*, that is, the study of the explicit doctrines or implicit stances of various philosophers, religious thinkers, and religious traditions toward other cultural traditions (Tracy 1990:15). In contrast to the other two approaches, this view implies that the comparative impulse comes from the religious thinkers or communities under study. Much of the debate that made the Chicago conferences so lively was caused by fundamental disagreements as to how to accent the very name of the discipline being constructed. But, more importantly, the rich cross-disciplinary fertilization that is revealed in the final papers results from a tacit agreement that these three perspectives should be held in "essential tension" (Kuhn 1977), a collective decision that allows for a "preventive pluralistic methodology" (Zilberman 1991:300) in which historians, philosophers, ethnographers, and theologians are all welcome.

A critical consequence of this debate over the definition of the discipline is the vital importance of the unifying recognition that the motive for comparison and construction of comparative discourse belong *both* to the work of analytical scholarship and to the world of philosophical and religious traditions being studied. At the obvious level, if we set out to compare the philosophy of religion articulated by, say, Hume and Hegel, it will be important to grasp the role of conclusions about comparative understanding found *in* their philosophical texts; at the less obvious level, if we are to compare the implicit philosophies of, say, medieval Islam and medieval Christianity, part of the task will be to discover the stances toward other religions embodied *in* these religious traditions.

This is not to say, of course, that our scholarly comparison will be identical, in intellectual motive or written discourse, to the comparative motives or discourses under study. While philosophers and religious traditions may provide modern scholars with useful tools for comparative analysis—the notions of analogy (Yearley 1990), metaphor (Poole 1986b; Schweiker 1992:271), and "superimposition" (Clooney n.d.:ch. 5), for example, have proven particularly helpful—I do not think that we can simply borrow *their* models of understanding as *our* models of understanding. To the degree that research increasingly reveals the richness of the interpretive, comparative, metapractical (Kasulis 1992), or metapragmatic (Silverstein 1993) resources of philosophical texts and religious traditions, this stricture becomes increasingly difficult to obey. Three options seem to be open to those who confront this dilemma: to appropriate local interpretive, comparative, and metapragmatic models as our analytical tools (e.g., using Thomistic analogy to understand Mencius); to take these local discourses under study as equal dialogic partners with reference to our analytical discourses (e.g., comparing their metaphors with our metaphors), ideally leading simultaneously to the "preservation" of the other's discourse (as Hallisey [1994] argues) and the sharpening of our conceptual tools; and to find in these local discourses necessary limitations and biases which in principle exclude them from sharing in the task of analysis yet which expand the range of things the analyst is forced to comprehend (Taylor 1985).

Why is it so dangerous to dignify local "theories" of comparison with the status of explanatory models? First, these kinds of local theories are often rationalizations, justifications, or secondary elaborations that must themselves be penetrated in the act of analysis. Second, they often lack time perspective and thus cannot begin to account for changes in either historical situations or ideological assumptions. Third, they tend to be decontextualized abstractions that "iron out" the contextual or indexical dimensions of experience, ignoring precisely those pragmatic aspects of philosophical reasoning and religious action that are subject to only limited self-awareness (Silverstein 1981a). Fourth, they often focus on semantic, propositional, or referential dimensions of discourse and miss the meaningfulness of rhetorical, organizational, and structural dimensions of texts and actions. Finally, they are inherently positional within society, whether the product of elites, radicals, or world renouncers, and need to be linked to alternative, competing, or contradictory theories from elsewhere in the heteroglossic social order. Taken together, all these conclusions point to the same general principle: to the degree that a philosophical or religious discourse approaches in either formal shape or declared purpose the status of being an abstract, complete, or true account of comparison, this discourse fails to achieve critical self-awareness of its own pragmatic features.

So comparative analytics and comparisons within traditions both have *pragmatic* dimensions that need to be critically identified. As a first approximation, several things might be included in an account of the pragmatics of any discourse: the personal motives or institutional interests behind the production of texts; the contextually grounded presuppositions and implications of texts; the strategic design or rhetorical organization of texts that contributes to their function or efficacy; the social dispersion of texts within a culture, such as the evaluative opposition between high and low culture, official and carnivalesque (Bakhtin 1968:9–10), or scholarly and popular (Gurevich 1983); explicit text-internal metapragmatic devices, such as performatives and *verba dicendi*, and implicit metapragmatic forms grounded in a discourse's textual properties, both of which provide a commentary on the function of the discourse in context;[6] the real-time dynamics of interpretive acts as socially realized practices; and the intertextual relationship among texts in a culture, including the chain of commentaries on texts (Doniger 1992:39–41). In sum, the pragmatics of discourse comprehends almost every kind of meaningfulness *other than* the decontextualized, distantiated, semantic meaning that Ricoeur (1984) labels the "said" of the text.

Despite the fact that many philosophical texts attempt to claim that they are decontextualized discourses asserting universal truths, just as many religious traditions claim unique access to the "really real," one of the jobs for analysts is to discover the pragmatics of these discourses or claims. But the analyst's discourse is not free from pragmatics! One of the great dangers of modern scholarship—and the discipline of the comparative philosophy of religion is no exception—is to assume that our own intellectual models, research techniques, and academic writings are not themselves subject to pragmatic considerations.[7] The ultimate irony of the position advocated here is that, although our scholarly acts of comparison can be fundamentally homologous to the comparative doctrines, stances, and encounters revealed in cross-cultural study, there is no reason in principle to model our comparative analytics on the *specific* comparative maneuvers we observe in religious or philosophical traditions. While the ubiquity of comparative discourse and cross-tradition interface can lead us to the universal set of pragmatic conditions and implications of comparison, our comprehension, though itself an act of comparison, is not compelled by any particular discoverable model.

Comparison and Interpretation as Practical Reason

At first glance, the application of the notion of "practical reason" to the field of religion seems to be an uneasy juxtaposition of opposites, since the division between religious practice and philosophical or theological discourse can correlate with the distinction between effective action and discursive reasoning. In other words, the field of religion seems to have pragmatics in the field of ritual and reason in the realm of doctrine or philosophical argumentation, thus leaving little room for a unified notion of practical reason. Furthermore, what is practical, namely, ritual action, is not particularly subject to efficient articulation or philosophical scrutiny. Also, *both* ritual, with its tendency toward decontextualized semiotic form (see Chapter 6) and religious discourse, with its attention to transcendent realities, often place religion at the opposite pole from the utilitarian or functional concerns of everyday life, which can be taken to be the locus of practical rationality (Maurice Bloch 1974:78).

On closer inspection, however, practical reason does play a critical role in religious traditions. Cross-culturally, religious phenomena that could be listed under the rubric of practical reason include: the embodiments of divinity in material tokens such as sacraments, amulets, icons, and masks; religious practices of socialization, indoctrination, initiation, and discipline; ritual acts with effective or even performative force, such as blessing, anathematization, and healing; rhetorical devices in religious communication, preaching, and conversion; the normative, ethical dimension of religious life and religious thinking; and the explicit philosophical expression of the religious validity of practical reason as an alternative to theoretical reason in notions such as mystical participation, *coincidentia oppositorum*, and the absurdity of belief.[8]

To this rather obvious list of dimensions of practical reason in religion needs to be added *comparison*, seen both as the historical interface of religious traditions and as a topic for philosophical and theological discourse about religion. In fact, if there is a tendency for the discipline of the comparative philosophy of religion to fission between the study of the cultural-historical dimension of religious traditions and the study of philosophical discourses about religion, careful attention to the importance of comparison can be a useful experiment in self-critical dialogue, since there appears to be a complex dialectic or reciprocal feedback between historical circumstances and philosophical reflections: on the one hand, the historical encounter between religious traditions can compel philosophical and theological theorizing about comparison; on the other hand, philosophical positions and theological doctrines can play powerful roles in prestructuring the experience of religious interface.

In commenting on her ethnographic fieldwork in New Guinea, where small-scaled societies live in close proximity with interlocking exchange relationships, Mead (1964:281) generalized:

> It can, I believe, be demonstrated that contiguity and close interrelationship between groups with differing communicational styles increase awareness that various aspects of the communicational system are learned, can be taught, and are transmissible to others who are not born with them.

This heightened sensibility to the conventionality of cultural systems as a result of historical encounter presents certain difficulties for religious and philosophical traditions, both of which, in many cases at least, try to make a claim of uniqueness and absoluteness. Thus, when religious traditions come into historical contact the encounter often becomes part of broader political and economic power relations put into play, though it is a mistake to analyze these situations solely from the point of view of the agency of the dominant force in the interface. The range of historical stances runs from fanatical exclusivism's dictating the rejection and condemnation of the Other so that no communication is deemed possible (Tillich 1963:31); to the zealous proselytizing of missions to convert the Other; to respectful juxtaposition facilitated by a thoroughgoing allegorizing of the Other's texts and doctrines in an effort to make the foreign seem "the same" (J. Z. Smith 1987:101); to creative forms of syncretism, blending, and hierachical layering; to efforts at multicultural dialogue predicated either on the relativist assumption of the formal equivalence of deities, cosmologies, or ritual practices or on the inclusivist assumption of the constructive benefit of modifying the "reading" of the local tradition through the perspective of an alien tradition (Clooney 1989:547; 1990).

Walker's (1994) analysis of al-Farabi, a tenth-century Islamic philosopher, illustrates a particularly clear case of comparison by hierarchical synthesis.[9] In the confrontation—real or hypothetical—between Greek philosophy, personified by Aristotle, and Islamic religion, epitomized by its founder Muhammad, al-Farabi maintains the formal identity of the great philosopher and the great religious founder, but only on the condition that each of the two roles operates according to the guidelines of "theoretical" reason, the principles of which were discovered by Aristotle. Theoretical reason leads to universal, logically demonstrated knowledge, while practical reason depends on the linguistic expressions, representational forms, and rhetorical techniques of particular cultures. Al-Farabi writes:

> There are two ways of making a thing comprehensible: first, by causing its essence to be perceived by the intellect, and second, by causing it to be imagined through the similitude that imitates it. . . . Now when one acquires knowledge of the beings or receives instruction in them, if he perceives their ideas themselves with his intellect, and his assent to them is by means of certain demonstration, then the science that comprises these cognitions is *philosophy*. But if they are known by imagining them through similitudes that imitate them, and assent to what is imagined of them is caused by persuasive methods, then the ancients call what comprises these cognitions *religion*. . . . In everything demonstrated by philosophy, religion employs persuasion. (al-Farabi 1962:44–45)

Thus, the philosopher and the religious leader are brought into a hierarchical relationship, since Aristotle and Muhammad can only enter into a nonlinguistic dialogue, that is, a kind of transparent communication anchored in universal knowledge. Several centuries later the vector of his hierarchy was severely challenged by Ibn Khaldûn, who argued that philosophers such as al-Farabi and Avicenna, in putting primacy on intellectual knowledge of corporeal existents, completely overlook "spiritual essences" (1967:402). Rather, argues Ibn Khaldûn,

> when Muhammad guides us toward some perception, we must prefer that to our own perceptions. We must have more confidence in it than in them. We must not seek to prove its correctness rationally, even if (rational intelligence) contradicts it. We must believe and know what we have been commanded (to believe and to know). We must be silent with regard to things of this sort that we do not understand. We must leave them to Muhammad and keep the intellect out of it. (Khaldûn 1967:390)

In contrast to this theoretical encompassment of Greek and Islamic traditions, Bantly's (1994) account of the loose synthesis of Buddhism and Confucianism in sixteenth-century China suggests that practical reason can also be a model for "conversation" across religious or philosophical systems. At the level of official doctrine, Buddhism's stress on monastic world-rejection and its location of the origin of suffering in human desire clearly contrast with Confucianism's focus on the world-affirming ritual conditioning for public life and its valorization of desire as a positive part of human nature. The synthesis of these two traditions attained in certain neo-Confucian schools of the Ming period, however, largely avoided theoretical dispute by formulating a response in terms of everyday social life, popular folklore, and literary forms. This uneasy synthesis combined a creative notion of desire as means for spiritual liberation with a claim that sagehood cannot be restricted to the ruling class. In this case, then, it is the concrete historical experience of Chinese Buddhism that provides a useful model for the "adventitious" quality of cross-cultural dialogue.

Several essays in this third volume explore a second dimension of the operation of practical reason in the philosophy of religion, namely, the dynamic process of *interpretation*. In some cases, this dynamism involves the historical trajectory of the "work" of hermeneutical practices; in other cases, the dynamism lies in the cultural attitudes toward history, time, and change entailed by philosophical positions or religious doctrines. What is remarkable, though, is that interpretive praxis is frequently a creative and structuring response to the comparative encounter, either with other religious traditions or with an earlier moment of the same tradition.[10]

Poole's account of the history of the Bimin-Kuskusmin's confrontation with the West details the powerfully conservative interpretive practices of ritual elders prior to the events of the "great destruction" of the 1940s (Poole 1986a; 1992). The elders were able to provide satisfying explanations of various experienced anomalies by relying on the rich metaphorical resources of their "mythic imagination": a strange phenomenon or threatening event that cannot be modeled by one of several existing plant metaphors (e.g., root as source, intertwining as intertextuality, and husk/core as shallow/deep meaning) is defined away as not culturally significant, that is, not leaving a "scar" on the culture's ritual "center place." This situation of interpretive adequacy changed dramatically after a group of ritual initiates burned to death in a fire at Telefolip and after the region experienced unusual sheet lightning. No longer able to maintain the position that anomalies do not scar the center, Trumeng, a prominent ritual elder, created a new mode of religious interpretation as a middle way between hermetic denial and cultural self-destruction (Poole 1994). In contrast to the previous hermeneutic of holism, Trumeng advocated a new interpretive method grounded in the assertion of the *analogy* of anomaly; that is, Trumeng found in the corpus of myths a dimension of historical praxis (including transformations, corruptions, and the progressive weakening of spirit) that was not previously focused on. The crisis situation of cultural encounter could now be modeled, since an anchored homology (or "indexical icon" [Silverstein 1981b]; see Chapter 4) can be established between the interpretation of praxis (the dynamism in the myths) and the praxis of interpretation (the hermeneutical actions of the ritual elders). In effect, Trumeng reasserted at a higher logical level the encompassment of history by the center place in his recognition that change is an essential feature of *both* traditional myth and current experience, yet still without admitting the possibility of the Other's power to forever scar the sacred center.[11]

Interestingly, this strongly pragmatic encompassment of history launched the Bimin-Kuskusmin elders on an interpretive path leading in the opposite direction—both geographically and semiotically. Now that the sacred site at Telefolip to the west had been tarnished, they worked to protect their own sacred site by severing ties with the wider interpretive community (by stopping the exchange of sacra and ritual personnel) and by elaborating an inward-looking, intentionally reflexive interpretive program. This, too, can be seen as an icon of the comparative situation, for the Bimin-Kuskusmin responded to the next historical incursion of missionaries with "philosophical" rather than ritual discourse.

In contrast to this analogical application of mythic metaphors, Patton's (1994) discussion of the history of commentaries on Veda 9.112 as a "practice of reading" within the Indian tradition illustrates a process involving both the making explicit of what was initially textually presupposed in the Vedic text and the recontextualization of the locus of textual performativity. The chant sets out multiple occupational roles (carpenter, physician, smith, miller, priestly poet) that strive with diverse means for the same ultimate goal, namely, gold or material wealth. Despite the overt parallelism and consequent equality of these paths toward wealth, the chant implies a fundamental hierarchy, since the utterance of *this mantra* in a sacrificial context (e.g., the pounding of Soma) is the performative means by which the priestly group gains its wealth and asserts its social preeminence.[12] Many centuries later one commentator counters the possible implication that members of the priestly or brahmanic caste might undertake different occupational activities by framing the mantra with the question about a hypothetical circumstance: what can priests legitimately do during a famine? An even later commentary continues this theme by adding the idea that the mantra was actually uttered "during" a drought, thus removing the text from its previous ritual context. In the first of these commentaries the performative force of the mantra is undermined by the process of literalizing the contextual presuppositions of the text; in the second, performativity is reintroduced when the commentator notes that the mantra is performed by priests who, having been forced into unbrahmanic labors, utter it to purify themselves. Finally, the diverse social roles mentioned in the Vedic mantra receive official codification in the *Laws of Manu*. Operating at a tangent to these legitimizing commentaries, however, are other occurrences of the theme of the "myth of exigency" in folklore and epic, which, as Patton argues, reverse the officializing tendency by narrating instances where other castes, even untouchables, can act toward the goal of ending the drought. As this case makes clear, the Indian tradition must be seen as a fundamentally diachronic (Vedic and post-Vedic) and essentially intertextual (mantra, commentary, statute, folktale, epic) field of interpretation.

Finally, Al-Azmeh's (1994) analysis of the hermeneutical parallels in medieval Arabic thought between the fields of religion and jurisprudence provides an excellent example of the linkage among practical reason, comparison, and interpretation. Theological interpretation is grounded in a genealogical typology whereby historical events are rendered significant by being considered replicas or simulacra of archetypal foundational acts; thus, chronological time is subsumed by salvation history in such a way as to deny the contingency, randomness, chaos, and uniqueness of instances, which are all brought into identity through their being performative results of the original types (Burkhalter 1985:245). In jurisprudence, the relationship between religious textual precedent and consequent legal judgment is, likewise, viewed as one of causal iconicity; and in situations where the particular case is not transparently assimilable under an explicit Koranic passage, a mechanism of analogy intervenes as an interpretive tool to "extend the purview of nomothetic discourse to previously uncharted domains" (Al-Azmeh 1986:87). The indexical ground of the analogical correlation of textual authority and particular judgment is not, however, located in either natural law or social convention, since only God's wisdom knows the causal relation between the two and since only God's command has true juridical force:

> Having no compelling necessity, the concordance of the one with the other, and the compulsion of the index linking the two in an analogical relation, is a matter which lies beyond rational certainty, but is guaranteed by the authority of the text and its hermeneutician. The final arbiter who decrees the ineffable to be operative is therefore equally the final cause of this decree; and the concordance which assures the assonance of humanity and divinity and thus

evades the horrors of infernal eternity is one whose custodian is the authority that decrees it. (Al-Azmeh 1986:91–92)

A consequence of these principles is that identical legal postulates found in non-Islamic cultures, or in Arabic societies prior to Islam, are by definition invalidated. In other words, a hermeneutic of total encompassment correlates with a comparative stance of radical exclusivism.

Directions for Future Research

By way of conclusion I point to two issues, one substantive and the other methodological, which might serve as a challenge for future research in the comparative philosophy of religion. After a careful review of the articles in the three edited volumes in this series, I think that more systematic attention needs to be directed to the bicausal relationship between philosophical discourse and the cultural traditions in which that discourse emerges. On the one hand, the surrounding tradition can provide an overarching, general ideology that influences the character of philosophical reasoning, as in the effect of evolutionary (if not imperialistic) ideologies on Hegel's typology of religions. Or, the existing social order might provide a foundation for intellectuals in certain social roles to think in similar ways, as in Humphreys' (1975:112) linkage of philosophies of transcendence and interstitial and solidary intellectuals, and as in J. Z. Smith's (1987:293) correlation of local notions of ritual as exact repetition with the social context of archaic urban elites. Or, there may be a patterned relationship between the predominance of implicit metapragmatic discourse and the non-scriptural basis of the religious tradition, and inversely, the development of explicit metapragmatics might correlate with scriptural literacy (Gellner 1988:75). One might, in this way, juxtapose the metapragmatic devices of the Bimin-Kuskusmin with the textually highlighted metapragmatic distinction between commonplace yet instructional language and abstract yet direct language in the Buddhist thinker Gurulogomi discussed by Hallisey.

On the other hand, it may well turn out, as Griffiths (1989:527–29) argues, that it is in the nature of philosophical reasoning to exist in a relatively decontextualized state, that is, not dependent upon cultural traditions, so that religious discourse responds to metaphysical commitments but not vice versa. This reversed causality would suggest research into the impact of philosophical discourse on religious traditions, along dimensions such as systematization (e.g., promoting local typologies of traditions in India), rationalization (e.g., the increasing attention to exegetical rules and interpretive principles in religious contexts), and regimentation (i.e., the development of official, standardized, or codified norms of religious practice, feeling, and expression). Of particular interest here would be to study changes in religious traditions across shifts in philosophical worldviews.

Second, in my opinion the comparative philosophy of religion needs to become clearer about its methodology of comparison, along at least three axes: modality, scope, and ground. By modality I refer to the status of the terms of comparison, whether imputed by the analyst, as in Schrempp's (1990) comparison of Maori cosmology and Kantian philosophy, Yearley's (1990) comparison of Mencius and Aquinas, and Patton's comparison of Benjamin's reading of Parisian arcades and Indian interpretations of Vedic mantras, or motivated by historical linkages, as is the case in the articles by Poole, Bantly, Al-Azmeh, and Stout (1994). The analyst must take extra care in making explicit the motivation for creating the artificial juxtaposition. Imputed comparison across cultural levels (India/Paris, Maori/Kant) and comparison between well-articulated systems (Plato/Kūkai, Mencius/Aquinas) are particularly difficult. By scope I mean the range of the units of comparison: are the units entire philosophical systems, key interpretive mechanisms (analogy, typology, metaphor), or specific religious doctrines or philosophical principles (good action, miracles)? Given that philosophical discourse tends toward systematic formulation, comparison operating at a lesser scope requires vigilance against atomization or fragmentation. Finally, by ground I mean the metric, criteria, or reason upon which the comparison is based. Whereas some authors take the ground from one of the units to be compared (usually from the Western one), others attempt comparative analysis without realizing, as the present commentary has insisted, that their scholarly activities have deep historical roots *and* find echoes in the traditions under study.

8 | Naturalization of Convention

> To become aware that one is following a tradition and is dependent on it can have a disturbing effect on persons who thought that they were free from it. Intellectual and literary traditions have much in common with substantive traditions. "Reason," "life," and "naturalness" appear differently when their proponents become conscious that these too are borne by tradition. Just as the argument that one's unquestioned beliefs were particular to one's own time and culture unsettled those who espoused them as universally valid, so the perception that the practice of reason and "naturalness" of conduct are traditional has a similar unsettling effect.
>
> —Edward Shils (1981:309)

Arbitrariness and Motivation

THE CONTRIBUTION OF received anthropological wisdom to the study of conventionality—wisdom I propose to challenge here—can be summarized as follows. From the external perspective of analytical reflection (philosophical, scientific, linguistic, or ethnographic) social convention appears arbitrary in stipulating a non-natural, socially derived relationship between a regulative or constitutive principle and its corresponding appropriate context (different nations prescribe driving on different sides of the road) or between an expressive sign and its signified meaning (*arbor* and *kerrekar* mean "tree" in different languages). But from the internal perspective of social actors these same conventions appear necessary: if I drive on the left side of the road in this country I will either be arrested or cause an accident; if I want to talk about trees in the Belauan language of Micronesia I must use the phonetic shape *kerrekar*. Indeed, because it would never occur to me to consider the possibility of an alternative practice, I do not imagine myself as following a rule at all as I drive or speak. As Benveniste (1971:44–46) points out in his critique of the Saussurean doctrine of the linguistic sign, there is no real contradiction here, since the external observer has the benefit of comparative knowledge of different societies, while the active participant is oriented toward achieving immediate communicational or pragmatic goals. Arbitrariness in these examples refers to the lack of natural or external motivation between rule and context or between signifier and signified and not, of course, to the random or free choice of individuals (cf. Hołowka 1981).[1] In fact, absence of motivation implies the complete responsibility of the community as the sole authority for acknowledging—or, as Kripke (1982:89) would say, applying justification conditions to—one of several possible alternative relationships (Barthes 1988a:155–56).

A paradoxical consequence of this maximal social constraint for maximally arbitrary rules is that individuals acting within a system have a tendency to regard conventions as naturally motivated, that is, as being *objective* rather than socially constituted, *invariant* rather than malleable, *autonomous* rather than dependent, *eternal* rather than historical, *universal* rather than relative, and *necessary* rather than contingent. This sense of convention as "second nature" focuses, thus, on the "presupposed" (Silverstein 1979:203), "habitual" (Whorf 1956), and "automatized" (Havránek 1964:9) character of socially legitimized rules. Furthermore, the intensity of this sense of naturalness is often proportional to the degree of systematicity of the convention in question. Rules that fit into elaborate, coordinated systems reinforce each other through mutual implication and have the potential to appear, like nature, as an autonomous, universal reality. In addition to language, ritual (Bell 1992:207), the commodity-form (Lukács 1971; Marx 1976:163–77; Simmel 1978:128–30; Habermas 1983:358; Baudrillard 1981:93), law (Balbus 1977; Gabel 1982), and naturalism in art (Krieger 1990) are cited in this regard, since each combines an extensive range of relevance with a high level of interlocking coherence and thus appears as a totalized, reified entity.

This tendency for naturalization is not without important consequences for the manipulation of power in society, for instituted conventions that enforce asymmetries of any sort—between chiefs and commoners, lords and peasants, older and younger, men and women—will continue to be reproduced (and thus to reproduce the asymmetry) if taken as natural. On the other hand, widespread awareness of the historical contingency of conventions and of the possibility of alternative institutional arrangements can lead to revolutionary challenges to the *status quo*. Bourdieu (1977:164–67) discusses this relationship among naturalization, systems of symbolic classification, and social power as follows:

> Every established order tends to produce . . . the naturalization of its own arbitrariness. Of all the mechanisms tending to produce this effect, the most important and the best concealed is undoubtedly the dialectic of the objective chances and the agents' aspirations, out of which arises the *sense of limits*, commonly called the *sense of reality*, i.e. the correspondence between the objective classes and the internalized classes, social structures and mental structures, which is the basis of the most ineradicable adherence to the established order. Systems of classification which reproduce, in their own specific logic, the objective classes, i.e. the divisions by sex, age, or position in the relations of production, make their specific contribution to the reproduction of the

power relations of which they are the product, by securing the misrecognition, and hence the recognition, of the arbitrariness on which they are based: in the extreme case, that is to say, when there is a quasi-perfect correspondence between the objective order and the subjective principles of organization (as in ancient societies) the natural and social world appears as self-evident. This experience we shall call *doxa*, so as to distinguish it from an orthodox or heterodox belief implying awareness and recognition of the possibility of different or antagonistic beliefs. Schemes of thought and perceptions can produce the objectivity that they do produce only by producing misrecognition of the limits of the cognition that they make possible, thereby founding immediate adherence, in the doxic mode, to the world of tradition experienced as a "natural world" and taken for granted. . . . The self-evidence of the world is reduplicated by the instituted discourses about the world in which the whole group's adherence to that self-evidence is affirmed. The specific potency of the explicit statement that brings subjective experiences into the reassuring unanimity of a socially approved and collectively attested sense imposes itself with the *authority* and *necessity* of a collective position adopted on data intrinsically amendable to many other structurations.

There is, however, another side to this issue which Bourdieu does not fully consider here, although he does address it in detail in his more recent work on "distinction" (Bourdieu 1984), namely, that conventions explicitly recognized by members of a society *as constituted* by the "established order" can serve as potent social indexes of the hierarchical distribution of power. In other words, within a given community there can be a continuum of conventionality such that those groups which execute rules with maximal delicacy or which are able to impose normative judgments upon the performance of others thereby reinforce their position of authority. Rather than contrive to perpetuate the "doxic mode" of unreflective, internalized acceptance, those in power celebrate their "typifying" power by constructing conventional rules which are exaggerated in complexity (e.g., poetry and ritual) or subject to rapid stylistic change (e.g., manners and fashion).

Furthermore, if social conventions do not always appear necessary from the actor's point of view, they are also not always regarded as arbitrary by outside, scientific observers. In fact, there is an important, if not dominant, trend in Western social theory to deny the historical, collective, and relative character of conventions by discovering various elements of motivation in these cultural constructs. This theoretical naturalization of convention involves (as will be detailed in the next section), for example, showing the deductive necessity of instituted rules, uncovering concealed practical rationality behind historically transmitted customs, or positing adaptive mechanisms as the real explanation of regular social practices. Far from transforming the advantage of a comparative perspective, what Benveniste (1971:44) calls the "impassive viewpoint of Sirius," into a vision of historical and cultural variability, these theories struggle to reintroduce universal explanatory principles in order to argue that existing conventions are the only possible arrangements.

These preliminary observations about the limitations of the received wisdom about conventionality are sufficient to point out the need to reopen the question of the relationship between nature and convention as a dynamic process in both social theory and social reality.

Naturalization in Social Theory

> Economists have a singular method of procedure. There are only two kinds of institutions for them, artificial and natural. The institutions of feudalism are artificial institutions, those of the bourgeoisie are natural institutions. In this they resemble the theologians, who likewise establish two kinds of religion. Every religion which is not theirs is an invention of men, while their own is an emanation from God. When the economists say that present-day relations—the relations of bourgeois production—are natural, they imply that these are the relations in which wealth is created and productive forces developed in conformity with the laws of nature. These relations therefore are themselves natural laws independent of the influence of time. They are eternal laws which must always govern society. Thus there has been history, but there is no longer any.
>
> —Karl Marx, 1847 (1963:120–21)

A central dynamic in modern Western culture involves, on the one hand, the insistence on the ability of individuals working together to rationally establish the conventions, rules, or laws which are the foundation of social order and, on the other hand, the attempt to ground these constructed principles in some suprahistorical, transcendent, or natural reality. That is, the social order is deemed rational when it is found to be the result of uncoerced, coordinated agreement of atomic individuals whose decisions are subject to no external constraints, but then the social order so constituted is legitimized by appeal to eternal, immutable postulates. To put it simply: the institutions of society are as they are because we agree to make them that way (the "conventional" moment) *and at the same time* our system of social practices could not possibly be other than it is (the "natural" moment).

This seemingly paradoxical dynamic corresponds to a paradoxical attitude toward the concept of conventionality itself. From one perspective, conventions are positively valued insofar as they register decision-making processes in which the only reason behind the agreed-upon rule is contributed *by* the participants involved. This ideal of presuppositionless agreement through the "marketplace of ideas" (Bosmajian 1984) repudiates all external or imposed restrictions and assumes that participants bring to negotiations identical rational equipment. In the words of Kant (1970:55), enlightenment consists of "the freedom to make *public use* of one's reason in all matters." Thus, actions regulated by conventions willfully and rationally undertaken are not seen as constrained, and those established conventions whose origin does not lie in explicit agreement persist only because of continued mutual consent (see, e.g., Lewis 1975:26). From a second perspective, however, conventions are negatively valued insofar as they appear to be historically transmitted formulas which confront rational actors as an oppressive burden from the past. Conventions in this sense channel thinking according to reasons *not* supplied freely by those in the present. Again Kant (1970:54–55): "Dogmas and formulas, these mechanical instruments for rational use (or rather misuse) of his natural endowments, are the ball and chain of his permanent immaturity."

Now the trouble lies in the obvious fact that conventions in the first "agreement" sense are destined to become conventions in the second "formula" sense, given the universal character of cultures to transmit symbolic constructs, including, for example, isolated semiotic types, patterns for action, artistic genres, and entire worldviews, rather than always invent them afresh.[2] There is, then, a tendency for positivistic modes of discourse to appeal to "nature" (in a number of senses) in order to justify inherited conventions as being, after all, in perfect harmony with some invariable, objective standard rather than as the result of coercive, unquestioned, and binding "tradition" (Acton 1952–53:5; Weber 1978:326). Accordingly, the category "nature" receives parallel alternative valuation. Nature is negatively valued if it is viewed as an external constraint on the exercise of individual rationality, and yet nature is positively valued as the source of validation that instituted conventions are the only ones possible.

To summarize: conventions as present agreements are seen as wholly arbitrary constructs, but conventions as historically transmitted formulas are taken as naturalized truths.

The opposition between convention and nature in Western social theory parallels the classical philosophical speculation on the character of language. The terms of these debates as established in Greek thought need only a brief review here. Using the then-standard contrast between the state of affairs in the natural world as it is as a matter of fact (*physei*) and the conventional institutions or opinions resulting from agreement, custom, or stipulation (*thesei*), Plato constructs the debate in the *Cratylus* between rival Heraclitean and Eleatic views, the former insisting that language has a built-in harmony with nature independent of human intervention and the latter arguing that words are appropriate for their meanings only by customary choice. Socrates, the mediating character in this dispute, shows how the relationship between various phonetic realizations and the corresponding "ideal name" is indeed conventional and arbitrary, while the relationship between the "ideal name" and the immutable world of form is natural and universal.

The poles of this debate about language mirror the distinction in classical political theory between inevitable "rules which are innate in nature" and adventitious "rules of the laws . . . created by covenant" (Antiphon in Gough 1936:10). That there is a constant interplay between the two terms is evident, for example, in hypothetical arguments about the way individuals, faced with competition and conflict in the state of nature prior to the establishment of law, covenant together to curb these natural tendencies. Society is, thus, an antinatural construction generated by the necessities of the natural order. As Plato (1961:606) synthesizes one such contractual theory:

> By nature, they say, to commit injustice is a good and to suffer it is an evil, but that the excess of evil in being wronged is greater than the excess of good in doing wrong, so that when men do wrong and are wronged by one another and taste of both, those who lack the power to avoid the one and take the other determine that it is for their profit to make a compact with one another neither to commit nor to suffer injustice, and that this is the beginning of legislation and of covenants between men.

This notion that legislative covenants protect individuals from the brute exercise of power is, of course, part of the charter myth of modern contractual theories of society, a myth which persists in recent philosophical theories of convention as coordinated agreement. Contractual theories of social origin often go hand in hand with conventional theories of language. Hobbes, for example, sees an analogy between the process by which individuals compact together in a commonwealth and the willful stipulation of the relationship between words and denoted reality. Society and language are both "artificial" constructs in contrast, respectively, to the state of nature and animal cries, which operate according to natural laws and do not involve conventional agreements of any sort. While bees and ants may form rudimentary societies, they do not constitute a commonwealth or speak a language, for they lack conventionality: "The agreements of these creatures is natural; that of men, is by covenant only, which is artificial" (Hobbes 1962:131). And yet for Hobbes both society and language are grounded in necessity. In the case of the commonwealth, individuals in the state of nature are compelled by dictates of reason to agree to give up their natural right to everything in order to protect their own interests. The original covenant which results in the submission of all to the sovereign does not presuppose some prior collective understanding; rather, it is the logical ground for all later sociability (Cassirer 1951:257). While the specific content of the contracts, covenants, and promises established by individuals in society varies widely, the inevitability of making them follows deductively from Hobbes's first principles about hedonistic determinism.

Similarly in language, words which we employ as mnemonic "marks" and communicative "signs" are, according to Hobbes, conventional along four dimensions: opacity (objects named do not display their natures in their names), mutability (new names are born daily), relativity (different words are in use in different nations), and noniconicity (there is no physical similarity between name and thing). And yet *that* we so invent words is a matter of necessity, due to the natural limitation of human memory and the physical separation between minds. As Hobbes (1981:195) argues: "Therefore, it is necessary for the acquisition of philosophy that there should be some signs by which what has been contrived by some might be disclosed and made known to others." Aware of the obvious problem that faces any theory of the conventional origin of names, that "it is incredible that men once came together to take counsel to constitute by decree what all words and all connexions of words would signify" (Hobbes 1978:38), Hobbes hypothesizes that the first individuals agree on names of only a few objects pointed out by God and then pass these names down through an ever-expanding tradition of naming conventions. What begins as a conventionalist approach to meaning ends up as a causal, mechanistic model of the development of language. For Hobbes, then, the artificiality of covenants and the conventionality of words are both anchored in necessity, since both are regimented by the fundamental notion that "reason is the law of nature" (Hobbes 1928:150; see also Habermas 1973:62–64). But as Sahlins (1976b:96) notes, Hobbes reproduces the historical specificity of market competition as the image of nature: "Since Hobbes, at least, the competitive and acquisitive characteristics of Western man have been confounded with Nature, and the Nature thus fashioned in the human image has been in turn reapplied to the explanation of Western man."

This tendency to locate a historically specific form of social relations in the state of nature characterizes the political philosophy of Locke as well. Locke defends an emergent bourgeois society against absolutist, noble, and feudal powers by arguing that state power's primary responsibility is to protect and legitimize those features of "civil society" which derive not from artificial, contractual causes but from aspects of the natural state. In particular, Locke attributes to this state of nature both the right to private property produced through individual labor and the right to unlimited accumulation made possible through money. Civil society thus appears to itself as a natural state, as a self-regulating, autonomous system requiring no arbitrary constructs to bring it into existence. The function of contracts becomes, then, not to constitute but rather to recognize already developing property relations (Rohbeck 1984:74).

A central opponent of this kind of contractual theory in the mid-nineteenth century was Henry Maine, who challenged the basic premise that the transition from the state of nature to civil society was accomplished through contractual agreements by pointing out that it is precisely this ability to make contracts that has to be explained historically. As Maine (1889:110–11) puts it: "Authority, Custom, or Chance are in fact the great source of law in primitive communities as we know them, not Contract." Equally forceful, however, is Maine's repudiation of natural-law theories which assumed that historically developed rules were "supposed to have been evolved from the unassisted contemplation of the conception of Nature" (Maine 1972:59). Rather, for Maine, the momentous invention that made state-level society (that is, based on territory rather than kinship) possible is "legal fiction," the artificial and conventional stipulation that a state of affairs exists when in fact it does not. Early states, for example, were based on the useful fiction that immigrant groups were genealogically related to the local population (Maine 1875:69). Legal fictions are more complex versions of fictions which create "definite social forms" such as the family, the tribe, and the village community out of "broken hordes, mere miscellanies of men" (Maine 1886:285). Once this convention was acknowledged and consecrated through common sacrifices, the "permanence and solidity" of the social order was assured. Thus, "the composition of the state, uniformly assumed to be natural, was nevertheless known to be in great measure artificial" (Maine 1972:77). This growth of legal fictions was the model for a constitutive openness which Maine sees as the distinguishing feature of modern society. Whereas in primitive societies a person's social position is naturally fixed by the irreversable assignment of status at birth, civilization developed the mechanism of contractual law through which a person could alter this natural state of affairs and "create it by himself by convention" (Maine 1972:183).

Whether in Hobbes's anchoring of the hypothetical original contract in natural law or in Maine's positive valuation of customary or legal conventions as diacritic of civilization, civil society is at one remove from bondage in nature, which is viewed either as the perpetual state of war or as the fixity of status. In other evolutionary theories, however, these terms are inverted, so that earlier states of society are explained by standards derived from the natural or practical logic of *contemporary* life. Maine's observation that advances in modes of legal reasoning are grounded in fictitious customs struck many nineteenth-century thinkers as a call for positivistic reform. The apparent irrationality of many customs, that is, the evident lack of means-ends appropriateness, should not be glorified but overcome, so that social conventions perpetuated through force of habit, while perhaps serving as "way-marks full of meaning" (Tylor 1871:16) for the expanding enterprise of developmental reconstruction, must in the end fall to the necessary logic of modern science. In place of Maine's recognition of the positive contribution of fictions, evolutionists such as E. B. Tylor and Lewis Henry Morgan endeavored to weed out unnecessary and irrational "survivals," that is, customs which have outlived their contextual appropriateness and practical motivation.

Morgan, for example, discovered an unexpected consistency in consanguineal kin terms of various American Indian societies. At first Morgan thought that these instances of the "classificatory system of relationship," that is, systems which lump under one linguistic label relations which our own system of terminology distinguishes (e.g., brother and male cousin), were, in the words of his friend and colleague the Rev. J. S. McIlvaine, "invented and wholly artificial" (Morgan in Kuper 1985:12). In contrast, the "descriptive systems" found in what Morgan and his contemporaries called "civilized" society "evidently follow the flow of blood" in supposedly providing a natural or objective match-up between biological and linguistic facts. Thanks to suggestive comments from McIlvaine, Morgan soon postulated a natural explanation for what he had earlier considered entirely artificial: the practice of brothers' having wives in common meant that no man could in principle distinguish his own from his brothers' children, so that the resulting classificatory pattern reflects a set of natural—though peculiar—facts. When J. F. McLennan, another important evolutionary theorist, attacked Morgan's explanation of classificatory kinship systems on the grounds that the evidence presented, namely, the extensive lists of kinship terms Morgan collected from all over the world, were ephemeral conventions of address, Morgan replied that the classificatory system is not at all "conventional," since it is based on "actual facts of social condition" and since it appears "identical in minute details over immense sections of the earth" (Morgan 1974:531).

Morgan assumed that the cultural practices of his own society are the result of logical, practical reflection on objective conditions of life (Sahlins 1976a:60). This state of self-evident objectivity then becomes the standard to render explicable diverse cultural practices at other stages on the evolutionary ladder. Moreover, Morgan is a paradigmatic case of the paradoxical attitude toward convention noted above. On the one hand, as we have just seen, he reduced artificial or customary classifications to their natural practicality. On the other hand, he thought that societies were entities constructed by the willful association of individuals, whether in the League of the Iroquois he made famous or in the less well-known Grand Order of the Iroquois, a fraternal order of gentlemen from western New York he helped found. For Morgan (1962:7) the confederacy was a clear historical example of convention by agreement: "Iroquois chiefs assembled in general congress, to agree upon the terms and principles of the compact, by which their future destinies were to be linked together." In 1845, in fact, Morgan and his brothers from the order were eyewitnesses to a ceremony reaffirming the charter of the Iroquois confederacy during which an Onondaga leader solemnly repeated, as one of the brothers reports, "the regulations adopted by the originators of the Confederacy, to render it stable and lasting" (Isaac Hurd in Bieder 1980:354).

A popular modern variant on Hobbes's reduction to mechanistic principles and Morgan's reduction to practical rationality is the sociobiological explanation of social behavior. Not content with dismissing the uniquely cultural content of institutions such as warfare, religion, and kinship, sociobiology's aim is to show the genetic basis for the general human ability to make conventions. The opposition between nature and convention, between genetic determination and cultural determination, is thus transcended. As Robin Fox (1980:185–86) puts it:

> If we can analyze society itself as a natural product of natural selection, then the categories arising from it are themselves products of the same process, deriving, certainly, not from "individual experience" but from the collective genetic experience of the group—its gene pool. They are thus at once both "social" and "innate." . . . Culture and society are natural phenomena, and concepts and categories, rules and emotions, have all developed together as interconnected responses to recognizable selection pressures. Conceptual thought and language, inhibitions by obedience to rules, emotional responses to objects of social and environmental classification, all developed together.

Since the tendency to follow social customs is itself genetically specified, conventions are rendered epiphenomenal, as merely linguistic labels for patterns of behavior regulated by noncultural factors.

In *The Red Lamp of Incest* (1980) Fox sets out to explain, among other things, one of the ur-conventions of anthropological discourse, namely, prescriptive marriage rules stipulating that individuals must find mates outside their own kin group yet from a specifically defined other group. At least since Morgan's time, nothing—language excepted—has more challenged our ability to construct universalistic explanations than the variety and complexity of documented patterns of marriage alliance, with corresponding systems of lineage organization and kin-term typologies. Fox argues that our early hominid ancestors faced an increasingly difficult time reconciling two needs, the need to maximize genetic replication through inbreeding and the need to maximize genetic strength through outbreeding. The solution to this dilemma was forced upon more developed *homo sapiens* when they began hunting for meat. With the males out hunting and the females out gathering, the sexes began to rely on each other not just for procreation but as exchange partners, so that rather than fight over women, men exchange near-kin among themselves, thereby establishing the category of "marriageable kin." In other words, a man does not marry his sister but rather is guaranteed the sexual services of a second or third cousin. Whereas hominid males had a "tendency to accumulate females" for breeding purposes, primitive hunting and gathering peoples maximized sexual capital through the "investment" in marriage. The parallel to the transition from mercantilist accumulation of wealth to capitalist investment is remarkable. Fox even phrases this development in terms of the switch from women as "use-values" to women as "exchange-values"! Instead of keeping females for themselves, dominant males in some groups began to exchange sisters; the perpetuation of this arrangement, called cross-cousin marriage, ensured the constant circulation of the most valued commodity, women.

But what happened to the notion of a marriage *rule*, if everything is determined in the end by the selective pressure? Fox's (1979:133–34) answer is, as he admits, "tedious":

> Our uniqueness lies not in having, recognizing, and behaving differentially to different kin (this happens throughout nature), it lies in giving this process names and rules of naming; in the classification not the kinship. . . . Kinship grouping and kin-derived behavior do not make us unique: the naming of kin does. In each case a universal, hence biological, feature is associated with a "cultural practice." But by the same logic, the cultural practice—ruling and naming, i.e., classification—if universal, must also be biological. Hence one set of biological features—the propensity to classify and regulate—comes into conjunction with two others: the propensity to outbreed and to behave differentially toward kin. All this is possible through the mediation of language. The latter, however, being universal, is also biological, and hence the unifying feature of the other two biological features is itself biological. Ergo, there is no nature-culture distinction, everything is natural-biological. Hence the argument that we cannot use analyses developed for nature to interpret culture fails since by its own logic the supposedly unique cultural features turn out to be natural.

Fox's just-so attack on conventionality is double-edged: the ability to make conventions, that is, to impose linguistic classification upon patterns of action, is merely the inconsequential labeling of already established practices. And because rules for kinship and marriage are found universally in human society they must be products of the same biological forces which determine the behavior they name. That is, conventions are either pointless or natural.[3]

Naturalization and Conventionalization in Social Reality

> Lastly we should realize that dancing in a partner's arms is a product of modern European civilization. Which shows you that things we find natural are historical. Moreover, they horrify everyone in the world but ourselves.
>
> —Marcel Mauss (1979:116)

> Thus, the concept of conventionality has in principle a relative, rather than absolute meaning: it is impossible to say that a given form is more conventional and another less conventional without taking into account how these forms function in the LANGUAGE under consideration, whether it is a natural language or a language of art.
>
> —Boris Uspensky (1976:82, n. 34)

We have seen that several strands of positivistic discourse, namely, Hobbes's deductive mechanics, Morgan's practical rationality, and Fox's sociobiological reductionism, posit the theoretical naturalness of social convention. Moreover, in this type of scientific metalanguage the codes and rules of social life are represented by an explanatory language which destroys the cultural specificity of its represented object. Conventions that could not be otherwise or which obey the requirements of some higher logic are, of course, no longer conventional. But this naturalization of convention can be observed in many places other than in the positivistic (mis)apprehension of cultural phenomena, namely, in the operation of societies themselves which regularly represent their conventions as necessary, immutable, or motivated constructs. If it can be documented that the naturalization of convention is itself a pervasive social phenomenon, then the theoretical arguments sketched above can be shown to be not only in principle incapable of accounting for this data but also understandable as merely another, unprivileged example of a widespread occurrence.

The crucial difference, however, between the naturalization of convention as part of a theoretical metalanguage and that as part of the data of social life is that only in the latter do the poles of nature and convention remain in a dynamic tension: in society, naturalization in fact perpetuates conventions by imputing powerful motivation to arbitrary constructs. My own cross-cultural reading and experience suggest that the social construction and function of the relationship between nature and convention can be as diverse as the different kinds of customs and rules often cited to prove the relativity of cultures. In order to move beyond the purely anecdotal I will present four ethnographic cases in order of increasingly explicit conventionality, that is, from examples where social conventions are relatively naturalized from the perspective of actors within the system to those where social rules confront actors as highly artificial, if not arbitrary, constructs.

Conventions, especially those dealing with norms of action, can operate hegemonically in a society by drawing into their scope groups which not only have no role in their construction but also become implicated in perpetuating their own subordination. Rebellion against disfranchisement is made difficult either because antinormative sentiments only incite strengthened authoritative pressure or because challenges presuppose the very conventions in dispute. In the case of the Baruya of New Guinea, as described by Godelier (1976, 1986), forms of domination of men over women are perpetuated by institutions and ideologies in which women become the principal agents of their own domination. To men are reserved the ownership of land, the knowledge of magic, the practice of warfare, the manipulation of sacred objects, and the control over affinal exchange. These objective manifestations of dominance are coupled with a difference in orientation of men and women, according to which men see their interests in terms of the tribe as a whole, while women, whose life course takes them from their fathers' houses to their husbands', view their sphere of activity as restricted to domestic space.

In contrast to the ten-year, intensive initiation process required for young boys, girls undergo brief, secret initiation lasting only two weeks, which nevertheless establishes powerfully the legitimacy of rules and concepts supporting masculine domination. During their initiation girls are instructed by female elders to obey certain behavioral conventions as necessary elements of the social order: for example, never resist your husband's sexual advances or cry out during intercourse, never cut your husband's sugarcane without his permission unless to serve his guests, never have sexual relations with visitors, and—this one to protect fragile male egos—never laugh if you catch sight of your husband's accidentially exposed genitals. After receiving these admonitions, the initiates ritually chew sugarcane, a crop planted only by men and symbolic of the penis, and whip themselves with stinging nettles (Godelier 1986:45–46). Having internalized these rules and experienced these hardships, the young girls are then taught that their subordinate position is not merely a matter of convention but is rooted in the "natural" differences between their bodies and sexual processes and those of men.

As Godelier (1976:284) concludes: "In a society without classes, the dominant ideas are the ideas of the dominant sex and the greatest force of domination is the consent of the dominated to their subordination." Without an independent set of concepts with which to confront their condition, the women are forced to use the symbolic language of the dominant males; and so as long as this condition prevails the men need only make minimal use of external forms of coercion (cf. Genovese 1982). The hegemonic function of social conventions has been cited frequently in recent discussion of the way linguistic categories perpetuate gender asymmetries. As Goldsmith (1980:182) remarks: "Therefore, when marginal people turn to the conventional language in an effort to interpret their suffering and devise valid means for altering their lives, at best they confront confusion and, at worst, they meet their own failure."

Rather than enforce oppressive conventions through the ruse of imputed naturalness, the Belauan culture of Micronesia—if I may turn briefly to my own ethnographic fieldwork—goes to no trouble to hide the fact that control over social conventions rests primarily in the hands of members of high-ranking or chiefly houses. In Belau conventions are called "paths," a term much like the Latin *via*, which refers not only to roads and sea lanes but to prescriptive channels of social relationships (e.g., the "path" between allied chiefly houses) and recognized strategies of political action (e.g., the "path of fire," a rhetorical technique involving heated threats). Although these relationships and strategies are widely known and actively discussed, the ability to have one's actions typified or categorized as being a token of a type and, more importantly, the power to create new "paths" which will be subsequently presupposed by others are guarded prerogatives of high rank. In the absence of writing (at least in traditional Belau) rules of customary behavior are codified only in oral traditions, including myths, historical narratives, and proverbs, and even then conventions are represented by exemplification rather than by a regimenting metalanguage. Taken together these traditions, called literally "words/deeds from ancient times," provide the most frequently cited reason for the existence of conventions. Interestingly, the origination of customs is almost invariably the act of mythological or heroic characters acting alone, in contrast to the myth of collective agreement in our own culture.

As an island society which existed in relative isolation for at least a millennium, Belau developed a strong sense of the coherence and self-sufficiency of its own culture. And Belau's experience as the object of powerful yet passing colonial regimes (Spanish, German, Japanese, and American) only served to intensify its sense of historical continuity, stability, and uniqueness. Although possessing the qualities of totality, consistency, and permanence, the category of culture in Belau is not interpreted in terms of a category of nature. In fact, the origin myth describes the transition from the amorphous depth of the sea to a land-based social existence as the creation of "paths" of migration (Parmentier 1987a:127–37). Belauan tradition is, thus, in total accord with Lévi-Strauss's (1969:8) dictum: "The absence of rules seems to provide the surest criterion for distinguishing a natural from a cultural process." Second, a pervasive dynamic of factionalism at all levels of social organization also contributes to the continued commitment to conventional behavior, since competition between rival segments normally presupposes rather than challenges social rules and understandings (Parmentier 1985c). Third, the systems of hierarchically ranked institutions interlock in such a fashion—with high-ranking titleholders heading high-ranking houses and these houses constituting high-ranking villages which in turn head political federations—that the exercise of typifying power constantly reinforces the institutional structure making it possible.

Acting according to conventional norms can signal to others one's knowledge of the convention, possession of a requisite level of skill for manipulating complex rules, and a positive valuation of the standard in question. But, in social contexts where there is a significant asymmetry in the power to establish conventions or in the availability of training to master them, conventional behavior can also index one's position in this institutionalized hierarchy. Distinction or differentiation in terms of conventions is one way that dominant groups can exercise what Bourdieu (1979) has termed "symbolic power," the ability to manipulate the arbitrariness of convention to set themselves apart from the general population, whose everyday behavior seems in contrast inflexible, rustic, and "natural."

An excellent example of this social-indexical function of convention is the French court of Louis XIV as described by Elias (1982, 1983). As Elias points out, the florescence of aristocratic court life corresponded to the rise of a middle class, or bourgeoisie, so that the fine gradations of rank found at court not only constituted a class-internal hierarchy but also distinguished courtly civility as a whole from lower strata of society. The courtly aristocracy is so much more sensitive to lower-class gestures than was the warrior nobility of the Middle Ages that it strictly and emphatically excludes everything "vulgar" from its sphere of life. Finally, this permanently smouldering social fear also constitutes one of the most powerful driving forces of the social control that members of this courtly upper class exert over themselves and other people in their circle. It is expressed in the intense vigilance with which they observe and polish everything that distinguishes them from people of lower rank: not only the external signs of status, but also their speech, their gestures, their social amusements and manners. The constant pressure from below and the fear it induces above are, in a word, one of the strongest driving forces—though not the only one—of that specifically civilized refinement which distinguishes the people of this upper class from others and finally becomes second nature to them (Elias 1982:304). There is, in fact, a contrast between the norms of sincerity, hard work, individualism, enrichment through education, in short, the idealization of "natural" behavior for the middle class, and the aristocratic pattern of artificially exaggerated manners, theatrical ceremonialism, and calculated control of affective impulses.[4] Court conventions concerning interpersonal etiquette, dress, and speech which might appear trivial, oppressive, or absurd to us constitute for those involved a coherent guide for establishing relational identity, as is shown in the following contemporary satirical passage cited by Elias:

> You require a doublet made of four or five layers of different taffetas; stocking such as you see, frieze and scarlet, accounting, I assure you, for eight ells of cloth at least; then you need boots, the flesh-side outermost, the heel very high, and spur-slippers also very high . . . the spurs must be gilded. . . . When, thus attired, you have arrived in the Louvre courtyard,—one alights between the guards, you understand—you begin to laugh at the first person you meet, you salute one, say a word to another: "Brother how you bloom, gorgeous as a rose. Your mistress treats you well; that cruel rebel has no arms against this fine brow, this well-curled moustache. And then this charming river-bank, one could die of admiration." This must be said while flinging the arms, agitating the head, moving from one foot to the other, painting with the hand now the moustache, now the hair. (Agrippa d'Aubigne in Elias 1983:230)[5]

Glossing this text, Elias notes a combination of fluctuating convention and the participants' high degree of commitment to their necessity:

> To keep one's place in the intense competition for importance at court, to avoid being exposed to scorn, contempt, loss of prestige, one must subordinate one's appearance and gestures, in short oneself, to the fluctuating norms of court society that increasingly emphasize the difference, the distinction of the people belonging to it. One *must* wear certain materials and certain shoes. One *must*

> move in certain ways characteristic of people belonging to court society. (Elias
> 1983:231–32)

And since the king and the palace at Versailles were the focal point of the entire
system, proper behavior of those at the lower reaches of the court hierarchy was
rendered meaningful by being oriented toward the same point as was the behavior of their superiors.

A final example of the institutional basis of conventionality comes from
Lotman's (1985) analysis of Russian culture in the eighteenth century, a case in
which the nobility went to extremes to highlight the hyper-conventionality of
their behavior. Lotman begins by locating the natural/conventional distinction
in two levels of behavior, everyday norms considered by members of society as
ordinary, instrumental and "natural," on the one hand, and ceremonial, ritual,
and nonpragmatic "poetic" behavior regarded as bringing to contexts of action
an independent signification, on the other hand. While both levels are, from the
point of view of an outside observer, fully conventional, the semiotic character
of the former level vanishes from the actors' point of view, or so Lotman claims:

> When a language is first recorded and studied, descriptions of everyday speech
> are generally oriented toward the external observer. This correlation is not co-
> incidental; like language, everyday behavior belongs to the sort of semiotic sys-
> tem that "native speakers" view as natural, a part of Nature and not Culture.
> Its semiotic and conventional character is apparent only to the external ob-
> server. (Lotman 1985:68)

As the data Lotman presents reveal, however, this "external" perspective is not
reserved for the theoretical observer but can characterize the perceptions of social
groups who experience some significant "other" as proof of the relativity of
custom.

From the period of Peter the Great, Lotman documents a process in which
the nobility increasingly adopted, even flaunted, behavior patterns borrowed
from the European middle class, to the degree that they acted like foreigners in
their own country. The motive for this seems to be that these nobles ensured that
their conventional behavior could resist being naturalized through repetition precisely because it appeared foreign, thereby demanding—in a perfect reversal of
Benveniste's argument—an attitude of externality. The resulting need for intensive instruction of children, the publication of manuals of polite conduct, and the
value placed on learning foreign languages further differentiated nobility and
peasants.

This "semiotization of everyday behavior" took many forms, from the
heightened theatricality of costume to the ritualization of what had previously
been "natural" activity. What all these "poetic" forms of behavior had in common was the availability of alternative norms or styles, again contrasting with
peasant behavior regulated by the invariable boundaries of the agricultural cycle.

(Curiously, but predictably, Peter himself inverted this inversion by displaying strikingly unaffected, "natural" behavior in ceremonial contexts.) The extremes to which this hyper-conventionality could run is illustrated by the case of one Vasilii Vasil'evich Golovin, a learned gentleman whose daily schedule was a cross between a theatrical performance and liturgical rite:

> If anything prevented the master from falling asleep right away, he did not stay in bed and was restless for the entire night. In this case, he would either begin reading aloud his favorite book, *The Life of Alexander the Great* by Quintus Curtius, or he would sit in a large armchair ... and intone the following words, now raising and now lowering his voice: "Satan, get thee to the barren places, to the thick woods and to the crevices of the earth, where the light of God's countenance shineth not. Satan, Enemy of Mankind, unhand me, get thee to the dark places, to the bottomless seas, to the shelterless uninhabited mountains of the wilderness where the light of God's countenance shineth not. Cursed wretch, be off to the Tartars! Be off, cursed wretch, to the inferno, to the eternal fire and appear to me no more. Thricedamned, thriceheathen and thricecursed! I blow on you and spit on you!" After finishing these exorcisms, he would rise from his chair and begin walking back and forth through all seven of his rooms shaking a rattle. These strange habits naturally provoked curiosity, and many of the servants peeked through the cracks to see what the master was doing. But this too was taken into account. The housemaids would begin shouting, employing various witticisms and proverbs, and pour cold water on the eavesdroppers from an upper window. The master approved all these actions, saying, "It serves the culprits right. Suffering means nothing to them, thricedamned, thriceheathen and thricecursed, untortured, untormented and unpunished!" Stamping his feet, he would repeat the same thing over and over again. (Quoted in Lotman 1985:79–80)

Lotman observes that this carnivalization of daily life implied not only that individuals played theatrical roles but also that life itself was viewed as a textual plot, often intentionally patterned after literary heroes (see also Lotman 1976).

Conclusion

> Philosophy commences when this immediate synthesis [of ethos and worldview] falls apart, when *physis* and *nomos* become distinguished and their relation is transformed into a *problem*. Its history is that of constant attempts both to reformulate this distinction and to construct a relation between the concepts distinguished. Its end is present when the relations between nature and convention, objects and values, facts and norms, science and morality, etc. are no longer seen as a meaningful problem.
>
> —György Márkus (1980:24)

The theoretical and ethnographic examples in the preceding sections are intended to challenge the simple idea that social conventions always appear arbitrary to analysts and necessary to actors. In fact, for an important part of Western social theory the positivist apprehension of convention involves the effort to reduce arbitrariness to rational (Hobbes), practical (Morgan), or adaptive (Fox) logic. As we have seen, naturalization of convention can be found even in theorists who stress the importance of unconstrained agreement as the foundation of social order. On the other hand, the ethnographic cases presented illustrate various modes of articulation of the natural and conventional poles within societies. Conventions of masculine domination operate hegemonically among the Baruya so that women are trained to accept their subordination as an immutable result of biological differentiation, while men concentrate on perpetuating the elaborate rituals of indoctrination that ensure their legitimizing power. In Belau, conventions are subject to hierarchical typification as a function of social rank; though accepted as given, stable, and binding, "paths" of convention are essentially cultural, without any naturalization to some extra-cultural standard. The French example shows that conventions stipulating courtly behavior are viewed as second nature by those who live and die by their social indexical implications. And finally in the Russian case, the aristocratic class presents itself to the larger society as if it were a foreign culture by adopting "poeticized" and idiosyncratic forms of behavior and thereby encourages a contrasting ideology of naturalness for rural, peasant life.

The tension between the naturalization of convention and the poeticization of convention exhibited within societies makes it impossible to adopt a theoretical stance which tries to reduce or transcend the opposition of nature and convention. In other words, there can be no strictly positivist theory of society which does not profoundly distort its object of investigation. Furthermore, arguments similar to that proposed by Roland Barthes (1967:89–98, 1972:115, 1983:285–86, 1988b:190), according to which the naturalization of convention is a process restricted to societies dominated by commodity fetishism, overlook the obvious fact that naturalization occurs in all types of social formations and, conversely, that conventions can appear as arbitrary, fabricated, or "semiotic" even in modern industrial societies (cf. Baudrillard 1981:158–59). There will always be, to return to Plato's *Cratylus*, those who insist that the basis of social convention is collective agreement and those who posit a natural or rational fitness in existing rules and customs. But so long as this tension continues to be observed by social theory we stand in little danger of the fate envisioned by Márkus for a philosophy which fails to see the nature/convention opposition as a problem.

Notes

1. Peirce Divested for Nonintimates

1. Exemplary summaries of Peirce's semiotic theory can be found in Fisch 1986; Oehler 1981; Randsell 1977; Savan 1987–88; and Tejera 1988.

2. The classical traditions are surveyed in Eco 1984:26–33; Kretzmann 1974; Telegdi 1982; and Todorov 1982:15–35. On Peirce's use of the Stoic tradition see Cosenza 1988.

3. I cite Peirce's writings using the abbreviations established in Fisch 1986:xi: CP: *Collected Papers of Charles Sanders Peirce* (1931–1958); MS: Peirce manuscripts in the collection of Harvard University, catalogued in Robin (1967); N: *Charles Sanders Peirce: Contributions to* The Nation (1975–1979); NEM: *The New Elements of Mathematics* (1976); SS: *Semiotic and Significs: The Correspondence between Charles S. Peirce and Victoria Lady Welby* (1977); W: *Writings of Charles S. Peirce: A Chronological Edition* (1982–).

4. It is erroneous to say, as several commentators do, that the icon is a First, the index a Second, and the symbol a Third. As signs, all three of these are triadic.

5. It is important not to think of icons, indices, and symbols as exclusive classes of signs. As Fisch (1986:333) helpfully explains: "We may therefore call a sign, for short, by the name of that element or aspect which is most prominent in it, or to which we wish to direct attention, without thereby implying that it has no element or aspect of the other two kinds."

6. For further discussion of Peirce's views on language see Brock 1981; Dewey 1946; Eco 1981; Jakobson 1980a; and Ransdell 1980.

2. Peirce's Concept of Semiotic Mediation

1. Several stylistic conventions need to be briefly noted. I use quotation marks to indicate the first occurrence of a technical term from Peirce's often bizarre semiotic vocabulary. (Peirce's own convention is to use capitalization). For bibliographic abbreviations see Note 3 in Chapter 1. Other studies of the development of Peirce's semiotic ideas include Deledalle 1986; Fisch 1986; Kloesel 1983; and Reiss 1984.

2. Peirce refined his definition of the sign constantly from 1867 to 1911. A few key references include: CP 1.541, 1903; CP 2.228, 1897; CP 2.230, 1910; CP 2.274, 1902; CP 5.484, c.1907; CP 8.177–85, 1902; NEM 3.233, 1909; NEM 4.239, c.1904; NEM 4.297; SS 31–33, 1904; SS 80–81, 1908; SS 196, 1906.

3. For "mediate determination" and "mediate representation" see, e.g., CP 1.553, 1867; CP 6.347, 1909; NEM 3.233, 1909; NEM 3.867, 1909; NEM 3.886, 1908; NEM 4.242, 1904; SS 80–81, 1908; MS 278a.10; MS 283.128.

4. Ayer (1968:161) argues that Peirce is confusing because he "conflates" the view of semiosis as an infinite series of sign production and the view of semiosis as an "infinite metalinguistic hierarchy." It seems to me that Peirce never doubted that these are equivalent conceptualizations.

5. For the definition of the *symbol* see, e.g., CP 2.222, 1903; CP 2.249, 1903; CP 2.274, 1902; CP 2.295, 1893; CP 2.297–302, 1895, CP 2.307, 1902; CP 3.360, 1885; CP 4.57, 1893; CP 4.500, 1903; CP 8.209, 1903; NEM 3.407, 1903; NEM 3.887, 1908; NEM 4.243, 1904; SS 33, 1906; SS 79, 1908; MS 7.7; MS 298.13, 1905.

6. The shape of the inverted Y figure is borrowed from illustrations Peirce himself uses to illustrate his manuscripts; see MS 7.13, CP 4.310, 1902, in which Peirce notes: "All that spring from the λ—an emblem of fertility in comparison to which the holy phallus of religion's youth is a poor stick indeed."

7. The use of the term "reason" in the first sentence of this quotation meaning "according to a principle" or "following a rule" is an important index of Peirce's gradually shifting perspective. In 1885 Peirce used the word "reason" to describe the relationship between sign and thing signified in the case of iconic signs, that is, as meaning a possible quality. In 1895 "reason" is equated with thought as genuine "triplicity" and as "mediating third" (MS 13).

8. There is a tendency, especially in Peirce's letters to Lady Welby, for confusion between marked and unmarked senses of the term "sign." In the marked sense, sign refers to the representamen or sign vehicle, that is, to the expressive and perceptible aspects of some object functioning semiotically; in the unmarked sense, sign refers to the complete sign relation taken as the irreducible triadic system of representamen, object, and interpretant.

9. On the dialogic nature of thought see CP 4.7, c.1906; NEM 3.835, 1905; NEM 3.866; NEM 3.407, 1903; MS 297.7; MS 296.11; MS 637.28: MS 803.3.

10. The doctrine of "medium of communication" is discussed additionally in SS 196, 1906; MS 283.105f, 1905–1906. In a review of Baldwin's *Thought and Things* Peirce notes that a sign is "the medium between two minds or between an object and an idea" (1907:204).

11. The same metaphor is used in another manuscript: "Thought is nothing but a tissue of signs. The objects concerning which thought is occupied are signs. To try to strip off the signs and get down to the very meaning itself is like trying to peel an onion and get down to the very onion itself" (MS 1334, 1905).

12. The etymology of "mediation," "middle," is not, however, linked to the verb "to mean" (Pelc 1982:7).

13. Peirce's enterprise reverses the Saussurean concept of proportionality of expression and sense. As Peirce noted: "Grammatical forms and logical forms are entirely different. The grammatical form depends on the expression; the logical form depends on the sense" (W 1.254, 1865).

3. Transactional Symbolism in Belauan Mortuary Rites

1. I adopt the convention of putting into quotation marks the initial occurrence of English words and phrases selected to gloss Belauan expressions. All subsequent uses of the English forms should be understood to stand for the Belauan words. Kinship terms, such as brother and sister, son and daughter, are to be taken in the Belauan sense and should not be thought to indicate a necessary biological link. Quotations from villagers are marked F and M for female and male. The ethnographic present is 1978–80.

2. Without broaching the complex question of whether to describe Belauan kinship in terms of matrilineages or according to the indigenous notion of "houses" (see Parmentier 1984), it is sufficient to note that there is a clear ranking of kinship ties among "offspring of women" (*ochell*) over ties among "offspring of men" (*ulechell*).

3. The ethnographic descriptions which follow are based on my own attendance at two funerals in Koror and six funerals in Ngeremlengui (located on the western coast of Babeldaob island) in 1978–80. Additional information on Belauan mortuary rites can be found in the ethnographic record covering the past two hundred years. The most important of these sources

are: Keate 1788:163–64 (based on Mr. Sharp's attendance at the funeral of the son of Rechucher of Koror in 1783); Barnard 1980:29 (based on his attendance at a funeral in Ngebiul in 1832); Semper 1982:87–91 (based on his attendance at the funeral for Mad's sister in Ngebuked, 1862), 175–76 (based on his observation of preparations for the funeral of Reklai Okerangel in Melekeok in 1862, which he did not himself attend); Kubary 1873:188, 230–31, 1885:57–58, 1900a (based on his participation in many funerals in Koror and Melekeok in 1871–72, during a devastating influenza epidemic, and in 1882–83); Krämer 1917–29, 3:350–59 (based on his attendance at the funeral of Adelbai, a low-ranking titleholder from Ngeremid, in 1909); Barnett 1949:135–49 (based on his attendance at the funeral of a ten-year-old boy from Chelab in 1948); and DeV. R. Smith 1983:277–300 (based on her participation in five funerals in Melekeok in 1972–73).

4. Close male friends of this eldest child often put out the announcement on behalf of "one of us." I was particularly struck by one such message issued by the surviving husband of a deceased woman, which made no direct mention of her death; rather, the message stated that the husband "had capsized."

5. Also, pulverized turmeric is used as a strength-inducing anointment for bodies of warriors (see Parmentier 1987a:282–83) as well as for young women during post-childbirth celebrations (see DeV. R. Smith 1983:171).

6. Force and Force (1972:108) describe an unusual situation they heard about in Ngchesar district, where a rival faction within a house interrupted the burial rite by violating the imposed silence; the disruption ended only when a titleholder from the other faction paid a male valuable to the rowdy group.

7. I saw these two words, along with the names of the givers, scribbled on food packages stacked in the cooking areas of mourning houses. It is not the case that all spouses of men bring *ngeliokl*, since the wives of the husband's brothers and the wives of his sons all contribute *chelungel*.

8. This procedure is labeled *merasm a bldokl*, after the word *rasm* "thatching needle."

9. Because of the extreme sacredness (*meang*) of this platform, it is never used twice but is taken to the mangrove channel, broken into pieces, and discarded.

10. Called the Tet (Handbag) of Olscheluib, this stone coffin rests today next to the Belau Museum in Koror.

11. There is understandable confusion in the ethnographic literature because this word, which is simply the term for boat or ship, resembles *dial*, the third-person-singular possessive of *dui* "title."

12. I never heard this word, *kekur*, yet I was told that it referred to a spoon made out of turtleshell.

13. For a remarkable photograph of the seating arrangement of a funeral in 1909 see Krämer 1917–29, 3:plate 20.

14. Cf. Krämer 1917–29, 3:354. The *mur*-feast and *orau*-valuable are allusions to two transactions in which a woman becomes the conduit of money from her husband to her brothers or mother's brother. A woman's social standing is, in part, measured by the value of these affinal contributions.

15. The symbolism here is complex. A male chiefly title is known as *dui*, which is the word for coconut frond, the idea being that a high-ranking man "carries the title" (*meluchel a dui*) on his head. In this portion of the rite, the coconut frond is wrapped in a wild taro leaf (*dudek el bisech*), since this is the same word for the white-tailed tropic bird (*dudek*), known to be a particularly strong flier. The connection between the bird and the title is made in a well-known story of a contest to seize the coconut frond title.

16. At one funeral I attended, the female children of the deceased woman also collected cash and contributed it as a lump sum to the total collected by the men.

17. Kubary adds that the spirit which caused the death carries off the *sis* plant.

18. Neither of these patterns is referred to as *omerodel* "adoption."

19. Barnett (1949:137) states that the term *badek* is extended to cover the funeral goods given to the spouses of men. I never heard this usage in Ngeremlengui.

20. These expressions of kinship solidarity contrast sharply with the extreme division between affinal sides described for the Dobuans (Fortune 1932:10–11).

21. See, e.g., Barton 1946:169–202; Blackwood 1935:487–502; Counts 1976–77; Fortune 1932:10–16; Furness 1910; Hudson 1966; Kaeppler 1978; Keesing 1982:143–67; Metcalf 1982; Poole 1984; Traube 1986:200–235; Volkman 1985:142–52; Weiner 1976:61–120.

4. The Political Function of Reported Speech

1. For comparative ethnographic data, see the papers collected in Bloch 1975; Brenneis and Myers 1984; and Paine 1981.

5. Tropical Semiotics

1. J. F. MacCannell (1981:296), writing about early modern Europe, notes that this process may have a third phase, the "revolution" that reinstates as arbitrary the fixed or naturalized metaphors of a society.

2. Weiner does not relate his analysis to the proposal by Schwimmer (1974:217) that there is an important difference between metaphoric and metonymic exchange objects.

3. This concentration on moral stories rather than charter myths might account for Weiner's failure to articulate his argument with recent work in the semiotics of myth. For examples of studies of myth with a semiotic focus see Barthes 1982; Casalis 1976; Drummond 1981; Greimas 1987; Ivanov and Toporov 1976; Liszka 1983, 1989; Lotman and Uspensky 1978; Ogibenin 1968; Schwimmer 1986; Semeka-Pankratov 1979; Shapiro and Shapiro 1988; Toporov 1974; Urban 1986; Zilberman 1984.

4. It is not clear whether to classify "The Hornbill Husband" as a moral story or as a serious myth. Williams points out that the Kutubu Foi version he collected suppresses the names of the characters and that the narrative serves as a charter for the "foundation" clan; Weiner, on the other hand, treats the Hegeso Foi version he recorded as a moral story without cultic relevance and without an associated magical spell.

5. Wagner has argued for one additional context, namely, the historical unfolding of epochal stages in the symbolism of a single cultural tradition. His analysis (1986b:96–125) of the transition from medieval to Reformation Christianity in terms of eucharistic ritual argues for the "temporal development of the Western core symbol as a process of tropic expansion and obviation."

6. Gurevich (1988:178–80) provides a brilliant critique of Bakhtin in suggesting that the medieval grotesque stands as a constant countertheme at both popular and high cultural levels rather than as a differentiating sign of that division.

6. The Semiotic Regimentation of Social Life

1. The argument here about "hyperstructure" is an extension of the aesthetic theory of Jan Mukařovský and Roman Jakobson.

2. My research has more recently expanded to include Old Sturbridge Village, Hancock Shaker Village, Old Deerfield, and Mystic Seaport, all constructed along the model of historical restoration pioneered at Colonial Williamsburg (Ainslie 1984:163). For the purpose of illustrating how a specific contextual *arrangement* of interpretants regiments tourists' experience

in ways that actually run counter to assorted textual forms of metasemiotic intent I will confine the discussion here to Colonial Williamsburg.

3. In the late 1980s, when officials of the Colonial Williamsburg Foundation realized that the "black experience" needed to be given more explicit attention, a grant from AT&T provided funds for tours and entertainment focused on Black History. And, conveniently, renewed excavation yielded additional artifacts to reflect the life of slaves.

4. Not content with the re-creation of the past, the Rockefellers were also the force behind the Museum of Modern Art in New York, which "promoted an image of glamorous modernity and liberalism that contrasted sharply with older types of museums and their nineteenth-century ideologies" (Duncan and Wallach 1978:33). And, as these authors demonstrate, the spatial organization of this museum regiments the visitor' experience of the enshrined objects.

5. See Fjellman's (1992:400) comments on "commodity fetishism" at Walt Disney World.

6. My argument here can be taken as an indirect criticism of Olson's (1987) more general discussion of "meta-television." Olson contends that television programming *about* television serves to undermine the conventions of "naturalness" as an arbitrary artifice. I would suggest, in contrast, that meta-television, like meta-advertising, reinforces the dominant rules of interpretation by including representations of them in the content of media messages.

7. Comparison, Pragmatics, and Interpretation

1. As the final presentation in the multiyear conference series, my discussant's task was to provide a general summary perspective on the issues of comparison and interpretation that would link the papers presented at this and at earlier conferences.

2. Taylor (1990:47) notes that the presence in the West of rational discourse about the equal value of other traditions seems to be an argument for the West's claim to cultural superiority, since this spirit of equality is missing in many other cultures.

3. For a record of penetrating discussions of the typology of comparison see Bantly 1990:3–21 (summary by Robert F. Campany), 123–44 (summary by Laurie L. Patton).

4. J. Z. Smith (1982:22) even postulates a typology of comparative thinking, in which various writers on religion are positioned relative to four types: ethnographic, encyclopedic, morphological, and evolutionary.

5. Cf. Gadamer's notion of "alienation," in Schweiker 1990:42.

6. This distinction comes from Silverstein's many lectures and papers on pragmatics and metapragmatics; see especially Silverstein 1993.

7. Two excellent recent demonstrations of the pragmatic background to comparative analytic work are J. Z. Smith 1990 and Eilberg-Schwartz 1990.

8. Several scholars have noted that comparison at the level of practical reason might help avoid the generalization that the more developed a philosophical theory is the more remote the chance of finding suitable comparative parallels in other theories (Kasulis 1982:403; Yearley 1990:179).

9. In the discussion of the conference paper in this and the following paragraphs I am primarily interested in drawing out material relevant to the joint theme of comparison and interpretation, which in several cases misses the authors' central concerns. Also, space restriction precludes dealing fully with all the conference papers here.

10. The argument proposed by MacIntyre (1988:357) that traditions are rational to the degree that they engage in historically layered self-criticism overlooks the important role of *cross*-cultural engagement.

11. The Bimin-Kuskusmin case is fruitfully compared to the myth of Hainuwele from Ceram analyzed by J. Z. Smith (1978:304; 1982:96–101), where the incongruity of the encounter with Europeans and foreign goods is coded by indigenous motifs in mythological narratives.

12. On this performative function see Clooney 1987:672.

8. Naturalization of Convention

1. The Saussurean theory that the relationship of "signification" in language is "radically arbitrary" and that "relative motivation" enters only along the axis of systemic "value" has received much recent criticism; for a summary see Friedrich 1979.

2. As Summers (1981:119) notes with respect to artistic convention: "Arbitrariness implies choice and judgment. But the choice of the builder or builders of the first fence is not the same as the choice of builders who come afterward. The potentially endlessly variable characteristics of the initial choice are magnified to the point of being qualitatively different from choices that come afterward; *this is because the first formulation defines the concept of a fence.*" Cf. Frye 1966:140.

3. For a mild critique of these ideas see Fortes 1983; for a stinging attack see Sahlins 1976b.

4. Elias (1983:230) notes, however, that a yearning for rural, natural life began to permeate the artistic conventions of the court, as evidenced in the development of landscape painting.

5. The gradation of court behavior echoes the linkage between social rank and ritualization of consumption in ancient Hawaii: "The consumption of this meat is never strictly profane but is ritualized to different degrees. Moreover, there is a complementarity between these degrees. In other words, it is precisely the extreme ritualization of the consumption of pork (as well as all other foods) by the ali'i [chiefs] that makes possible the lesser ritualization of its consumption by those of inferior rank. Thus the meals of the people of different rank form an ideal series: closer to the gods, an ali'i of high rank takes the first step in the process of approaching them, and this step makes all the others possible, whether they are directly associated (but in a subordinate position) with the ali'i's meal or are separate from it" (Valeri 1985:126).

References

Acton, H. B. 1952–53. Tradition and Some Other Forms of Order. *Proceedings of the Aristotelian Society* 53:1–28.

Ainslie, Michael L. 1984. Historic Preservation in the United States: A Historical Perspective. In Yudhishthir Raj Isar, ed., *The Challenge to Our Cultural Heritage: Why Preserve the Past?* pp. 163–68. Washington, D.C.: Smithsonian Institution Press.

Al-Azmeh, Aziz. 1986. *Arabic Thought and Islamic Societies.* London: Croom Helm.

———. 1992. Barbarians in Arab Eyes. *Past and Present* 134:3–18.

———. 1994. Practical Reason and Myths of Origin: A Study in the Clerico-Legal Appropriation of the World in an Islamic Tradition. In Frank E. Reynolds and David Tracy, eds., *Religion and Practical Reason.* Albany: State University of New York Press.

Alexander, Jeffrey C. 1986. The "Form" of Substance: The Senate Watergate Hearings as Ritual. In Sandra J. Ball-Rokeach and Muriel G. Cantor, eds., *Media, Audience, and Social Structure,* pp. 243–51. Newbury Park, Calif.: Sage Publications.

Al-Farabi. 1962. The Attainment of Happiness. In *Alfarabi's Philosophy of Plato and Aristotle,* pp. 11–50. Trans. Muhsin Mahdi. New York: The Free Press of Glencoe.

Aoyagi, Machiko. 1987. Gods of the Modekngei Religion in Belau. In Iwao Ushijima and Ken-ichi Sudo, eds., *Cultural Uniformity and Diversity in Micronesia,* pp. 339–61. Senri Ethnological Studies 21. Osaka: National Museum of Ethnology.

Ardener, Edwin. 1975. Belief and the Problem of Women. In Shirley Ardener, ed., *Perceiving Women,* pp. 1–17. London: J. M. Dent and Sons.

Ayer, A. J. 1968. *The Origins of Pragmatism: Studies in the Philosophy of Charles Sanders Peirce and William James.* San Francisco: Freeman, Cooper and Company.

Babcock, Barbara A. 1978. Too Many, Two Few: Ritual Modes of Signification. *Semiotica* 23(3/4):291–302.

Bakhtin, Mikhail M. 1968 [1965]. *Rabelais and His World.* Trans. Hélène Iswolsky. Cambridge, Mass.: M.I.T. Press.

———. 1981. *The Dialogic Imagination: Four Essays.* Ed. Michael Holquist. Trans. Caryl Emerson and Michael Holquist. University of Texas Press Slavic Series no. 1. Austin: University of Texas Press.

———. 1986. *Speech Genres and Other Late Essays.* Ed. Caryl Emerson and Michael Holquist. Trans. Vern W. McGee. University of Texas Press Slavic Series no. 8. Austin: University of Texas Press.

Balbus, Isaac D. 1977. Commodity Form and Legal Form: An Essay on the "Relative Autonomy" of the Law. *Law and Society Review* 11:571–88.

Bantly, Francisca Cho. 1994. The Fear of *Qing*: Confucian and Buddhist Discourses on

Desire. In Frank E. Reynolds and David Tracy, eds., *Religion and Practical Reason.* Albany: State University of New York Press.

Bantly, Francisca Cho, ed. 1990. *Deconstructing/Reconstructing the Philosophy of Religions.* Chicago: The Divinity School, University of Chicago.

Barnard, Edward C. 1980. *"Naked and a Prisoner": Captain Edward C. Barnard's Narrative of Shipwreck in Palau, 1832–1833.* Ed. Kenneth R. Martin. Sharon, Mass.: Kendall Whaling Museum.

Barnett, Homer G. 1949. *Palauan Society: A Study of Contemporary Native Life in the Palau Islands.* Eugene: University of Oregon Publications.

Barthes, Roland. 1967 [1964]. *Elements of Semiology.* Trans. Annette Lavers and Colin Smith. New York: Hill and Wang.

———. 1972 [1957]. *Mythologies.* Trans. Annette Lavers. New York: Hill and Wang.

———. 1982 [1956]. Myth Today. In Susan Sontag, ed., *A Barthes Reader,* pp. 93–149. New York: Hill and Wang.

———. 1983 [1967]. *The Fashion System.* Trans. Matthew Ward and Richard Howard. New York: Hill and Wang.

———. 1986 [1967]. The Discourse of History. In *The Rustle of Language,* pp. 127–40. Trans. Richard Howard. New York: Hill and Wang.

———. 1988a [1973]. Saussure, the Sign, Democracy. In *The Semiotic Challenge,* pp. 151–56. Trans. Richard Howard. New York: Hill and Wang.

———. 1988b [1964]. Semantics of the Object. In *The Semiotic Challenge,* pp. 179–90. Trans. Richard Howard. New York: Hill and Wang.

Barton, R. F. 1946. *The Religion of the Ifugaos.* American Anthropological Association Memoir Series no. 65. Menasha, Wis.: American Anthropological Association.

Baudrillard, Jean. 1981 [1972] *For a Critique of the Political Economy of the Sign.* Trans. Charles Levin. St. Louis: Telos Press.

———. 1982. The Beaubourg-Effect: Implosion and Deterrence. *October* 20:3–13.

———. 1990 [1970]. Mass Media Culture. In *Revenge of the Crystal: Selected Writings on the Modern Object and Its Destiny, 1968–1983,* pp. 63–98. Ed. Paul Foss and Julian Pefanis. London: Pluto Press.

Bauman, Richard. 1986. *Story, Performance, and Event: Contextual Studies of Oral Narrative.* Cambridge Studies in Oral and Literate Culture no. 10. Cambridge: Cambridge University Press.

Bauman, Zygmunt. 1968. Semiotics and the Function of Culture. *Social Science Information* 7(5):69–80.

Bell, Catherine. 1992. *Ritual Theory, Ritual Practice.* New York: Oxford University Press.

Benveniste, Emile. 1971 [1939]. The Nature of the Linguistic Sign. In *Problems in General Linguistics,* pp. 43–48. Trans. Mary Elizabeth Meek. Miami Linguistic Series no. 8. Coral Gables, Fla: University of Miami Press.

Bernal, Martin. 1987. *Black Athena: The Afroasiatic Roots of Classical Civilization,* vol. 1: *The Fabrication of Ancient Greece 1795–1985.* New Brunswick, N.J.: Rutgers University Press.

Bieder, Robert E. 1980. The Grand Order of the Iroquois: Influences on Lewis Morgan's Ethnology. *Ethnohistory* 27:349–61.

Black, J. A. 1981. The New Year Ceremonies in Ancient Babylon: "Taking Bel by the Hand" and a Cultic Picnic. *Religion* 11:39–59.

Blackwood, Beatrice. 1935. *Both Sides of Buka Passage: An Ethnographic Study of So-*

cial, Sexual, and Economic Questions in the North-Western Solomon Islands. Oxford: Clarendon.

Bloch, Marc. 1967 [1928]. A Contribution Towards a Comparative History of European Societies. In *Land and Work in Mediaeval Europe*, pp. 44–81. Trans. J. E. Anderson. New York: Harper Torchbooks.

Bloch, Maurice. 1974. Symbols, Song, Dance and Features of Articulation: Is Religion an Extreme Form of Traditional Authority? *Archives Européenes de sociologie* 15:55–81.

———. 1982. Death, Women and Power. In Maurice Bloch and Jonathan Parry, eds., *Death and the Regeneration of Life*, pp. 211–30. Cambridge: Cambridge University Press.

Bloch, Maurice, ed. 1975. *Political Language and Oratory in Traditional Society*. London: Academic Press.

Bloch, Maurice, and Jonathan Parry. 1982. Introduction: Death and the Regeneration of Life. In Maurice Bloch and Jonathan Parry, eds., *Death and the Regeneration of Life*, pp. 1–44. Cambridge: Cambridge University Press.

Boon, James A. 1982. *Other Tribes, Other Scribes: Symbolic Anthropology in the Comparative Study of Cultures, Histories, Religions, and Texts*. Cambridge: Cambridge University Press.

———. 1984. Folly, Bali, and Anthropology, or Satire across Cultures. In Edward M. Bruner, ed., *Text, Play, and Story: The Construction and Reconstruction of Self and Society*, pp. 156–77. 1983 Proceedings of The American Ethnological Society. Washington, D.C.: American Ethnological Society.

———. 1990. *Affinities and Extremes: Crisscrossing the Bittersweet Ethnology of East Indies History, Hindu-Balinese Culture, and Indo-European Allure*. Chicago: University of Chicago Press.

Boorstin, Daniel J. 1961. *The Image: A Guide to Pseudo-Events in America*. New York: Harper and Row.

Bosmajian, Haig. 1984. The Metaphoric Marketplace of Ideas and the Pig in the Parlor. *The Midwest Quarterly* 26:44–62.

Bourdieu, Pierre. 1977 [1972]. *Outline of a Theory of Practice*. Trans. Richard Nice. Cambridge: Cambridge University Press.

———. 1979 [1977]. Symbolic Power. Trans. Richard Nice. *Critique of Anthropology* 4:77–85.

———. 1984 [1979]. *Distinction: A Social Critique of the Judgement of Taste*. Trans. Richard Nice. Cambridge, Mass.: Harvard University Press.

———. 1987. The Force of Law: Toward a Sociology of the Juridical Field. *The Hastings Law Journal* 38:201–48.

Bourdieu, Pierre, and Jean-Claude Passeron. 1977 [1970]. *Reproduction in Education, Society and Culture*. Trans. Richard Nice. London: Sage Publications.

Boyer, Pascal. 1990. *Tradition as Truth and Communication: A Cognitive Description of Traditional Discourse*. Cambridge Studies in Social Anthropology no. 68. Cambridge: Cambridge University Press.

Brenneis, Donald Lawrence, and Fred R. Myers, eds. 1984. *Dangerous Words: Language and Politics in the Pacific*. New York: New York University Press.

Brock, Jarrett E. 1981. An Introduction to Peirce's Theory of Speech Acts. *Transactions of the Charles S. Peirce Society* 17(4):319–26.

Bruss, Elizabeth W. 1978. Peirce and Jakobson on the Nature of the Sign. In R. W. Bailey, L. Matejka, and P. Steiner, eds., *The Sign: Semiotics around the World*, pp. 81–98. Ann Arbor: Michigan Slavic Publications.

Buczynska-Garewicz, Hanna. 1978. Sign and Continuity. *Ars Semiotica* 2:3–15.

———. 1979. Peirce's Method of Triadic Analysis of Signs. *Semiotica* 26:251–59.

———. 1984. Peirce's Idea of Sign and the Cartesian Cogito. In Jerzy Pelc et al., eds., *Sign, System and Function: Papers of the First and Second Polish-American Semiotics Colloquia*, pp. 37–47. Berlin: Mouton.

Burkert, Walter. 1987. *Ancient Mystery Cults*. Cambridge, Mass.: Harvard University Press.

Burkhalter, Sheryl. 1985. Completion in Continuity: Cosmogony and Ethics in Islam. In Robin W. Lovin and Frank E. Reynolds, eds., *Cosmogony and Ethical Order: New Studies in Comparative Ethics*, pp. 225–50. Chicago: University of Chicago Press.

Campany, Robert F. 1990. "Survival" as an Interpretive Strategy: A Sino-Western Comparative Case Study. *Method and Theory in the Study of Religion* 2(1):2–26.

Casalis, Matthieu. 1976. The Dry and the Wet: A Semiological Analysis of Creation and Flood Myths. *Semiotica* 17(1):35–67.

Cassirer, Ernst. 1951 [1932]. *The Philosophy of the Enlightenment*. Trans. Fritz C. A. Koelln and James P. Pettegrove. Princeton: Princeton University Press.

Clooney, Francis X. 1987. Why the Veda Has No Author: Language as Ritual in Early Mimamsa and Post-Modern Theology. *Journal of the American Academy of Religion* 55:659–84.

———. 1989. Evil, Divine Omnipotence, and Human Freedom: Vedānta's Theology of Karma. *Journal of Religion* 69:530–48.

———. 1990. Reading the World in Christ: From Comparison to Inclusivism. In Gavin D'Costa, ed., *Christian Uniqueness Reconsidered: The Myth of a Pluralistic Theology of Religions*, pp. 63–80. Maryknoll, N.Y.: Orbis Books.

———. n.d. *Theology after Vedānta*. Manuscript.

Comaroff, John. 1975. Talking Politics: Oratory and Authority in a Tswana Chiefdom. In Maurice Bloch, ed., *Political Language and Oratory in Traditional Society*, pp. 140–61. London: Academic Press.

Cosenza, Giovanna. 1988. Peirce and Ancient Semiotics. Trans. Susan Petrilli. *Versus: Quaderni di Study Semiotici* 50–51:159–74.

Cotter, John L. 1970. Exhibit Review: Colonial Williamsburg. *Technology and Culture* 11:417–27.

Counts, David R. 1976–77. The Good Death in Kaliai: Preparation for Death in Western New Britain. *Omega* 7:367–72.

Counts, Dorothy Ayers, and David R. Counts, eds. 1985. *Aging and Its Transformations: Moving toward Death in Pacific Societies*. Lanham, Md.: University Press of America.

Culler, Jonathan. 1981. Semiotics of Tourism. *American Journal of Semiotics* 1(1/2):127–40.

Daniel, E. Valentine. 1984. *Fluid Signs: Being a Person the Tamil Way*. Berkeley: University of California Press.

———. 1989. The Semiosis of Suicide in Sri Lanka. In Benjamin Lee and Greg Urban, eds., *Semiotics, Self, and Society*, pp. 68–100. Approaches to Semiotics no. 84. Berlin: Mouton de Gruyter.

Danks, Benjamin. 1892. On Burial Customs of New Britain. *Journal of the Anthropological Institute* 21:348–56.

Deledalle, Gerard. 1986. La Sémiotique Peircienne Comme Métalangage: Éléments Théorique et Esquisse D'une Application. In Jonathan D. Evans and André Helbo, eds., *Semiotics and International Scholarship: Towards a Language of Theory*, pp. 49–63. Dordrecht: Martinus Nijhoff.

Dewey, John. 1946. Peirce's Theory of Linguistic Signs, Thought, and Meaning. *Journal of Philosophy* 43:85–95.

Doniger, Wendy. 1992. Rationalizing the Irrational Other: "Orientalism" and the *Laws of Manu*. *New Literary History* 23:25–43.

Drummond, Lee. 1981. The Serpent's Children: Semiotics of Cultural Genesis in Arawak and Trobriand Myth. *American Ethnologist* 8(3):633–60.

Dumézil, Georges. 1970 [1966]. *Archaic Roman Religion*. 2 vols. Trans. Philip Krapp. Chicago: University of Chicago Press.

———. 1988 [1948]. *Mitra-Varuna: An Essay on Two Indo-European Representations of Sovereignty*. Trans. Derek Coltman. New York: Zone Books.

Duncan, Carol, and Alan Wallach. 1978. The Museum of Modern Art as Late Capitalist Ritual: An Iconographic Analysis. *Marxist Perspectives* (Winter):28–51.

Eco, Umberto. 1975. Looking for a Logic of Culture. In Thomas A. Sebeok, ed., *The Tell-Tale Sign: A Survey of Semiotics*, pp. 9–17. Lisse: Peter De Ridder Press.

———. 1981. Peirce's Analysis of Meaning. In Kenneth L. Ketner et al., eds., *Proceedings of the C. S. Peirce Bicentennial International Congress*, pp. 179–93. Lubbock: Texas Tech Press.

———. 1984. *Semiotics and the Philosophy of Language*. Bloomington: Indiana University Press.

Eilberg-Schwartz, Howard. 1990. *The Savage in Judaism: An Anthropology of Israelite Religion and Ancient Judaism*. Bloomington: Indiana University Press.

Eliade, Mircea. 1954 [1949]. *The Myth of the Eternal Return: Or, Cosmos and History*. Trans. Willard R. Trask. Bollingen Series no. 46. Princeton: Princeton University Press.

Elias, Norbert. 1982 [1939]. *The Civilizing Process*, vol. 2: *Power and Civility*. Trans. Edmund Jephcott. New York: Pantheon Books.

———. 1983 [1969]. *The Court Society*. Trans. Edmund Jephcott. New York: Pantheon Books.

Esposito, Joseph L. 1979. On the Origins and Foundations of Peirce's Semiotic. *Peirce Studies* 1:19–24.

Fernandez, James W. 1986. *Persuasions and Performances: The Play of Tropes in Culture*. Bloomington: Indiana University Press.

Fisch, Max H. 1986 [1978]. Peirce's General Theory of Signs. In *Peirce, Semeiotic, and Pragmatism: Essays by Max H. Fisch*, pp. 321–55. Ed. Kenneth Laine Ketner and Christian J. W. Kloesel. Bloomington: Indiana University Press.

Fjellman, Stephen M. 1992. *Vinyl Leaves: Walt Disney World and America*. Boulder, Colo.: Westview Press.

Force, Roland W., and Maryanne Force. 1972. *Just One House: A Description and Analysis of Kinship in the Palau Islands*. Bishop Museum Bulletin no. 235. Honolulu: Bishop Museum Press.

———. 1981. The Persistence of Traditional Exchange Patterns in the Palau Islands, Micronesia. In Roland W. Force and Brenda Bishop, eds., *Persistence and Exchange: A Symposium*, pp. 77–89. Honolulu: Bishop Museum Press.

Fortes, Meyer. 1983. *Rules and the Emergence of Society*. Occasional Paper no. 39. London: Royal Anthropological Institute of Great Britain and Ireland.

Fortier, John. 1979. Thoughts on the Re-creation and Interpretation of Historical Environments. In *Third Conference Proceedings 1978, International Congress of Maritime Museums*, pp. 251–62. Mystic, Conn.: Mystic Seaport Museum.

Fortune, Reo. 1932. *Sorcerers of Dobu: The Social Anthropology of the Dobu Islanders of the Western Pacific*. London: George Routledge and Sons.

Foster, Robert J. 1989. Thick beyond Description: Ethnography and Culture as Trope. *Oceania* 45:148–56.

Foucault, Michel. 1978 [1976]. *The History of Sexuality*, vol. l: *An Introduction*. Trans. Robert Hurley. New York: Vintage Books.

———. 1980 [1976]. Two Lectures. In *Power/Knowledge: Selected Interviews and Other Writings, 1972–1977*, pp. 78–108. Ed. Colin Gordon. Trans. Kate Soper. New York: Pantheon Books.

Fox, James J. 1973. On Bad Death and the Left Hand: A Study of Rotinese Symbolic Inversions. In Rodney Needham, ed., *Right and Left: Essays on Dual Symbolic Classification*, pp. 342–68. Chicago: University of Chicago Press.

Fox, Robin. 1979. Kinship Categories as Natural Categories. In Napoleon A. Chagnon and William Irons, eds., *Evolutionary Biology and Human Social Behavior: An Anthropological Perspective*, pp. 132–44. North Scituate, Mass.: Duxbury Press.

———. 1980. *The Red Lamp of Incest*. New York: E. P. Dutton.

Friedrich, Paul. 1979 [1978]. The Symbol and Its Relative Non-Arbitrariness. In *Language, Context, and the Imagination*, pp. 1–61. Stanford: Stanford University Press.

Frye, Northrop. 1966. Reflections in a Mirror. In Murray Krieger, ed., *Northrop Frye in Modern Criticism*, pp. 133–46. New York: Columbia University Press.

Furness, William Henry. 1910. *The Island of Stone Money: Uap of the Carolines*. Philadelphia: J. B. Lippincott.

Gabel, Peter. 1982 [1981]. Reification in Legal Reasoning. In Piers Beirne and Richard Quinney, eds., *Marxism and Law*, pp. 262–78. New York: John Wiley and Sons.

Gadamer, Hans-Georg. 1979. Practical Philosophy as a Model of the Human Sciences. Trans. James Risser. *Research in Phenomenology* 9:74–85.

Geertz, Clifford. 1973. *The Interpretation of Cultures*. New York: Basic Books.

———. 1983 [1976]. Art as a Cultural System. In *Local Knowledge: Further Essays in Interpretive Anthropology*, pp. 94–120. New York: Basic Books.

———. 1986. The Uses of Diversity. *Michigan Quarterly Review* 25(1):105–23.

Gellner, Ernest. 1988. *Plough, Sword, and Book: The Structure of Human History*. Chicago: University of Chicago Press.

Genovese, Eugene D. 1982 [1976]. The Hegemonic Function of the Law. In Piers Beirne and Richard Quinney, eds., *Marxism and Law*, pp. 239–94. New York: John Wiley and Sons.

Giesey, Ralph E. 1985. Models of Rulership in French Royal Ceremonial. In R. Sean Wilentz, ed., *Rites of Power: Symbolism, Ritual, and Politics since the Middle Ages*, pp. 41–64. Philadelphia: University of Pennsylvania Press.

Ginzburg, Carlo. 1991 [1989]. *Ecstasies: Deciphering the Witches' Sabbath*. Trans. Raymond Rosenthal. New York: Pantheon Books.

Godelier, Maurice. 1976. Le sexe comme fondement ultime de l'ordre social et cosmique chez les Baruya de Nouvelle-Guinée. In Armando Verdiglione, ed., *Sexualité et pouvoir*, pp. 268–306. Paris: Payot.

——. 1986 [1982]. *The Making of Great Men: Male Domination and Power among the New Guinea Baruya*. Trans. Rupert Swyer. Cambridge Studies in Social Anthropology no. 56. Cambridge: Cambridge University Press.

Goldschläger, Alain. 1982. Towards a Semiotics of Authoritarian Discourse. *Poetics Today* 3:11–20.

Goldsmith, Andrea. 1980. Notes on the Tyranny of Language Usages. *Women's Studies International Quarterly* 3:179–91.

Goody, Jack. 1977. *The Domestication of the Savage Mind*. Cambridge: Cambridge University Press.

Gough, John Wiedhofft. 1936. *The Social Contract: A Critical Study of Its Development*. Oxford: Clarendon Press.

Gould, Stephen Jay. 1989. *Wonderful Life: The Burgess Shale and the Nature of History*. New York: W. W. Norton.

Grady, Susan E., and Michael B. Feinman. 1983. Advertising and the FTC: How Much Can You "Puff" Until You're Legally Out of Breath? *Administrative Law Review* 36:399–411.

Greimas, Algirdas Julien. 1987 [1963]. Comparative Mythology. In *On Meaning: Selected Writings in Semiotic Theory*, pp. 3–16. Trans. Paul H. Perron and Frank H. Collins. Theory and History of Literature no. 38. Minneapolis: University of Minnesota Press.

Griffiths, Paul J. 1989. Buddha and God. *Journal of Religion* 69:502–29.

——. 1990. Denaturalizing Discourse: Ābhidhārmikas, Propositionalists, and the Comparative Philosophy of Religion. In Frank E. Reynolds and David Tracy, eds., *Myth and Philosophy*, pp. 57–94. Albany: State University of New York Press.

Gurevich, Aaron I. 1988. *Medieval Popular Culture: Problems of Belief and Perception*. Trans. János M. Bak and Paul A. Hollingsworth. Cambridge Studies in Oral and Literate Culture no. 14. Cambridge: Cambridge University Press.

——. 1983. Popular and Scholarly Medieval Cultural Traditions: Notes in the Margin of Jacques Le Goff's Book. *Journal of Medieval History* 9:71–90.

Habermas, Jürgen. 1971 [1968]. *Knowledge and Human Interests*. Trans. Jeremy J. Shapiro. Boston: Beacon Press.

——. 1973 [1971]. *Theory and Practice*. Trans. John Viertel. Boston: Beacon Press.

——. 1983 [1981]. *The Theory of Communicative Action*, vol. 1: *Reason and the Rationalization of Society*. Trans. Thomas McCarthy. Boston: Beacon Press.

Hallisey, Charles. 1994. In Defense of Rather Fragile and Local Achievement: Reflections on the Work of Gurulogomi. In Frank E. Reynolds and David Tracy, eds., *Religion and Practical Reason*. Albany: State University of New York Press.

Handler, Richard. 1986. Authenticity. *Anthropology Today* 2(1):2–4.

——. 1987. Overpowered by Realism: Living History and the Simulation of the Past. *Journal of American Folklore* 100:337–41.

Hanks, William F. 1989. Texts and Textuality. *Annual Review of Anthropology* 18:95–127.

——. 1990. *Referential Practice: Language and Lived Space among the Maya*. Chicago: University of Chicago Press.

Hanson, F. Allan, and Louise Hanson. 1981. The Cybernetics of Cultural Communication. In Richard T. De George, ed., *Semiotic Themes*, pp. 251–73. University of Kansas Humanistic Studies no. 53. Lawrence: University of Kansas Publications.

———. 1983. *Counterpoint in Maori Culture*. London: Routledge and Kegan Paul.

Harris, Roy. 1984. The Semiology of Textuality. *Language Sciences* 6(2):270–86.

Havránek, Bohuslav. 1964 [1932]. The Functional Differentiation of the Standard Language. In Paul L. Garvin, ed., *A Prague School Reader on Esthetics, Literary Structure, and Style*, pp. 3–16. Washington, D.C.: Georgetown University Press.

Heesterman, J. C. 1985. *The Inner Conflict of Tradition: Essays in Indian Ritual, Kingship and Society*. Chicago: University of Chicago Press.

Hegel, Georg Wilhelm Friedrich. 1987. *Lectures on the Philosophy of Religion*, vol. 2: *Determinate Religion*. Ed. Peter C. Hodgson. Berkeley: University of California Press.

Heimann, Betty. 1957. The Supra-Personal Process of Sacrifice. *Revista degli Studi Orientali* 32:731–39.

Herder, Johann Gottfried. 1988 [1773]. Correspondence on Ossian and the Songs of Ancient Peoples. In David Simpson, ed., *The Origins of Modern Critical Thought: German Aesthetic and Literary Criticism from Lessing to Hegel*, pp. 71–76. Cambridge: Cambridge University Press.

Herodotus. 1987. *The History*. Trans. David Grene. Chicago: University of Chicago Press.

Herzfeld, Michael. 1986. Meta-Anthropology: Semiotics In and Out of Culture. In Jonathan D. Evans and André Helbo, eds., *Semiotics and International Scholarship: Towards a Language of Theory*, pp. 209–21. Dordrecht: Martinus Nijhoff.

———. 1992. Metapatterns: Archaeology and the Uses of Evidential Scarcity. In Jean-Claude Gardin and Christopher S. Peebles, eds., *Representations in Archaeology*, pp. 66–86. Bloomington: Indiana University Press.

Hidikata, Hisakatsu. 1973 [1956]. *Stone Images of Palau*. Micronesian Area Research Center Publication no. 3. Agana, Guam: Garrison and McCarter.

Hobbes, Thomas. 1928. *The Elements of Law, Natural and Politic*. Ed. Ferdinand Tönnies. Cambridge: Cambridge University Press.

———. 1962 [1651]. *Leviathan*. Ed. Michael Oakeshott. New York: Collier Books.

———. 1978 [1658]. *De Homine*. In *Man and Citizen*, pp. 33–85. Ed. Bernard Gert. Trans. Charles T. Wood, T. S. K. Scott-Craig, and Bernard Gert. Gloucester, Mass.: Peter Smith.

———. 1981 [1655]. *Computatio Sive Logica*. Ed. Isabel C. Hungerland and George R. Vick. Trans. Aloysius Martinich. New York: Abaris Books.

Hołowka, Teresa, 1981. On Conventionality of Signs. *Semiotica* 33(1/2):79–86.

Hudson, A. B. 1966. Death Ceremonies of the Maanyan Dayaks. *Sarawak Museum Journal* 13:341–416.

Humphreys, S. C. 1975. Transcendence and the Intellectual Roles: The Ancient Greek Case. *Daedalus* 104:91–118.

Isaac, Rhys. 1982. *The Transformation of Virginia, 1740–1790*. Chapel Hill: University of North Carolina Press.

Ivanov, V. V., and V. N. Toporov. 1976. The Invariant and Transformation in Folklore Texts. Trans. Nancy Fowler. *Dispositio* 1(3):263–70.

Jakobson, Roman. 1980a. A Few Remarks on Peirce, Pathfinder in the Science of Language. In *The Framework of Language*, pp. 31–38. Ann Arbor: Michigan Studies in the Humanities.

————. 1980b [1956]. Metalanguage as a Linguistic Problem. In *The Framework of Language*, pp. 81–92. Ann Arbor: Michigan Studies in the Humanities.

————. 1985 [1972]. Language and Culture. In *Selected Writings*, vol. 7: *Contributions to Comparative Mythology, Studies in Linguistics and Philology, 1972–1982*, pp. 101–12. Ed. Stephen Rudy. Berlin: Mouton.

————. 1987 [1960]. Linguistics and Poetics. In *Language in Literature*, pp. 62–94. Ed. Krystyna Pomorska and Stephen Rudy. Cambridge, Mass.: Harvard University Press.

Jameson, Fredric R. 1979. Marxism and Historicism. *New Literary History* 11(1):41–73.

————. 1982. Beyond the Cave: Modernism and Modes of Production. In Paul Hernandi, ed., *The Horizon of Literature*, pp. 157–82. Lincoln: University of Nebraska Press.

Jappy, A. G. 1984. Peirce's Third Trichotomy and Two Cases of Sign Path Analysis. *Semiotica* 49:15–26.

Kaeppler, Adrienne L. 1978. *Me'a faka'eiki*: Tongan Funerals in a Changing Society. In Niel Gunson, ed., *The Changing Pacific: Essays in Honour of H. E. Maude*, pp. 174–202. Melbourne: Oxford University Press.

Kant, Immanuel. 1970 [1784]. An Answer to the Question: "What is Enlightenment?" In Hans Reiss, ed., *Kant's Political Writings*, pp. 54–60. Trans. H. B. Nisbet. Cambridge: Cambridge University Press.

Kasulis, Thomas P. 1982. Reference and Symbol in Plato's *Cratylus* and Kūkai's *Shōjijissōgi*. *Philosophy East and West* 32(4):393–405.

————. 1985. The Incomparable Philosopher: Dogen on How to Read the *Shobogenzo*. In William R. LaFleur, ed., *Dogen Studies*, pp. 83–98. Honolulu: University of Hawaii Press.

————. 1992. Philosophy as Metapraxis. In Frank E. Reynolds and David Tracy, eds., *Discourse and Practice*, pp. 169–95. Albany: State University of New York Press.

Keate, George. 1788. *An Account of the Pelew Islands . . . from the Journals and Communications of Captain Henry Wilson, 1783*. London: G. Nichol.

Keesing, Roger M. 1982. *Kwaio Religion: The Living and the Dead in a Solomon Island Society*. New York: Columbia University Press.

Kertzer, David I. 1988. *Ritual, Politics, and Power*. New Haven: Yale University Press.

Kesolei, Katherine, ed., 1971. *Palauan Legends*, no. 1. Koror: Palau Community Action Agency.

Khaldûn, Ibn. 1967. *The Muqaddimah: An Introduction to History*. Trans. Franz Rosenthal. Princeton: Princeton University Press.

Kitcher, Philip. 1985. *Vaulting Ambition: Sociobiology and the Quest for Human Nature*. Cambridge, Mass.: M.I.T. Press.

Kloesel, Christian J. W. 1983. Peirce's Early Theory of Signs (1863–1885): The First Barrier. *American Journal of Semiotics* 2(1/2):109–20.

Kluckhohn, Clyde. 1960. The Use of Typology in Anthropological Theory. In Anthony F. C. Wallace, ed., *Men and Cultures: Selected Papers of the Fifth International Congress of Anthropological and Ethnological Sciences*, pp. 134–40. Philadelphia: University of Pennsylvania Press.

Krämer, Augustin. 1917–29. *Palau*. 5 vols. In G. Thilenius, ed., *Ergebnisse der Südsee-Expedition, 1908–1910*. Hamburg: Friederichsen.

Kretzmann, Norman. 1974. Aristotle on Spoken Sound Significant by Convention. In

John Corcoran, ed., *Ancient Logic and Its Modern Interpretations*, pp. 3–21. Synthese Historical Library no. 9. Dordrecht: Reidel.

Krieger, Murray. 1990. The Semiotic Desire for the Natural Sign: Poetic Uses and Political Abuses. In David Carroll, ed., *The States of "Theory": History, Art, and Critical Discourse*, pp. 221–53. New York: Columbia University Press.

Kripke, Saul A. 1982. *Wittgenstein on Rules and Private Language: An Elementary Exposition*. Cambridge, Mass.: Harvard University Press.

Kubary, J. S. 1873. Die Palau-Inseln in der Südsee. *Journal des Museum Godeffroy* 1:177–238.

———. 1885. Die sozialen Einrichtungen der Pelauer. In *Ethnographische Beiträge zur Kenntnis der Karolinischen Inselgruppe und Nachbarschaft*, pp. 35–150. Berlin: Asher.

———. 1895. Die Industrie der Pelau-Insulaner. In *Ethnographische Beiträge zur Kenntnis des Karolinen Archipels*, pp. 118–299. Leiden: P. W. M. Trap.

———. 1900a [1885–86]. Die Todten-Bestattung auf den Pelau-Inseln. In A. Bastian, ed., *Die Mikronesischen Kolonien aus ethnologischen Gesichtspunkten*, vol. 2, pp. 37–48. Berlin: Asher.

———. 1900b. Das Verbrechen und das Strafverfahren auf den Pelau-Inseln. In A. Bastian, ed., *Die Mikronesischen Kolonien aus ethnologischen Gesichtspunkten* vol. 2, pp. 1–36. Berlin: Mittler.

———. 1969 [1888]. *The Religion of the Palauans*. Woodstock, Md.: Micronesian Seminar.

Kuhn, Thomas S. 1977. *The Essential Tension: Selected Studies in Scientific Tradition and Change*. Chicago: University of Chicago Press.

Kuhrt, Amelie. 1987. Usurpation, Conquest and Ceremonial: From Babylon to Persia. In David Cannadine and Simon Price, eds., *Rituals of Royalty: Power and Ceremonial in Traditional Societies*, pp. 20–55. Cambridge: Cambridge University Press.

Kuipers, Joel C. 1990. Talking about Troubles: Gender Differences in Weyéwa Ritual Speech Use. In Jane Monnig Atkinson and Shelly Errington, eds., *Power and Difference: Gender in Island Southeast Asia*, pp. 153–75. Stanford: Stanford University Press.

Kuper, Adam. 1985. The Development of Lewis Henry Morgan's Evolutionism. *Journal of the History of the Behavioral Sciences* 21:3–22.

Larson, Mildred Lucille. 1978. *The Functions of Reported Speech in Discourse*. Dallas: Summer Institute of Linguistics and University of Texas at Arlington.

Lears, T. J. Jackson. 1983. From Salvation to Self-realization: Advertising and the Therapeutic Roots of the Consumer Culture, 1880–1930. In Richard Wightman Fox and T. J. Jackson Lears, eds., *The Culture of Consumption: Critical Essays in American History, 1880–1980*, pp. 1–38. New York: Pantheon Books.

Leiss, William, Stephen Kline, and Sut Jhally. 1990. *Social Communication in Advertising: Persons, Products and Images of Well-Being*. 2nd ed. New York: Routledge.

Leone, Mark P. 1981a. The Relationship between Artifacts and the Public in Outdoor History Museums. *Annals of the New York Academy of Sciences* 376:301–14.

———. 1981b. Archaeology's Material Relationship to the Present and the Past. In Richard A. Gould and Michael B. Schiffer, eds., *Modern Material Culture: The Archaeology of Us*, pp. 5–14. New York: Academic Press.

———. 1987. The Archaeology of the DeWitt Wallace Gallery at Colonial Williamsburg. Manuscript.

Lévi-Strauss, Claude. 1967 [1955]. The Structural Study of Myth. In *Structural Anthropology*, pp. 202–28. Trans. Claire Jacobson and Brooke Grundfest Schoepf. New York: Basic Books.

———. 1969 [1967]. *The Elementary Structures of Kinship*. Ed. Rodney Needham. Trans. James Harle Bell and John Richard von Sturmer. Boston: Beacon Press.

———. 1976 [1960]. Structure and Form: Reflections on a Work by Vladimir Propp. In *Structural Anthropology*, vol. 2, pp. 115–45. Trans. Monique Layton. New York: Basic Books.

Lewis, David. 1975. Languages and Language. In Keith Gunderson, ed., *Language, Mind, and Knowledge*, pp. 3–35. Minnesota Studies in the Philosophy of Science, vol. 7. Minneapolis: University of Minnesota Press.

Lincoln, Bruce. 1991. *Death, War, and Sacrifice: Studies in Ideology and Practice*. Chicago: University of Chicago Press.

Liszka, James Jakób. 1981. Peirce and Jakobson: Toward a Structuralist Reconstruction of Peirce. *Transactions of the Charles S. Peirce Society* 17:41–61.

———. 1983. A Critique of Lévi-Strauss' Theory of Myth and the Elements of a Semiotic Alternative. In John N. Deely and Margot D. Lenhart, eds., *Semiotics 1981*, pp. 459–72. New York: Plenum Press.

———. 1989. *The Semiotic of Myth: A Critical Study of the Symbol*. Bloomington: Indiana University Press.

Littleton, C. Scott. 1974. Georges Dumézil and the Rebirth of the Genetic Model: An Anthropological Appreciation. In Gerald James Larson, ed., *Myth in Indo-European Antiquity*, pp. 169–79. Berkeley: University of California Press.

Lotman, J. M. 1976 [1974]. Theatre and Theatricality in the Order of Early Nineteenth-Century Culture. In Henryk Baron, ed., *Semiotics and Structuralism: Readings from the Soviet Union*, pp. 33–63. White Plains, N.Y.: International Arts and Sciences Press.

———. 1985 [1977]. The Poetics of Everyday Behavior in Eighteenth-Century Russian Culture. In Alexander D. Nakhimovsky and Alice Stone Nakhimovsky, eds., *The Semiotics of Russian Cultural History*, pp. 67–94. Trans. Andrea Beesing. Ithaca: Cornell University Press.

———. 1990. *Universe of the Mind: A Semiotic Theory of Culture*. Trans. Ann Shukman. Bloomington: Indiana University Press.

Lotman, J. M., and B. A. Uspensky. 1978 [1973]. Myth—Name—Culture. *Semiotica* 22(3/4):211–34.

Lowenstein, Daniel Hays. 1988. "Too Much Puff": Persuasion, Paternalism, and Commercial Speech. *University of Cincinnati Law Review* 56:1205–49.

Lukács, Georg. 1971 [1922]. Reification and the Consciousness of the Proletariat. In *History and Class Consciousness: Studies in Marxist Dialectics*, pp. 83–222. Trans. Rodney Livingstone. Cambridge, Mass.: M.I.T. Press.

MacCannell, Dean. 1976. *The Tourist: A New Theory of the Leisure Class*. New York: Schocken Books.

MacCannell, Juliet Flower. 1981. The Semiotic of Modern Culture. *Semiotica* 35(3/4):287–301.

———. 1985. Towards a Theory of Metaphor and Ideology. In John Deely, ed., *Semiotics 1984*, pp. 450–61. Lanham, Md.: University Press of America.

MacDonald, Margaret. 1935. Charles S. Peirce on Language. *Psyche* 15:108–28.

————. 1936. Language and Reference. *Analysis* 4:33–41.

MacIntyre, Alasdair. 1988. *Whose Justice? Which Rationality?* Notre Dame: University of Notre Dame Press.

MacKinnon, Catharine A. 1987. *Feminism Unmodified: Discourses on Life and Law.* Cambridge, Mass.: Harvard University Press.

Maine, Henry Sumner. 1875. Kinship as the Basis of Society. In *Lectures on the Early History of Institutions*, pp. 64–97. New York: Henry Holt and Company.

————. 1886. *Dissertations on Early Law and Custom.* New York: Henry Holt and Company.

————. 1889. *Village-Communities in the East and West.* New York: Henry Holt and Company.

————. 1972 [1861]. *Ancient Law.* New York: Dutton.

Márkus, György. 1980. Practical-Social Rationality in Marx: A Dialectical Critique— Part 2. *Dialectical Anthropology* 5:1–31.

————. 1984 [1980]. The Paradigm of Language: Wittgenstein, Lévi-Strauss, Gadamer. In John Fekete, ed., *The Structural Allegory: Reconstructive Encounters with the New French Thought*, pp. 104–29. Theory and History of Literature no. 11. Minneapolis: University of Minnesota Press.

Martens, Ekkehard. 1981. C. S. Peirce on Speech Acts. In Kenneth L. Ketner et al., eds., *Proceedings of the C. S. Peirce Bicentennial International Congress*, pp. 289–92. Lubbock: Texas Tech Press.

Marx, Karl. 1963 [1847]. *The Poverty of Philosophy.* New York: International Publishers.

————. 1976 [1867]. *Capital*, vol. 1. Trans. Ben Fowkes. New York: Vintage Books.

Mauss, Marcel. 1979 [1935]. Body Techniques. In *Sociology and Psychology*, pp. 95–119. Trans. Ben Brewster. London: Routledge and Kegan Paul.

McKeon, Richard. 1946. Aristotle's Conception of Language and the Arts of Language. *Classical Philology* 41:193–206, 42:21–50.

Mead, Margaret. 1964. Vicissitudes of the Study of the Total Communication Process. In Thomas A. Sebeok et al., eds., *Approaches to Semiotics*, pp. 277–87. The Hague: Mouton.

Meletinski, E. M. 1984. The Semantic Organization of the Mythological Narratives. *Cahiers Roumains d'Etudes Litteraires* 1:60–68.

Mertz, Elizabeth. 1985. Beyond Symbolic Anthropology: Introducing Semiotic Mediation. In Elizabeth Mertz and Richard J. Parmentier, eds., *Semiotic Mediation: Sociocultural and Psychological Perspectives*, pp. 1–19. Orlando, Fla.: Academic Press.

Mertz, Elizabeth, and Richard J. Parmentier, eds. 1985. *Semiotic Mediation: Sociocultural and Psychological Perspectives.* Orlando, Fla.: Academic Press.

Mertz, Elizabeth, and Bernard Weissbourd. 1985. Legal Ideology and Linguistic Theory: Variability and Its Limits. In Elizabeth Mertz and Richard J. Parmentier, eds., *Semiotic Mediation: Sociocultural and Psychological Perspectives*, pp. 261–85. Orlando, Fla.: Academic Press.

Metcalf, Peter. 1982. *A Borneo Journey into Death: Berawan Eschatology from Its Rituals.* Philadelphia: University of Pennsylvania Press.

Moore, Sally Falk. 1987. Explaining the Present: Theoretical Dilemmas in Processual Ethnography. *American Ethnologist* 14(4):727–36.

Morgan, Lewis Henry. 1962 [1851]. *League of the Iroquois.* New York: Corinth Books.

———. 1974 [1877]. *Ancient Society*. Ed. Eleanor Burke Leacock. Gloucester, Mass.: Peter Smith.

Morson, Gary Saul, and Garyl Emerson. 1990. *Mikhail Bakhtin: Creation of a Prosaics*. Stanford: Stanford University Press.

Motomitsu, Uchibori. 1983. The Ghosts Invited: The Festival for the Dead among the Iban of Sarawak. *East Asian Cultural Studies* 23:93–128.

Mukařovský, Jan. 1977a [1936]. Art as a Semiotic Fact. In *Structure, Sign, and Function*, pp. 82–88. Ed. John Burbank and Peter Steiner. Trans. Wendy Steiner. New Haven: Yale University Press.

———. 1977b [1938]. Poetic Designation and the Aesthetic Function of Language. In *The Word and Verbal Art*, pp. 65–73. Ed. and trans. John Burbank and Peter Steiner. New Haven: Yale University Press.

Munn, Nancy. 1970. The Transformation of Subjects into Objects in Walbiri and Pitjantjatjara Myth. In Ronald M. Berndt, ed., *Australian Aboriginal Anthropology*, pp. 141–63. Nedlands: University of Western Australia Press.

Murphey, Murray G. 1961. *The Development of Peirce's Philosophy*. Cambridge, Mass.: Harvard University Press.

Oehler, Klaus. 1981. An Outline of Peirce's Semiotics. In Martin Krampen et al., eds., *Classics of Semiotics*, pp. 1–21. New York: Plenum Press.

O'Flaherty, Wendy Doniger. 1986. The Uses and Misuses of Other Peoples' Myths. *Journal of the American Academy of Religion* 54:219–39.

———. 1988. *Other Peoples' Myths: The Cave of Echoes*. New York: Macmillan.

Ogibenin, B. L. 1968. Myth Message in Metasemiotic Research. *Social Science Information* 5:87–93.

Oliver, Richard L. 1979. An Interpretation of the Attitudinal and Behavioral Effects of Puffery. *Journal of Consumer Affairs* 13:8–27.

Olson, Scott R. 1987. Meta-television: Popular Postmodernism. *Critical Studies in Mass Communication* 4:284–300.

Osborne, Douglas. 1966. *The Archaeology of the Palau Islands: An Intensive Survey*. Bishop Museum Bulletin no. 230. Honolulu: Bishop Museum Press.

———. 1979. *Archaeological Test Excavations, Palau Islands, 1968–1969*. *Micronesica*, Supplement 1.

Paine, Robert, ed. 1981. *Politically Speaking: Cross-Cultural Studies of Rhetoric*. Philadelphia: Institute for the Study of Human Issues.

Pallis, Svend Aage. 1926. *The Babylonian Akitu Festival*. Historisk-filologiske Meddelelser no. 12, 1. Copenhagen: Andr. Fred. Host and Son.

Parmentier, Richard J. 1984. House Affiliation Systems in Belau. *American Ethnologist* 11(4):656–76.

———. 1985a. Signs' Place *in Medias Res*: Peirce's Concept of Semiotic Mediation. In Elizabeth Mertz and Richard J. Parmentier, eds., *Semiotic Mediation: Sociocultural and Psychological Perspectives*, pp. 23–48. Orlando, Fla.: Academic Press. [Chapter 2]

———. 1985b. Semiotic Mediation: Ancestral Genealogy and Final Interpretant. In Elizabeth Mertz and Richard J. Parmentier, eds., *Semiotic Mediation: Sociocultural and Psychological Perspectives*, pp. 359–85. Orlando, Fla.: Academic Press.

———. 1985c. Diagrammatic Icons and Historical Processes in Belau. *American Anthropologist* 87:1–13.

————. 1986. Tales of Two Cities: Narratives of Rank in Ngeremlengui, Belau. *Journal of Anthropological Research* 42:161–82.

————. 1987a. *The Sacred Remains: Myth, History, and Polity in Belau*. Chicago: University of Chicago Press.

————. 1987b. Peirce Divested for Non-intimates. *RS/SI* 7:19–37. [Chapter 1]

————. 1989. Naturalization of Convention: A Process in Social Theory and in Social Reality. *Comparative Social Research* 11:279–99. [Chapter 8]

————. 1991. The Rhetoric of Free Association and Palau's Political Struggle. *Contemporary Pacific* 3:146–58.

————. 1993a. The Political Function of Reported Speech: A Belauan Example. In John A. Lucy, ed., *Reflexive Language: Reported Speech and Metapragmatics*, pp. 261–86. Cambridge: Cambridge University Press. [Chapter 4]

————. 1993b. The Semiotic Regimentation of Social Life. *Semiotica* 95(3/4):357–95. [Chapter 6]

Patton, Laurie L. 1994. Dis-solving a Debate: Toward a Practical Theory of Myth. In Frank E. Reynolds and David Tracy, eds., *Religion and Practical Reason*. Albany: State University of New York Press.

Peirce, Charles Sanders. 1891. The Architecture of Theories. *The Monist* 1:161–76.

————. 1931–58. *Collected Papers of Charles Sanders Peirce*. 8 vols. Ed. Charles Hartshorne, Paul Weiss, and Arthur W. Burks. Cambridge, Mass.: Harvard University Press.

————. 1975–79. *Charles Sanders Peirce: Contributions to* The Nation. 3 vols. Comp. Kenneth Laine Ketner and James Edward Cook. Lubbock: Texas Tech Press.

————. 1976. *The New Elements of Mathematics*. 4 vols. Ed. Carolyn Eisele. The Hague: Mouton.

————. 1977. *Semiotic and Significs: The Correspondence between Charles S. Peirce and Victoria Lady Welby*. Ed. Charles S. Hardwick. Bloomington: Indiana University Press.

————. 1982–. *Writings of Charles S. Peirce: A Chronological Edition*. 4 vols. Ed. C. Kloesel. Bloomington: Indiana University Press.

Pelc, Jerzy. 1982 [1981]. Semiotic and Nonsemiotic Concepts of Meaning. *American Journal of Semiotics* 1(4):1–19.

Plato. 1961. *Republic*. In *The Collected Dialogues of Plato*, pp. 575–844. Ed. Edith Hamilton and Huntington Cairns. Trans. Paul Shorey. New York: Pantheon Books.

Ponzio, Augusto. 1984. Semiotics between Peirce and Bakhtin. *RS/SI* 4(3/4):273–92.

Poole, Fitz John Porter. 1984. Symbols of Substance: Bimin-Kuskusmin Models of Procreation, Death, and Personhood. *Mankind* 14:191–216.

————. 1986a. The Erosion of a Sacred Landscape: European Exploration and Cultural Ecology among the Bimin-Kuskusmin of Papua New Guinea. In M. Tobias, ed., *Mounain People*, pp. 169–82. Norman: University of Oklahoma Press.

————. 1986b. Metaphors and Maps: Towards Comparison in the Anthropology of Religion. *Journal of the American Academy of Religion* 54(3):411–57.

————. 1992. Wisdom and Practice: The Mythic Making of Sacred History among the Bimin-Kuskusmin of Papua New Guinea. In Frank E. Reynolds and David Tracy, eds., *Discourse and Practice*, pp. 13–50. Albany: State University of New York Press.

————. 1994. The Reason of Myth and the Rationality of History: The Logic of the Mythic in Bimin-Kuskusmin "Modes of Thought." In Frank E. Reynolds and David

Tracy, eds., *Religion and Practical Reason*. Albany: State University of New York Press.

Posner, Roland. 1988. Semiotics vs. Anthropology: Alternatives in the Explication of "Culture." In Henry Broms and Rebecca Kaufmann, eds., *Semiotics of Culture*, pp. 151–83. Helsinki: Arator.

———. 1989. What Is Culture? Toward a Semiotic Explication of Anthropological Concepts. In Walter A. Koch, ed., *The Nature of Culture*, pp. 240–95. Bochum Publications in Evolutionary Semiotics no. 12. Bochum: Studienverlag Dr. Norbert Brockmeyer.

Preston, Ivan L. 1975. *The Great American Blow-Up: Puffery in Advertising and Selling*. Madison: University of Wisconsin Press.

———. 1989. False or Deceptive Advertising under the Lanham Act: Analysis of Factual Findings and Types of Evidence. *Trademark Reporter* 79:508–53.

Pridgen, Dee, and Ivan L. Preston. 1980. Enhancing the Flow of Information in the Marketplace: From Caveat Emptor to *Virginia Pharmacy* and Beyond at the Federal Trade Commission. *Georgia Law Review* 14:635–80.

Propp, Vladimir. 1968 [1957]. *Morphology of the Folktale*. Ed. Louis A. Wagner. Trans. Laurence Scott. Indiana University Research Center in Anthropology, Folklore, and Linguistics Publication no. 10. Austin: University of Texas Press.

———. 1984. *Theory and History of Folklore*. Ed. Anatoly Liberman. Trans. Ariadna Y. Martin and Richard P. Martin. Theory and History of Literature no. 5. Minneapolis: University of Minnesota Press.

Ransdell, Joseph. 1977. Some Leading Ideas of Peirce's Semiotic. *Semiotica* 19(3/4):157–78.

———. 1980. Semiotic and Linguistics. In Irmengard Rauch and Gerald F. Carr, eds., *The Signifying Animal: The Grammar of Language and Experience*, pp. 135–85. Bloomington: Indiana University Press.

Rappaport, Roy A. 1979 [1974]. The Obvious Aspects of Ritual. In *Ecology, Meaning, and Religion*, pp. 172–221. Richmond, Calif.: North Atlantic Books.

———. 1980. Concluding Comments on Ritual and Reflexivity. *Semiotica* 30:181–93.

———. 1992. Ritual, Time, and Eternity. *Zygon* 27:5–30.

Reiss, Timothy J. 1984. The Young Peirce on Metaphysics, History of Philosophy and Logic. *RS/SI* 4:24–47.

Reynolds, Frank E., and David Tracy, eds. 1990. *Myth and Philosophy*. Albany: State University of New York Press.

———. 1992. *Discourse and Practice*. Albany: State University of New York Press.

———. 1994. *Religion and Practical Reason*. Albany: State University of New York Press.

Richards, Jef I., and Richard D. Zakia. 1981. Pictures: An Advertiser's Expressway through FTC Regulation. *Georgia Law Review* 16:77–134.

Ricoeur, Paul. 1967. *The Symbolism of Evil*. Trans. Emerson Buchanan. Boston: Beacon Press.

———. 1974a. *The Conflict of Interpretations: Essays in Hermeneutics*. Ed. Don Ihde. Evanston: Northwestern University Press.

———. 1974b. Metaphor and the Main Problem of Hermeneutics. *New Literary History* 6:95–110.

——. 1976. *Interpretation Theory: Discourse and the Surplus of Meaning*. Fort Worth: Texas Christian University Press.

——. 1984 [1971]. The Model of the Text: Meaningful Action Considered as a Text. *Social Research* 51:185–218.

——. 1991 [1971]. What Is a Text? In *From Text to Action: Essays in Hermeneutics, II*, pp. 105–24. Trans. Kathleen Blamey and John B. Thompson. Evanston: Northwestern University Press.

Robin, Richard S. 1967. *Annotated Catalogue of the Papers of Charles S. Peirce*. Amherst: University of Massachusetts Press.

Rochberg-Halton, Eugene. 1985. The Fetishism of Signs. In John Deely, ed., *Semiotics 1984*, pp. 409–18. Lanham, Md.: University Press of America.

Rohbeck, Johannes. 1984. Property and Labour in the Social Philosophy of John Locke. *History of European Ideas* 5:65–77.

Rome, Edwin P., and William H. Roberts. 1985. *Corporate and Commercial Speech: First Amendment Protection of Expression in Business*. Westport, Conn.: Quorum Books.

Rosensohn, W. L. 1974. *The Phenomenology of Charles S. Peirce: From the Doctrine of the Categories to Phaneroscopy*. Amsterdam: B. R. Gruener.

Rotfeld, Herbert H., and Ivan L. Preston. 1981. The Potential Impact of Research on Advertising Law: The Case of Puffery. *Journal of Advertising Research* 21:9–18.

Rotfeld, Herbert H., and Kim B. Rotzoll. 1980. Is Advertising Puffery Believed? *Journal of Advertising* 9(3):16–20.

——. 1981. Puffery vs. Fact Claims—Really Different? In James H. Leigh and Claude R. Martin, Jr., eds., *Current Issue and Research in Advertising 1981*, pp. 85–103. Ann Arbor: Graduate School of Business Administration, University of Michigan.

Rousseau, Jean-Jacques. 1984 [1753]. *A Discourse on Inequality*. Trans. Maurice Cranston. London: Penguin Books.

Sahlins, Marshall. 1976a. *Culture and Practical Reason*. Chicago: University of Chicago Press.

——. 1976b. *The Use and Abuse of Biology: An Anthropological Critique of Sociobiology*. Ann Arbor: University of Michigan Press.

Sanches, Mary. 1975. Metacommunicative Acts and Events: Introduction. In Mary Sanches and Ben G. Blount, eds., *Sociocultural Dimensions of Language Use*, pp. 163–76. New York: Academic Press.

Saussure, Ferdinand de. 1954. Notes inédites de F. de Saussure. *Cahiers Ferdinand de Saussure* 12:49–71.

——. 1959 [1916]. *Course in General Linguistics*. Trans. Wade Baskin. New York: McGraw-Hill.

——. 1974. *Cours de linguistique générale*. Critical edition by Rudolf Engler. 4 vols. Wiesbaden: Otto Harrassowitz.

Savan, David. 1987–88. *An Introduction to C. S. Peirce's Full System of Semiotics*. Monograph Series of the Toronto Semiotic Circle no. 1. Toronto: Victoria College in the University of Toronto.

Schmidt, Richard M., Jr., and Robert Clifton Burns. 1988. Proof or Consequences: False Advertising and the Doctrine of Commercial Speech. *University of Cincinnati Law Review* 56:1273–94.

Schrempp, Gregory. 1990. Antinomy and Cosmology: Kant among the Maori. In Frank

E. Reynolds and David Tracy, eds., *Myth and Philosophy*, pp. 151–80. Albany: State University of New York Press.

Schweiker, William. 1990. *Mimetic Reflections: A Study in Hermeneutics, Theology and Ethics*. New York: Fordham University Press.

———. 1992. The Drama of Interpretation and the Philosophy of Religions: An Essay on Understanding in Comparative Religious Ethics. In Frank E. Reynolds and David Tracy, eds., *Discourse and Practice*, pp. 263–94. Albany: State University of New York Press.

Schwimmer, Erik. 1974. Objects of Mediation: Myth and Praxis. In Ino Rossi, ed., *The Unconscious in Culture: The Structuralism of Claude Lévi-Strauss in Perspective*, pp. 209–37. New York: E. P. Dutton.

———. 1977. Semiotics and Culture. In Thomas A. Sebeok, ed., *A Perfusion of Signs*, pp. 153–79. Bloomington: Indiana University Press.

———. 1983. The Taste of Your Own Flesh. *Semiotica* 46(2/4):107–29.

———. 1986. Icons of Identity. In Paul Bouissac, Michael Herzfeld, and Roland Posner, eds., *Iconicity: Essays on the Nature of Culture*, pp. 359–84. Tübingen: Stauffenburg Verlag.

Segal, Charles. 1983. Greek Myth as a Semiotic and Structural System and the Problem of Tragedy. *Arethusa* 16:173–98.

Seitel, Peter. 1977. Saying Haya Sayings: Two Categories of Proverb Use. In J. David Sapir and J. Christopher Crocker, eds., *The Social Use of Metaphor: Essays on the Anthropology of Rhetoric*, pp. 75–99. Philadelphia: University of Pennsylvania Press.

Semeka-Pankratov, Elena. 1979. A Semiotic Approach to the Polysemy of the Symbol *nāga* in Indian Mythology. In Irene Portis Winner and Jean Umiker-Sebeok, eds., *Semiotics of Culture*, pp. 237–90. The Hague: Mouton.

Semper, Karl. 1982 [1873]. *The Palau Islands in the Pacific Ocean*. Trans. Mark L. Berg. Guam: Micronesian Area Research Center, University of Guam.

Shapiro, Michael, and Marianne Shapiro. 1988. Semiosis in Myth: The Slavic Witch, Baba-Jaga. In *Figuration in Verbal Art*, pp. 237–66. Princeton: Princeton University Press.

Sherzer, Joel. 1983. *Kuna Ways of Speaking: An Ethnographic Perspective*. Austin: University of Texas Press.

Shils, Edward. 1981. *Tradition*. Chicago: University of Chicago Press.

Shimp, Terence A. 1978. Do Incomplete Comparisons Mislead? *Journal of Advertising Research* 18:21–27.

Silverstein, Michael. 1976. Shifters, Linguistic Categories and Cultural Description. In Keith H. Basso and Henry A. Selby, eds., *Meaning in Anthropology*, pp. 11–55. Albuquerque: University of New Mexico Press.

———. 1977. Cultural Prerequisites to Grammatical Analysis. In Muriel Saville-Troike, ed., *Linguistics and Anthropology*, pp. 139–51. Georgetown University Round Table on Languages and Linguistics 1977. Washington, D.C.: Georgetown University Press.

———. 1979. Language Structure and Linguistic Ideology. In Paul R. Clyde, William F. Hanks, and Carol L. Hofbauer, eds., *The Elements: A Parasession on Linguistic Units and Levels*, pp. 193–247. Chicago: Chicago Linguistics Society.

———. 1981a. The Limits of Awareness. *Working Papers in Sociolinguistics*, no. 84. Austin: Southwest Educational Development Laboratory.

———. 1981b. Metaforces of Power in Traditional Oratory. Lecture, Department of Anthropology, Yale University.

———. 1981c. Who Shall Regiment Language? Intuition, Authority, and Politics in Linguistic Communication. Matthew Vassar Lecture, Vassar College.

———. 1985a. Language and the Culture of Gender: At the Intersection of Structure, Usage, and Ideology. In Elizabeth Mertz and Richard J. Parmentier, eds., *Semiotic Mediation: Sociocultural and Psychological Perspectives*, pp. 219–59. Orlando, Fla.: Academic Press.

———. 1985b. The Functional Stratification of Language and Ontogenesis. In James V. Wertsch, ed., *Culture, Communication, and Cognition: Vygotskian Perspectives*, pp. 205–35. Cambridge: Cambridge University Press.

———. 1987a [1980]. The Three Faces of "Function": Preliminaries to a Psychology of Language. In Maya Hickmann, ed., *Social and Functional Approaches to Language and Thought*, pp. 17–38. Orlando, Fla.: Academic Press.

———. 1987b. Monoglot "Standard" in America: Standardization and Metaphors of Linguistic Hegemony. *Working Papers and Proceedings of the Center for Psychosocial Studies*, no. 13. Chicago: Center for Psychosocial Studies.

———. 1992. The Indeterminacy of Contextualization: When Is Enough Enough? In Peter Auer and Albo Di Luzio, eds., *The Contextualization of Language*, pp. 55–76. Amsterdam: John Benjamins.

———. 1993. Metapragmatic Discourse and Metapragmatic Function. In John A. Lucy, ed., *Reflexive Language: Reported Speech and Metapragmatics*, pp. 33–58. Cambridge: Cambridge University Press.

Simmel, Georg. 1978 [1907]. *The Philosophy of Money*. Trans. Tom Bottomore and David Frisby. Boston: Routledge and Kegan Paul.

Singer, Milton. 1984 [1978]. For a Semiotic Anthropology. In *Man's Glassy Essence: Explorations in Semiotic Anthropology*, pp. 33–52. Bloomington: Indiana University Press.

Skidmore, Arthur. 1981. Peirce and Semiotics: An Introduction to Peirce's Theory of Signs. In Richard T. De George, ed., *Semiotic Themes*, pp. 32–50. University of Kansas Humanistic Studies no. 53. Lawrence: University of Kansas Publications.

Smith, Arthur L. 1972. Filming the Past at Colonial Williamsburg. *Film and History* 5:1–9.

Smith, Brian K. 1980. The Unity of Ritual: The Place of the Domestic Sacrifice in Vedic Ritualism. *Indo-Iranian Journal* 29:79–96.

Smith, DeVerne Reed. 1983. *Palauan Social Structure*. New Brunswick: Rutgers University Press.

Smith, Jonathan Z. 1978. Map Is Not Territory. In *Map Is Not Territory: Studies in the History of Religions*, pp. 289–309. Leiden: E. J. Brill.

———. 1982. *Imagining Religion: From Babylon to Jonestown*. Chicago: University of Chicago Press.

———. 1987. *To Take Place: Toward Theory in Ritual*. Chicago: University of Chicago Press.

———. 1990. *Drudgery Divine: On the Comparison of Early Christianities and the Religions of Late Antiquity*. Chicago: University of Chicago Press.

Sopher, David E. 1964. Indigenous Uses of Turmeric (*Curcuma domestica*) in Asia and Oceania. *Anthropos* 59:93–127.

Steiner, Peter. 1981. In Defense of Semiotics: The Dual Asymmetry of Cultural Signs. *New Literary History* 12:415–35.

Stocking, George W., Jr. 1987. *Victorian Anthropology*. New York: Free Press.

Stout, Jeffrey. 1994. Kuhn and Comparative Ethics. In Frank E. Reynolds and David Tracy, eds., *Religion and Practical Reason*. Albany: State University of New York Press.

Summers, David. 1981. Conventions in the History of Art. *New Literary History* 13:103–25.

Tambiah, Stanley J. 1985a [1968]. The Magical Power of Words. In *Culture, Thought, and Social Action*, pp. 17–59. Cambridge, Mass.: Harvard University Press.

———. 1985b [1981]. A Performative Approach to Ritual. In *Culture, Thought, and Social Action*, pp. 123–66. Cambridge, Mass.: Harvard University Press.

Taylor, Charles. 1985. Understanding and Ethnocentrism. *Philosophical Papers*, vol. 2, *Philosophy and the Human Sciences*, pp. 116–33. Cambridge: Cambridge University Press.

———. 1990. Comparison, History, Truth. In Frank E. Reynolds and David Tracy, eds., *Myth and Philosophy*, pp. 37–56. Albany: State University of New York Press.

Tejera, V. 1988. *Semiotics from Peirce to Barthes: A Conceptual Introduction to the Study of Communication, Interpretation and Expression*. Leiden: E. J. Brill.

Telegdi, Zsigmond. 1982 [1976]. On the Formation of the Concept of "Linguistic Sign" and on Stoic Language Doctrine. In Ferenc Kiefer, ed., *Hungarian General Linguistics*, pp. 537–88. Amsterdam: John Benjamins.

Thibault, Paul J. 1991. *Social Semiotics as Praxis: Text, Social Meaning Making, and Nabokov's Ada*. Theory and History of Literature no. 74. Minneapolis: University of Minnesota Press.

Tillich, Paul. 1963. *Christianity and the Encounter of the World Religions*. New York: Columbia University Press.

Todorov, Tzvetan. 1971. The Principles of Narrative. Trans. Philip E. Lewis. *Diacritics* 1(1):37–44.

———. 1982 [1977]. *Theories of the Symbol*. Trans. Catherine Porter. Ithaca: Cornell University Press.

Toporov, V. N. 1974. On the Typological Similarity of Mythological Structures among the Ket and Neighboring Peoples. *Semiotica* 10:19–42.

Tracy, David. 1990. On the Origins of Philosophy of Religion: The Need for a New Narrative of Its Founding. In Frank E. Reynolds and David Tracy, eds., *Myth and Philosophy*, pp. 11–36. Albany: State University of New York Press.

Traube, Elizabeth G. 1980. Affines and the Dead: Mambai Rituals of Alliance. *Bijdragen tot Taal-, Land- en Volkenkunde* 136:90–115.

———. 1986. *Cosmology and Social Life: Ritual Exchange among the Mambai of East Timor*. Chicago: University of Chicago Press.

Turner, Victor. 1969. *The Ritual Process: Structure and Anti-Structure*. Chicago: Aldine.

———. 1977. Sacrifice as Quintessential Process: Prophylaxis or Abandonment? *History of Religions* 16(3):189–215.

Tushnet, Mark. 1982. Corporations and Free Speech. In David Kairys, ed., *The Politics of Law: A Progressive Critique*, pp. 253–61. New York: Pantheon Books.

Tylor, E. B. 1871. *Primitive Culture*, vol. l. London: John Murray.

Urban, Greg. 1986. The Semiotic Function of Macro-parallelism in the Shokleng Origin Myth. In Joel Sherzer and Greg Urban, eds., *Native South American Discourse*, pp. 15–57. Berlin: Mouton de Gruyter.

Uspensky, Boris. 1976 [1971]. *The Semiotics of the Russian Icon*. Ed. Stephen Rudy. Lisse: Peter de Ridder Press.

Valeri, Valerio. 1985. *Kingship and Sacrifice: Ritual and Society in Ancient Hawaii*. Trans. Paula Wissing. Chicago: University of Chicago Press.

———. 1990. Both Nature and Culture: Reflections on Menstrual and Parturitional Taboos in Huaulu (Seram). In Jane Monnig Atkinson and Shelly Errington, eds., *Power and Difference: Gender in Island Southeast Asia*, pp. 235–72. Stanford: Stanford University Press.

Volkman, Toby Alice. 1985. *Feasts of Honor: Ritual and Change in the Toraja Highlands*. Illinois Studies in Anthropology no. 16. Urbana: University of Illinois Press.

Vološinov, V. N. 1973 [1929]. *Marxism and the Philosophy of Language*. Trans. Ladislav Matejka and I. R. Titunik. New York: Seminar Press.

Wagner, Roy. 1972. *Habu: The Innovation of Meaning in Daribi Religion*. Chicago: University of Chicago Press.

———. 1974. Are There Social Groups in the New Guinea Highlands? In Murray Leaf, ed., *Frontiers of Anthropology*, pp. 95–122. New York: Van Nostrand.

———. 1977a. Speaking for Others: Power and Identity as Factors in Daribi Mediummistic Hysteria. *Journal de la Société des Océanistes* 56/57:145–52.

———. 1977b. Scientific and Indigenous Papuan Conceptualizations of the Innate: A Semiotic Critique of the Ecological Perspective. In Timothy P. Bayliss-Smith and Richard G. Feachem, eds., *Subsistence and Survival: Rural Ecology in the Pacific*, pp. 385–410. London: Academic Press.

———. 1978. *Lethal Speech: Daribi Myth as Symbolic Obviation*. Ithaca: Cornell University Press.

———. 1981. *The Invention of Culture*. 2nd ed. Chicago: University of Chicago Press.

———. 1983. Visible Ideas: Toward an Anthropology of Perceptive Values. *South Asian Anthropologist* 4(1):1–7.

———. 1986a. *Asiwinarong: Ethos, Image, and Social Power among the Usen Barok of New Ireland*. Princeton: Princeton University Press.

———. 1986b. *Symbols That Stand for Themselves*. Chicago: University of Chicago Press.

———. 1988. Foreword to James F. Weiner, *The Heart of the Pearl Shell*. Berkeley: University of California Press.

Walker, Paul E. 1993. Al-Farabi on Religion and Practical Reason. In Frank E. Reynolds and David Tracy, eds., *Religion and Practical Reason*. Albany: State University of New York Press.

Wallace, Michael. 1986a. Visiting the Past: History Museums in the United States. In Susan Porter Benson, Stephen Brier, and Roy Rosenzweig, eds., *Presenting the Past: Essays on History and the Public*, pp. 137–61. Philadelphia: Temple University Press.

———. 1986b. Reflections on the History of Historic Preservation. In Susan Porter Benson, Stephen Brier, and Roy Rosenzweig, eds., *Presenting the Past: Essays on History and the Public*, pp. 165–99. Philadelphia: Temple University Press.

Weber, Max. 1978 [1956]. *Economy and Society*, vol. 1. Ed. Guenther Roth and Claus Wittich. Berkeley: University of California Press.

Weiner, Annette B. 1976. *Women of Value, Men of Renown: New Perspectives in Trobriand Exchange*. Austin: University of Texas Press.

———. 1992. *Inalienable Possessions: The Paradox of Keeping-While-Giving*. Berkeley: University of California Press.

Weiner, James F. 1986. Men, Ghosts and Dreams among the Foi: Literal and Figurative Modes of Interpretation. *Oceania* 57:114–27.

———. 1988. *The Heart of the Pearl Shell: The Mythological Dimension of Foi Sociality*. Berkeley: University of California Press.

Wheelock, Wade T. 1982. The Problem of Ritual Language: From Information to Situation. *Journal of the American Academy of Religion* 50:49–71.

Whorf, Benjamin Lee. 1956 [1939]. The Relation of Habitual Thought and Behavior to Language. In *Language, Thought, and Reality*, pp. 134–59. Ed. John B. Carroll. Cambridge, Mass.: M.I.T. Press.

Wild, John. 1947. An Introduction to the Phenomenology of Signs. *Philosophy and Phenomenological Research* 8:217–44.

Williams, Francis Edgar. 1977 [1940–1942]. Natives of Lake Kutubu, Papua. In *'The Vailala Madness' and Other Essays*, pp. 161–330. Ed. Erik Schwimmer. Honolulu: University Press of Hawaii.

Winner, Irene Portis. 1988. Research in Semiotics of Culture. In Thomas A. Sebeok and Jean Umiker-Sebeok, eds., *The Semiotic Web 1987*, pp. 601–36. Berlin: Mouton de Gruyter.

Yearley, Lee H. 1990. *Mencius and Aquinas: Theories of Virtue and Conceptions of Courage*. Albany: Sate University of New York Press.

Zakia, Richard D. 1986. Adverteasement. *Semiotica* 59:1–11.

Zilberman, David S. 1984. Semantic Shifts in Epic Composition (On the 'Modal' Poetics of *The Mahābhārata*). In Morris Halle et al., eds., *Semiosis: Semiotics and the History of Culture*, pp. 267–99. Ann Arbor: University of Michigan Press.

———. 1991. Understanding Cultural Traditions through Types of Thinking. In *The Birth of Meaning in Hindu Thought*, pp. 299–329. Ed. Robert S. Cohen. Dordrecht: D. Reidel.

Index

Advertising: pragmatic function, 142, 143, 145, 153; agencies, 143, 151; language of, 143, 145, 148, 153; deceptive, 144, 146, 147, 148, 153, 154; formal structure, 145; ideology of, 145, 149; regulation of, 146–55 passim. *See also* Meta-ads; Visual images
Aesthetic function, 131
Analogy, 112, 160, 166, 171, 172
Arbitrariness: of convention, 107, 173, 188; of the sign, 169, 197n6, 198nn1,2
Archaeology, historical, 141
Aristotle, 3, 42
Authoritative speech, 70–72, 79, 92
Awareness, 111, 145, 166, 167, 177
Ayer, A. J., 193n4

Bakhtin, Mikhail M., 70, 71, 92, 123, 159, 196n6
Baldwin, James M., 194n10
Barthes, Roland, 141
Baruya, 130, 132, 186, 187
Belau: funerals, 47–69 passim, 194n3, 195n6; burial practices, 49–50, 54, 56; social organization, 49, 63, 187; titles, 49, 50, 56, 60, 77, 195nn11,15; rank, 56, 187, 188; religion, 56, 75, 77, 95; kinship, 63, 69, 194n2; ethnographic background, 73–78; history, 73, 74, 188; political factions, 74, 188, 195n6; language, 76, 194n1; political rhetoric, 78; rules of speaking, 87, 90, 94, 96
Benveniste, Emile, 175, 177, 190
Bimin-Kuskusmin, 170, 171, 173, 198n11
Boon, James, 123
Bourdieu, Pierre, 123, 176, 177, 188
Bourgeois society, 181, 188
Buddhism, 170, 173

Carter's Grove Plantation, 138, 139
Caveat emptor tradition, 143, 144, 145, 150, 153

Classification: symbolic, 176; kinship, 182, 183, 185; linguistic, 184
Code, cultural, xiii, xiv, 121, 122, 126, 127
Collectivizing symbolization, 105, 109. *See also* Symbolic obviation
Colonial Williamsburg, 135–42, 196n2
Commercial speech, 143, 145, 148–53
Commodity: magical spells as, 121; historical reproductions, 141, 142, 143; embodiment of social value, 150, 184; form, 176; fetishism, 192, 197n5
Communication, by signs, 3
Comparison: as metalanguage, 159, 160, 171; genetic, 160, 161, 163; historical stances, 160, 166, 169, 173; cross-cultural, 161, 162, 197n4; methodology, 163, 174, 197n7; local models, 166, 167; pragmatics of, 167; typology of, 197n4
Connotation, 30, 31, 105, 154
Confucianism, 170
Consumption, culture of, 142, 145
Context: and indexicality, xv; of performance, xvi, 96, 101, 128, 129; entailment, 96, 122
Contextualization: of ritual, 68; of sign systems, 125; institutional, 126
Contract, social theory of, 180, 182
Conventionality, 19, 133, 169, 177, 178, 185
Conventions: normative, 107, 118; Peircean, 107; social, 171, 172, 175, 176, 187, 189; agreement, 175, 179; and arbitrariness, 175; artistic, 176, 198n2; relativity, 186; of naturalness, 197n6
Cosmogony, 134
Creativity, semiotic, 14, 72, 123
Cultural semiotics, xiv, 108, 109

Decontextualization, xvii, 103, 130, 131, 132
Decontextualized discourse, xvi, 166, 167, 173
Degeneracy, in sign relation, 35–38
Demythologization, 164

RICHARD J. PARMENTIER, Associate Professor of Anthropology at Brandeis University, is the author of *The Sacred Remains: Myth, History, and Polity in Belau* and articles on Pacific ethnography, anthropological linguistics, and semiotic theory. He is coeditor, with Elizabeth Mertz, of *Semiotic Mediation: Sociocultural and Psychological Perspectives.*